The Iron Men of Metz:

Reflections of Combat with the 95th Infantry Division

Tobias O. Vogt

Aventine Press

Published by Aventine Press
1023 4th Ave #204
San Diego CA, 92101
www.aventinepress.com

ISBN: 1-59330-277-0

Library of Congress Control Number: 2005926637
Library of Congress Cataloging-in-Publication Data
The Iron Men of Metz

Printed in the United States of America

Dedicated to:

The 6,591 Iron Men who made
the ultimate sacrifice.

Acknowledgements

First, and foremost, I would like to thank my Grandparents for the inspiration and guidance that they have provided throughout my lifetime. My Grandfather's mentorship and "War Stories" have greatly influenced many of my personal choices. Without them my life would have been much different. I would also like to thank my wife for her loving support, encouragement and assistance during this project and while I was deployed to Operations Enduring and Iraqi Freedom, I know this sacrifice was very hard on her; my Father, whose motivation and assistance were outstanding. The families of the Iron Men were a great help; I offer my sincere appreciation for all their support. Thanks to the 95th Division (Institutional Training) memorial staff for their help with digital photos from *Victory* and *The 377th Infantry Regiment, 95th Division*. Professionally I would like to thank the Special Operations community and a few of my brothers in arms, namely Ashton Naylor, Bill Shaw and Jerry Torres for their friendship and support throughout my endeavors. Academically, I would especially like to thank the faculty of the Hawaii Pacific University Master of Arts in Diplomacy and Military Studies program. Under their diligent guidance I was able to develop academically, and achieve the skills necessary to complete this demanding project. Thank you Dr. Pavkovic, Dr. Juarez, Dr. Primm, Dr. Madison, Dr. Foweraker, General Bramlett and Ambassador Salmon. Finally, I would like to thank the Iron Men for sharing their time, assistance and memories with us. It is, after all, their actions and reflections that made this project possible.

Forward

There are many opinions of history, what it is and what it is not. As I have studied different areas of history through the years I couldn't help but to form strong opinions of my own as to the possible errors and shortfalls of certain topics. In areas of study predating the written word my mind immediately begins to cast doubt on the question of "how historians really know what happened in centuries long past." Is there anyone that can verify the literature professor's interpretations of such classic works as the *Iliad* or the *Odyssey*, or the historian's theories of tactical and strategic goals of the same time period? In my opinion it is difficult to stand before an audience and lecture on what was and was not, in such time periods even as recent as Medieval or Early Modern Europe. Because of these doubts, I have always been more attracted to authors such as Stephen Ambrose and his many works on the Second World War. For reasons of clarity, accuracy and personal interest I have therefore looked to the 20th Century for the majority of my historical studies. With the aid of excellent documentation and participant interviews it is thoroughly enjoyable for me to learn about the events that have recently shaped the world within which we live. When dealing with an issue that encompasses an enormous portion of the world's population, such as the total mobilization for World War II, almost every member of what Tom Brokaw called the *Greatest Generation* has an enormous amount of information to share with future generations.

A finite resource, the world is losing these instruments of history at an alarming rate. The length of a normal life span makes the task of the budding historian that much more difficult, as human sources begin to pass away and memories begin to cloud. Returning to the issue of accuracy, it is important to note that no two accounts of any one incident will ever be exactly the same. Human beings sense and interpret information differently, and by so doing can provide an excellent, well rounded account if questioned in appropriate depth. Time is also the great enemy of accuracy, with each passing day, and in this instance years, the mind has a way of selectively recalling and altering past events. Just as initial trauma or bravado can distort accounts, so too does time tend to interfere with the accurate recollection of historic events. The noted historian John Keegan in his first book, *The Face of Battle*, covers many of the distorting elements of history. For those interested in the area of historiography (The study of history), Dr. Keegan can add quite a bit of clarity to the necessities of thorough research and educated deduction. For reasons unknown to the individual, unit or commander, Dr. Keegan identified that an unfortunate result of battlefield recording and literature is often inflation or skewed accounts of glory and grandeur in the favor of the victor. With this in mind, common sense must be employed when reviewing even the generally accurate accounts of participants. Although it's extremely easy for us to forget, the legendary heroes and figures that fill the pages of history were nothing more than human beings, living their lives much the same as you are now.

For the men of the 95th Infantry Division, their war took place almost sixty years ago. For some the memories and emotions are as clear as if they happened earlier in the day. For others, memories may have faded into the realm of a story that they have been asked to recite repeatedly throughout the past decades. And as with anything, there are those that fall in the middle, having moments of clarity and emotion intermingled with their well-rehearsed stories of battles long gone by.

This project was never envisioned as a definitive account of strategy at the highest levels or an academic review of the division's performance. There have been more than enough works describing the Generals and their elaborate plans. Instead, the primary focus was to share the experiences of a few great Iron Men. The historical outline and annexes are meant to paint the larger picture for the World War II novice. The complete Oral Histories facilitate a personal relationship between the reader and each Iron Man as they make their way across Europe and into the pages of history.

Table of Contents

Preface..1
I. The Road to War..5
II. Baptism by Fire...69
III. Continued Resistance..211
IV. Change of Mission...263
Annexes:..307
    A. 95th Infantry Division Organization.............................307
    B. 95th Infantry Division roll-up..308
    C. Biographical Summaries...310
Selected Bibliography..321

The rifleman fights without promise of either reward or relief. Behind every river there's another hill- and behind that hill, another river. After weeks or months in the line only a wound can offer him the comfort of safety, shelter and a bed.

Those who are left to fight, fight on, evading death but knowing that with each day of evasion they have exhausted one more chance for survival. Sooner or later, unless victory comes this chase must end on the litter or in the grave.

General Omar Bradley

Preface

The history of the 95th Division's activation, initial training and deployment, is much like any other division's history from the World War II time period. The division was briefly activated for World War I (September to December 1918) but was never fully formed before deactivation. The 95th was kept as a part of the reserve force during the interwar period until it was activated again for duty in March 1942. Major General Harry L. Twaddle was named the division commander at that time with a formal reactivation ceremony held at Camp Swift, Texas, on July 15, 1942. The initial enlisted cadre was incorporated from the 7th Infantry Division. The officers came from all walks of life, arriving from various officer candidate programs, and the reserve and active duty forces. The initial troops also came from every source available, with a heavy emphasis on selective service draftees from the Midwest. A good portion of the division originated from the Chicago area, with later replacements assigned from the greater United States.

As with other early World War II divisions, the soldiers of the 95th were indoctrinated into Army life with basic individual training. Marching, obstacle courses, weapons familiarization and qualification, map reading, long conditioning and tactical movements and bivouacs were all in days work for the new inductees. The next step in the two-year preparation period was unit training in the United States and England. The division moved from Camp Swift to training areas near Fort Sam Houston, Texas. The degree of training difficulty increased here as the troops trained on advanced weapons systems and demolitions as they attacked mock-ups of North African and German villages, performed river crossings and conducted force on force maneuvers. Next they moved to the Louisiana maneuver area where the men battled the environment as much as their opposing forces. Following the Louisiana maneuvers the division garrisoned at Camp Polk, Louisiana. The division's time at Polk was cut short as they were ordered to take part in more maneuvers in the California desert, based at Camp Coxcomb. One of the key advantages to the new California training area was the use of live ammunition. At Camp Coxcomb the troops had the opportunity to see the devastating effects of demolitions and the indirect fire that supported their maneuvers. A change in scenery, living conditions and proximity to the European Theater was next on tap for the 95th when they were ordered to Indiantown Gap Military Reservation, Pennsylvania.

Although the men had to endure the shock of rapidly moving from the pleasant California climate to the below freezing temperatures of Pennsylvania winter, they now had access to several of the United States largest cities during their limited off time. West Virginia would be the next host for training. The West Virginia training consisted of the normal combat team exercises as well as advanced training in military mountaineering, and pack and assault climbing courses for selected individuals. Adding to the difficulty of the maneuvers was the mountainous terrain and a large influx of new recruits in preparation for embarkation. In close proximity to the nations' capital, the division also played host to ranking officials and took part in ceremonies and celebrations, all while contemplating their impending deployment to combat. On June 25, 1944, the division's advanced party embarked for Europe. The main body moved further north to a staging area at Camp Miles Standish, Massachusetts, just outside of Boston. After crossing the Atlantic by troop ship, on the *USS West Point*, the 95th fully closed on Liverpool, England by August 17, 1944.

Initially housed in Winchester, in Hampshire, the division continued to train and enjoy what precious little off time there was in England for the next month. [On September 14, 1944, the last of the boats carrying the men of the 95th sailed across the English Channel for Normandy. The division debarked at Omaha beach, the earlier location of fierce resistance on D-day, but now a staging area for the massive influx of personnel and supplies. Upon arrival the division became part of Lieutenant General George Patton's Third Army, and bivouacked near Norriey-Le-Sec prior to pushing forward to the front line. On October 19th, 1944, the 95th Infantry Division moved further into France, taking up positions in the Moselle River bridgehead sector, east of Moselle and south of the famed fortified city of Metz. The moment of truth was now upon the men of the 95th; two years of training could not quell questions of personal combat performance and the horrors of a war in which they were about to partake. It would not be long until these young Americans would have the answers to there questions, and along the way earn the accolades of such cherished names as "The Iron Men of Metz" and "The Bravest of the Brave," coming face to face with the realities of 145 days of combat in Europe.]

I. The Road to War

Many historians argue that World War II is simply an extension of World War I. This is an argument that is often used in classrooms as students are taught about the United States Army Dough Boys that broke the back of the Kaiser and almost immediately loaded transports for home. To many Americans the departure of the United States Army clearly signifies the end of the First World War. Prior to the American commitment to the First World War, Europe had been engulfed in total war since 1914. By the time the United States Army arrived in 1917 they were responsible for providing the final push that drove the battered German Army from its trenches. Following the 1918 armistice, the United States Army returned to a thriving economy in a beautiful nation that hadn't been touched by the realities of five-years of trench warfare. Europe on the other hand had been devastated. An entire generation of young men lie face down in the mud never to rise again. France, who had bore the brunt of the German war machine, now played host to an elaborate series of trenches and destruction that had no value in times of peace. England, in addition to the sacrifice of men and material, went deep into debt to finance the Great War. Nonetheless, the allies had at least emerged victorious. For Germany, not even the final outcome could be placed in the credit column of its accounting ledger. While sacrificing an enormous amount of men and material, Germany would soon find itself a broken republic subject to every demand of the victors.

American President Woodrow Wilson, full of determination and forethought, sailed for Europe following the war. He had outlined his fourteen points and fathered his dream of a united entity, whose objective was to prevent future wars, it was called the League of Nations. Unfortunately for Wilson, America, with full the support of the congress, wanted to return to her principles of isolationism. Europe too wanted something different, revenge and reparations. As a result of the differing objectives the League of Nations would be doomed to failure before it began, and the resulting Treaty of Versailles, an event in which the defeated Germans weren't even invited to participate in, would punish Germany for her atrocities and prevent the country from any possibility of democratic rebirth or recovery. While the traditional European balance of power had been destroyed and the flow of world trade had been severely disrupted, America, in spite of the nuisance of the war, prepared to launch into the roaring twenties.

Post-World War I

While America was busy avoiding prohibition and making overnight millionaires in the stock market, Europe was attempting to recover from the destruction of a continent. Great Britain, formerly the world's banker, was now reduced to the status of a debtor nation. France had been ravaged to the point that it was no longer a first-rate power in the eyes of the world. On the periphery, Russia had become the Union of Soviet Socialist Republics (USSR) and was locked firmly in the throws of Communism. A little known player in the Pacific, Japan, had on the other hand benefited greatly from the war. Fighting on the side of the Allies, Japan had received the former German possessions in Asia following the war. Firmly establishing the small island nation as the principal power in the Pacific. Adhering to George Washington's isolationist theories America had withdrawn from international life. Congressional leaders attempted to avoid the quagmire that was post-World War I Europe.

In Germany the Kaiser was banished to neutral Holland and replaced by the doomed Weimar Republic. The economic embargo that had killed 800,000 German citizens in the last two years of the war was not lifted until the treaty had been signed and the Allied powers had had the opportunity to capitalize on the absence of Germany. The treaty itself was designed to keep Germany weak and exact enormous payment from the broken nation. The vanquished country forfeited all of her overseas colonies, to include the "Polish Corridor" and the "buffer states," demilitarized west of the Rhine, and was reduced militarily to a small internal force. Austria, Hungary, Czechoslovakia and Yugoslavia were formed from former German territories. More importantly, Germany was forced to acknowledge responsibility for the war as a basis for future reparations, later calculated in excess of 33 billion dollars. In the fertile post-war German soil of defeat, with its extreme poverty, despair and no hope for the future, were the seeds of Hitler's Nazi party.

Born to Austrian parents on April 20, 1889, Adolf Hitler was the opposite of the Aryan race that he so cherished. An average man with dark broad features, he lived his young adult life in Vienna. Most historians are in agreement that young Adolf formed his racist views of the world at an early age and that he also served honorably during the Great War. Not wanting to fight the First World War with an inferior Austrian Army, Hitler moved to Munich and enlisted in the Army of the Kaiser. He served in the World War I trenches, rising to the rank of corporal and was decorated for valor before the war's end. Following the war, hungry and unemployed like the rest of the German people, Hitler became the seventh member of a little known group named the German Workers Party. He quickly rose to the helm of the rapidly expanding organization, and assumed control of the newly named National Socialist Workers Party (the German acronym for the party is "NAZI") almost from the beginning. By 1923, membership in the party had gone from seven to 70,000. While the party thrived, the economy, if there was such a thing at the time, hit rock bottom. France invaded the industrial heartland of Germany because the Germans could not pay the excessive reparations placed on them. Workers routinely refused to work in occupied territories and the German mark was almost completely worthless.

In the same year Hitler and his Nazi party attempted to orchestrate a coup, the "Beer Hall Putsch." Unfortunately Hitler's partners were less enthusiastic and it failed. As a result of the failed coup Hitler found himself in prison, but capitalized on his thirteen-months of confinement by beginning to write his plan of action, *Mein Kampf* (My Struggle). Meanwhile, the republic continued to deteriorate and the Nazi's changed their tactics to gain control of Germany. The party now looked to the electoral process as their vehicle of ascension, with Hitler seated firmly behind the wheel. By 1933, the Nazi party controlled forty percent of the total popular vote and an aging and quite possibly senile Paul von Hindenburg, the president of Germany, named Adolph Hitler as Chancellor. Hitler immediately began to consolidate his power. By 1934, he had purged the German republic, the Nazi party, and demanded total allegiance to the *Fuhrer*, his self-proclaimed position as leader of the German people. His newfound leadership had a dramatic effect on the German people. Suddenly, after years of persecution and hardship, it was once again an honor to declare oneself a German citizen. Hitler fostered national pride and began an immediate economic turn around as he re-militarized the German nation, refused to pay reparations and began to assert himself in international politics.

France was outraged at Hitler's actions, but in her weakened condition during the German resurgence there was little that could be done unilaterally. The French strategy resulting from World War I was one of defense. Although the French had occupied the Ruhr in 1923, invasion was no longer an option. Since the German's had begun to falter on their payments the French government was forced to pay war debts from its own treasury. There was only a finite amount of money to rebuild France. The bulk of the national defense monies, nearly a half-billion United States dollars, went to build the Maginot Line, an amazing series of underground fortifications that stretched from Switzerland to just shy of the Ardennes forest in Belgium. Unfortunately, the massive defensive line did not include the Ardennes, an oversight that left open a high-speed avenue of approach for future attack. France was forced to watch and wait with great apprehension as Hitler shook his fist at the world.

Great Britain of the thirties was in no position to assist Continental Europe, regardless of the imposing and rapidly increasing German threat. Although more kind and understanding in their post-World War I treatment of Germany, the English had to adjust to their reduced status in international affairs. Saddled with massive war debt, England also depended on German reparations to assist in payments to the United States. The British Prime Minister, Neville Chamberlain, understood all too well the mounting German threat and intentions, but was politically and economically unable to avert possible military actions in Europe. Britains were not ready to sacrifice another generation of men to fight in Continental Europe, nor were they prepared to fight a war that new technology could possibly bring to their doorstep. Remarkable strides in transportation had been made since the First World War, namely the perfection of the airplane and with it the debated potential for airpower to single handedly bring a nation to its knees. The English Channel would no longer isolate the British Isles from war in Europe. Even if it were possible to use the threat of force, the British expected their representatives to avoid war at all costs. Demonstrating this viewpoint was the British Prime Minister who attempted to secure "peace in our time." Chamberlain secured the peace by appeasing Hitler in Munich following the German annexation of the *Sudetenland* region of Czechoslovakia and Austria. Unfortunately, peace in Neville Chamberlain's time amounted to nothing more than a hollow promise from Hitler, a promise that the German *Fuhrer* never intended to honor.

Europe Ignites

After formally withdrawing from the League of Nations and rearming Germany following his rise to power, Hitler, contrary his peace treaty with Chamberlain or his later nonaggression pact of convenience with Stalin, was looking to test his forces. [The Spanish Civil War provided Hitler and his military planners, as well as other European powers, with an appropriate arena to test their men and equipment. With his *Wehrmacht* (Armed Forces) hardened, Hitler now deemed his country ready to reclaim the territory and prestige befitting the *Reich*. Hitler began by annexing Czechoslovakia and Austria, before making his intentions all too clear by invading Poland in 1939. Resistance was minimal as the German *Wehrmacht* performed to perfection, conquering Poland in a matter of days. Scrambling into action the Soviets entered Poland and Finland to secure their boarders prior to the diplomatic maneuverings that would undoubtedly follow Germany's actions. In Finland, the ill-prepared Soviet forces were stiffly resisted and greatly delayed as the fierce Finnish fighters attacked using guerilla warfare techniques to severely attrit the superior Red Army. The German High Command watched as the Red Army was temporarily paralyzed in the frozen Finish forest, clearly demonstrating their ineptness as an early fighting force.

Because of treaty obligations with Poland the begrudging nations of Great Britain and France were forced to declare war on Germany following the invasion. For the next year a "phony war" raged in Europe as neither of the countries were prepared to go to battle with the mighty German war machine. Hitler invaded Norway and Denmark next, experiencing a greater deal of resistance from the Norwegian forces and later guerilla forces in contrast to the complete capitulation of the Danish King. England and France were still in a state of denial, preparing but not prepared to confront Hitler, as their forces quickly evacuated Norway. Well

aware of the famed French Maginot Line, Germany proceeded
to conduct a *blitzkrieg* (lightning war) through the Netherlands,
Belgium and Luxembourg. They avoided the infamous line in favor
of the impenetrable Ardennes. The British were forced to hastily
evacuate from continental Europe at Dunkirk as the *Wehrmacht*
raced for Paris. Hitler's forces entered the city on June 14, 1940,
with the formal signing of the German-French Armistice occurring
a few days later. Luckily for Great Britain, Hitler had not prepared
his Navy as he had his Army. In fact, many historians view the
Battle of Britain almost as an after thought, with no formal plans
prior to the fall of France. Instead, the task would fall to Reichs
Marshal Hermann Goering's *Luftwaffe* (Air Force) as the Army staff
hastily prepared a plan of attack, Operation Sea Lion. The Battle
of Britain was Hitler's first taste of defeat. Goering's *Luftwaffe* was
unable to bring England to her knees and Operation Sea Lion was
the operation that never was.

Not to be out done, Italy under Benito Mussolini looked
to capitalize on her gain of Ethiopia from 1935. The Italians
attacked into British Somaliland, Egypt and Greece, as German
forces under their esteemed commander General, and later Field
Marshal, Erwin Rommel took part in the North Africa Campaign.
Yugoslavia and Crete would also feel the full extent of Axis power,
with the latter being the victim of a massive German airborne
assault. Although the Axis powers were in concept a coalition
force, actual coordination and communication between Mussolini
and Hitler was all but non-existent. This lack of a combined
effort would also be identified between Japan and Germany as
the Japanese, like the Italians, conducted unilateral operations in
support of a separate political objective. Also of importance is
the airborne invasion of Crete. For the watchful eye of American
planners the successful use of airborne troops on Crete validated
the concept of the paratrooper, but for Germany, the horrific loses
of this invasion caused Hitler to redesign the airborne concept of
the German Army.

Based on several factors, including Hitler's desire to destroy the Bolshevist state, Germany invaded Russia on June 22, 1941. With his decision to open the Russian front, Hitler would follow in Napoleon's tragic footsteps of defeat. The decision appeared far less foolish at the time. Hitler and the majority of his generals believed because of their inability to invade England, the demonstration of Soviet weakness in Finland and the retarded status of Soviet mobilization, that the annexation of European Russia was the next logical move. Operation Barbarossa, as it was known, was originally planned to commence six weeks earlier, but the *Wehrmacht* was delayed by action in the Baltics. Unlike the *blitzkrieg* through Western Europe, the German invasion of the Soviet Union was not supported by a developed infrastructure, nor was it confined to a manageable area of operations. The Russian landscape was vast and unimproved, thus adding a significant natural obstacle belt for the mobile German forces. As the *Wehrmacht* ranged further and further from its sources of supply, every little bit of Soviet resistance put them even more behind on their time schedule. Like Napoleon's *Grande Armee*, the German *Wehrmacht* would face its better in the form of the brutal Russian winter. By December 6, 1941, the date of the Russian counter attack that marked the turn of the operation, the Germans had crossed the scorched Russian countryside to within forty miles of Moscow. Hitler ordered his commanders to come back victorious or not at all, a decision that would waste vast quantities of irreplaceable men and material. Even as Hitler was sacrificing nearly a million men in Russia, he remained extremely cautious when dealing with the United States. He continued to instruct his Navy to be careful not to sink American vessels, attempting to avoid repeating the potential for war that had followed the sinking of the *Athenia* in 1939. As with the Great War, America was slow to again enter the fight "over there" as Hitler emerged two decades later. It would take a major event to awake the sleeping giant, so far removed from the ravages of war.

The Pacific

Truly a world war, the Axis and Allied powers were about to do battle around the globe. From the waters of the Americas, to Asia, Africa and Europe, the world would brace as its fate was decided in the factories, on the battlefields and across the oceans of the planet. Following the gains of her early expansion, the Russo-Japanese War and WWI, Japan continued her expansion that had begun a century before during the Meji period. By 1941 Japan was the undisputed power of the Pacific, but her expansion came at a price. The United States invoked trade embargos in an attempt to deprive the island nation of the necessary natural resources that had to be imported. Building on the lack of Axis communication and coordination, Japan embarked on an escalation of hostilities that would have dire consequences for the Axis powers. Without the consent, or even the knowledge, of Hitler or Mussolini, Japan formulated and executed a plan designed to cripple the American Navy, not yet formally in the war, with one devastating blow. On December 7, 1941, "a date that will live in infamy", the Japanese attacked Pearl Harbor on the island of Oahu. The surprise attack on the United States Navy was just the incident necessary to wake the American giant.

Until Pearl Harbor, the isolationist viewpoint had prevailed within the United States. President Roosevelt had gradually taken steps to prepare for war, but similar to the English and French early attitudes, Americans were not willing to sacrifice more lives for another war on foreign soil. Although the lend-lease concept, as well as several other pro-Ally actions, had been in effect for a few years, Americans were not prepared to move past the stage of material commitment. The Great Depression had retarded the American industrial base and caused the populace, and the majority of their elected representatives, to focus almost completely on domestic issues. While partial mobilization and increased foreign trade stimulated the depressed economy, most citizens felt that world war certainly would not. Regardless of opinion prior to the attack on Pearl Harbor, December 7th awoke the sleeping giant and provided President Roosevelt the freedom to conduct the war with total support.

Although an extremely damaging attack, the Japanese objective to destroy the American Navy in Pearl Harbor had not been accomplished. In addition to several ships being deployed from the harbor, the Japanese strategists failed to correctly estimate the resolve and industrial strength of the United States. The Japanese desire to fight a limited war and quickly sue for the *status quo* would not come to be. Instead, with their single act of aggression, they had officially begun what could truly be defined as world war. Following the surprise attack the United States did not delay in formally declaring war on Japan. Because of treaty requirements, the European Axis powers were also drug into the war with America. Upholding their agreement with Japan, Germany and Italy begrudgingly declared war on the United States. The American Navy, much like the Army, quickly repaired and expanded to accommodate the total war effort. Anticipating the impending American entrance, the Allies designed a new strategy for the war in the winter and spring of 1941. During staff conversations between America, Britain and Canada, known as the ABC talks, the Allies decided to confront the Axis in both theaters. The general military strategy named the European Theater as the primary theater of operations. It called for the Allies to treat the Pacific Theater as a secondary theater, initially fighting defensive actions, until the assets of both theaters could be consolidated following victory in Europe. While this strategy was questioned from time to time, the Pacific remained the secondary effort fought primarily by the United States Navy, with soldiers supplementing Marine forces for amphibious assaults.

The Japanese had created a spectacular defensive belt in the Pacific comprised of strategic garrisons reinforced by naval and air assets. The Japanese soldiers were well trained, equipped and quickly earned the well-deserved reputation as ferocious, and fanatical fighters. The Japanese armed forces had the advantage of combat experience in the initial days of the war, but their limited industrial resources of the home islands and lack luster operational security would prove decisive in their defeat. Aiding the Allied war effort in the destruction of the Japanese Navy was their inability to secure lines of communication. From the outset of the Pacific fight, the Allies had the benefit of access to intercepted Japanese transmissions; a process known as "Magic", provided Allied commanders with Japanese intentions and even exact battle plans. This poor security would eventually allow the Americans to ambush and kill the head of the Japanese Navy, Isoroku Yamamoto, as he flew forward to inspect his men. Ironically the "Iron Admiral" killed in this aerial ambush was a former naval attaché to the United States, and had disagreed with his countrymen when they stated the United States would be a soft target.

Intercepted transmissions also played a key role in the turning battle of the Pacific Theater, Midway. The Allies began the war in the Pacific slowly, initially conducting smaller operations against the Marshalls, Wake and Marcus Islands, and air operations against Tokyo and Rabaul. As the Allies built combat power in theater and prepared for their second phase, the Japanese struck out to expand their Pacific perimeter and destroy Allied lines of communication. Their efforts culminated in failure during the battles of the Coral Sea and Midway. As a result of these battles, the Japanese dominance of the Pacific came to an end, passing the advantage to the Allied forces in the spring of 1942. With their powerful Navy and Air Force greatly reduced, the Japanese now moved to a war of attrition. While the Japanese prepared for their new defensive strategy, the Allies prepared to embark on the historical Pacific island-hopping campaigns. General MacArthur and Admiral Nimitz had designed the island-hopping strategy earlier in the war, but the conditions had not been set until a massive amount of destruction was inflicted on the Japanese at Midway.

The idea behind the successive amphibious assaults was to seize the most important, not necessarily the most difficult, islands and to by-pass the less strategic islands. This would limit unneeded loss of Allied lives and equipment, and allow the Japanese to rot in isolation while the Allies blazed a trail to Tokyo. Guadalcanal and Papua marked the beginning of the offensive campaign that continued all the way to Okinawa. While each island had its own story and defensive network, the Allies quickly discovered that the Japanese reputation of fighting to the death was in fact reality. Nevertheless, the strategy limited the effectiveness of numerous land locked Japanese garrisons, expedited the campaign, and allowed for an economy of force to be employed in the theater. By mid-1944, after a long debate over the merits of the Formosa vs. Philippine route to Japan, plans were in full swing for the invasion of the latter. The campaign that would fulfill General MacArthur's historic promise to return to the Philippines began on October 20, 1944, with the assault on Leyte.

European Theater thru October 1944

While Pacific planners were feverishly working over their maps of the Philippines, European planners were doing the same in preparation for the amphibious assault of France. As planners were preoccupied with their enormous task, front line forces were dying in large numbers. The Russians were battling a desperate fight that was gradually turning in their favor as 1942 was ushered in. The Allies knew that a cross-channel invasion was necessary, but at this early stage of American entry into the war, the men, material and experience were not yet available. As a result of numerous factors, the operation that would eventually be named Overlord, was postponed from year to year until conditions permitted the landings at Normandy on June 6, 1944, and the supporting landings on August 15th, code named Dragoon. The latter originally being designed to jointly clear the Germans from southern France.

In the meantime the Allied leaders understood the importance of taking the fight to the Axis forces. It was decided at the Anaconda Conference following Pearl Harbor that an Allied, Anglo-American, force would attack in North Africa in an attempt to work from the softer periphery to the hardened interior forces.

Just as the Russians had begun to take the initiative, so had the English with their success against the Italians in Egypt. The *Afrika Korps* received new leadership in early February 1942, as the esteemed "Desert Fox," General Erwin Rommel, arrived in Tripoli to assume command of the German forces. With the introduction of the Americans, in addition to the massive amounts of material support previously provided, the Allied coalition would eventually overwhelm the isolated Axis forces. The Allies, commanded by Lieutenant General Dwight D. Eisenhower, with the famous Brit Lieutenant General Bernard Law Montgomery leading the Eighth Army, were about to be introduced to the horrors of war. Despite initial success by the Rommel's forces, the Allies quickly learned how to survive, and more importantly win in combat. With the Axis forces cornered in North Africa, it was time to decide on the next course of action for the Allies. At Casablanca President Roosevelt was again confronted with the fact that an invasion of continental Europe was still not possible. Although unable to attend, Soviet Premier Joseph Stalin continued to call for a second front in Europe, but to Churchill's chagrin the Allies were faced with the realities of the European forces remaining idol for another year until an invasion force could be readied, or conducting a smaller attack in the Mediterranean. The Mediterranean would have to do. It was also at Casablanca that Roosevelt and Churchill declared the Allied political objective of "unconditional surrender." Scholars have debated that this may have prolonged the war, but regardless of duration, a clear political objective had been established for the militaries to support. With Sicily firmly in their sights, the two major forces in Allied direction, Roosevelt and Churchill, dispatched their troops in support of operation Husky. Building on the rapid success of Husky, General Eisenhower was instructed to quickly transition to operation Avalanche.

The Allies steadily increased offensive air operations in support of their eventual cross-channel invasion into France. The American and British air commands worked out a continuous bombing scenario designed to weaken the German industrial capacity and will to fight. While the focus on attriting German industrial output was eventually accomplished, the constant attacks on German citizens, in conjunction with the anticipated reprisals of unconditional surrender, only strengthened their resolve during the latter part of the war. The British focus of night carpet-bombing complemented the American daylight precision bombing concept. This bombing strategy would be gradually increased in Europe, with a similar unilateral strategy used by the Americans against the "paper cities" of Japan in the Pacific Theater. To the dismay of interwar air strategist, air power alone, while playing a vital role in strategic bombing and tactical support, could not win the war.

In an attempt to maintain the victorious momentum in southern Europe, the Allied staff designed a plan to shift to an amphibious assault on the Italian mainland, operation Avalanche. As the Allies hit the shores of Italy the "soft underbelly" of the Axis coalition, Mussolini tumbled from power quickly, but the subsequent surrender negotiations cost the invasion valuable time. Sweeping from the north the Germans refused to sacrifice the Italian peninsula. Their vicious counter-attack nearly pushed the Allies back into the sea, but by late 1943, Allied forces had begun to push steadily through Italy. At the same time, November 1943, the leaders of the United States, England and Russia met in Teheran. This was the first meeting where all three would be together. Stalin, who was unable to attend the other conferences, was now able to steal away from the war effort since the Germans were no longer threatening the gates of Moscow. He took advantage of the personal interaction with Roosevelt and Churchill to push hard for a definitive answer on when the second front would be opened and who would command it. At the conclusion of the conference, it was decided that General Eisenhower would be the Supreme Commander, Allied Expeditionary Force, with a tentative date of May 1, 1944, set for the invasion at that time. The Allies were bogged down in Italy, but with Eisenhower's departure command passed to the British. With the help of Churchill, who personally stopped on the peninsula following the Teheran Conference, the 30 Allied divisions committed to operation Avalanche were eventually rallied forward to victory. It would require direct input from the prime minister, a daring assault on Anzio, and several more months of hard fighting before the Allies entered Rome on June 4, and then attacked the Gothic Line on August 25, 1944.

In England, operation Roundup, the cross-channel invasion plan that called for a three-division front, was renamed operation Overlord and increased to a five-division front. The mutual Allied air effort was increased as troops were massed in English holding areas for the principal Allied amphibious assault of the war. German planners were faced with the overwhelming task of defending a massive amount of French coastline. The German command anticipated the assault would take place at Pas de Calais, a narrow portion of the English Channel, and had designed a defense based on rapid reaction forces instead of attempting to stop the impending amphibious assault on every beach. The Allies were quick to expand on elaborate deception measures that reinforced German suspicions of Pas de Calais when they discovered the Axis plans and preparations. This strategy was later changed in late 1943, when Field Marshal Erwin Rommel was named as the commander of Army Group B. He immediately attempted to fortify key beaches because he did not believe that the German forces would have the freedom of maneuver, based on Allied air superiority, to execute the existing defense.

"Too little, too late" can be said for the new German defensive plan. The Allies named June 1, 1944, as the new D-day, but based on weather Eisenhower was forced again to postpone the assault.

On June 6, 1944, a large portion of the German commanders, to include Rommel who was attending his wife's birthday party in Germany, were away from their posts to participate in war games, ironically focused on the possibility of a French invasion. Unlike the German command, the Allies were present for duty on the night of June 5, 1944. An invasion fleet of 2,700 ships steamed for the Normandy coast as thousands of Allied paratroopers soared overhead. The landing sites were broken down into three separate areas, with the Americans responsible for two and a joint Anglo-Canadian assault force responsible for the third which was further subdivided into landing sites Gold, Juno and Sword. Omaha, one of the American beaches, happened to be heavily fortified and well defended. An extra German division was even on site for training as Rangers scaled the rocky cliffs of Pointe du Hoc. Assaulting infantrymen and combat engineers, who were lucky enough to make it to the beach alive, crawled exposed across the open strip of death and complete mayhem. The other two beaches were less bloody. An error in navigation accounted for a delay on the second American beach, Utah. Meanwhile, the British contingent made a remarkable seven miles inland towards the village of Caen, even after stopping for a spot of tea. By nightfall the Allied forces had pushed off the beaches and into an even worse obstacle that had not been identified during the intelligence preparation, they were the accursed Normandy hedgerows.

The Allies were contained in the hedgerows for the next few months as the existing obstacles were reinforced by Rommel's outstanding command of the German defense. By chance, the Field Marshal's staff car was attacked by an American fighter plane, seriously wounding Rommel, who would commit suicide a few days later as a result of being implicated in a failed assassination attempt on Hitler. With American ingenuity and a less able German commander, the Allied forces began to make headway in late July. While the combat troops were fighting inland, the Allied support troops were feverishly massing men and material on the

Normandy lodgment sites for the eventual breakthrough of the hedgerows. On the same day that the Allies attacked the Gothic Line in Italy, August 25, 1944, portions of the Allied continental forces marched into Paris. The Allies were assaulting deeper into continental Europe in the late summer and early fall of 1944. By October the Allies had stretched their supply lines to their absolute limit. The First Army crossed into Germany and attacked the outlying portions of the Siegfried Line. The Seventh Army had made it to Belfort Gap while Patton's Third Army was pushing into Luxembourg and Alsace-Lorraine. With the lack of supplies halting the Allies, the Germans were able to take advantage of the lull by regrouping their forces and further fortifying their defensive positions.

After two years of training, the 95th Infantry Division was finally ordered to transports in early September. By mid-September, the Allies had launched Operation Market-Garden and the last of the transports carrying the Victory Division had sailed for Normandy. The 95th disembarked at Omaha beach, the site of the fiercest fighting on D-day just two months past. Upon arrival, the division participated briefly in the Red Ball Express prior to moving further into France by truck and train, and eventually staged near Norriey-Le-Sec in preparation to be pushed forward. Only twenty miles from the city, they were close enough to hear the bombardment of Metz through the night, realizing that soon they would experience the direct fire battle. The division was now part of the XX Corps, more specifically, part of General Patton's famous Third Army. The Third Army, under the command of "Old Blood and Guts" was one of the driving forces in maintaining the Allied momentum in the face of stiff German opposition. Patton wasted no time in sharing his vision of maneuver with all the field grade officers, and one officer and noncommissioned officer from each company in the division. Marching fire in support of a continued advance would be one of the general's first lessons for the untested leadership of the 95th Infantry Division. Patton opposed digging

in, and instead informed his attentive audience that contrary to
Army field manuals, he expected his subordinates to continue
forward behind the cover of their weapon systems.

Charles R. Fowler
Artillery Officer and Infantry Rifle Platoon
Leader 377th Infantry Regiment

My name is Charles Fowler. My first military experience was in
1938 when I joined the National Guard, Battery B, 45th Division in
Anadarko, Oklahoma. It was a 105mm Howitzer unit. We went to
training one summer at Camp Bullis, Texas when General Patton
was in charge of the training. During the last day of the training
exercise I had my appendix removed at Brooks General Hospital
when it was just two years old. It didn't have air conditioning
then. They just had big windows and fans in the hospital. When
I was through at the hospital they shipped me by train back to
Oklahoma. In September of 1939 I went to Oklahoma A&M
College in Stillwater, Oklahoma. They later changed it to Oklahoma
State University. I took advanced Reserve Officer Training Corps
training while the war was on. They called the National Guard up,
but the executive officer didn't call me from college because he had
a volunteer to take my place. Instead I stayed in ROTC. Before
we graduated in the spring of 1943 the ROTC people went to Fort
Sill, Oklahoma in March to get all our clothing and everything.
When we graduated in May we were sent to Fort Benning, Georgia
where we took the officer's training course.

They did not give us 2nd Lieutenant out of college then. We
were mixed with Ohio State University students and sergeants
that were sent to the school. Approximately twenty to twenty-five
percent of them didn't make it. I had friends that didn't make it.
After I was commissioned I was sent to Camp Blanding in Florida
to teach basic training. I was only down there for two or three
months before they sent me to Spartanburg, South Carolina for

training. I went to school for the 105mm Canon, I forget where it was at, maybe it was a t Fort Benning. Anyway, I was sent to the 95th Division at Indiantown Gap, Pennsylvania in early 1944. While there I was sent to mule-packing school in West Virginia and then the division maneuvered in West Virginia. I vividly remember crossing the Black Water Canyon for some reason. Then we were sent to a staging area in Massachusetts and shipped to England. We were in England for two or three weeks until the division went across and landed at Omaha beach. They were short of help, and I remember that since I had worked in an oil field that I went down and helped them hook up the trucks and the guns to lift them out of the hole.

William Lake
Anti-Tank Infantryman 377th Infantry Regiment

My name is William Lake, Private First Class of tank company 377th Infantry Regiment of the 95 Infantry Division. I was drafted at the age of 18 in to the United States Army at Fort Sheridan, Illinois. We stayed there probably three days and got issued military clothing. I don't recall getting any inoculations and we did not get GI haircuts, never did. They put us on a train at Pullman and although the Army had strict regulations about two men even sitting on the same bed playing cards, the lower bunks had two men in them. Nothing seemed to be a miss. We were on the train quite a bit because we went 450 or 500 miles. We had at least one overnight and I can't remember if there was a second, but I can remember being in Kentucky and the next thing I knew we got the train stopped and we heard some trucks, and everybody was asking: "Where are we?" Some of the drivers said, "This is the 95th Infantry Division, Camp Indiantown Gap, Pennsylvania", which was located near Harrisburg. Then morale started falling, because so many of us had fair education and myself I had been working in the aircraft industry and naturally I wanted to be with aircraft.

We got to the unit there and they isolated us into separate barracks, so we wouldn't contaminate the regulars that were already there. It was wintertime in Pennsylvania when we took approximately eight-weeks of basic training and this is when the Army was giving 19-weeks in the basic training replacement centers. They sent us to our assigned companies and we got advanced training there. Mine was an anti-tank company; we had a 57mm towed gun and a ton and a half truck that pulled it. It weighed about 2000-pounds and it was flat trajectory and it was thought to be a wonderful weapon until somebody discovered that German tanks were made out of steel. High explosive rounds were ineffective except on church people, but you couldn't very well shoot at church people, because the gun wouldn't elevate. The Armor piercing shells were a special shell that the British had devised, and having never shot at a German vehicle, I don't know if they were effective or not.

A rifle company had 186 people roughly and an anti-tank company was only about 130-135 but we had the same number of officers. All our officers were 90-day wonders, including the Captain I think. Now Captain Rosoff was from I think Philadelphia and may have gotten ROTC out of college because he had been preparing himself to be a lawyer. We had one Lieutenant from Wisconsin and one from Oregon State and one from Texas. Mine was from Georgia. Most of our people were Midwesterners. The Army later disbanded these companies, especially during the battle of the Bulge, when they needed more people.

I only went on one 25-mile road march that was all that was offered. Sometimes if you're on KP you get out of details. I went through eight-weeks of basic and shot sharp shooter on the rifle range; I think I was three points below expert. I didn't think about it at the time, but I'm glad I didn't make expert, because that's where they selected their snipers. I didn't know that at the time. I carried and M1 until the day we lost three people. I turned my rifle in and got a 45 pistol after that. I had moved up in the chain of the gun squadron. Even my squad leader didn't have a pistol, he had to carry a carbine. A pistol was sort of a status symbol.

But back to my training; then we went out to West Virginia, for so-called mountain maneuvers, where we learned to rappel down cliff sides, with a little rope under your rear end you kicked yourself away from the hill and rappelled down. We learned to survive in the pathways; they weren't roads they were pathways in the West Virginia hills. There were snakes, rain and mud, and everybody was lost because we had no maps. It didn't last very long, it was only maybe two-weeks and here was another one of those fast decisions: "Grab all your gear and get on the vehicles" and we went back to Indiantown Gap. We cleaned up the equipment and turned part of it in and by then they had orders for seven-days leave. We went home on the trains and of course troop trains; all trains in those days were overcrowded, like you would see sometimes in movies where everybody is crowded together in the walkways.

When we got back we didn't stay very long, maybe one or two days and then we got on a troop train to Camp Myles Standish in Dobbins, Massachusetts south of Boston. There we got in the water using the buddy system and tried to ensure that everybody could at least keep himself above the water. I got the inoculations and I don't really know what, but we did some things that kept us busy for about a week. We got some passes to go into town, I was 18-years old, not allowed to drink, not allowed to buy cigarettes and I was fighting for democracy. I can remember I went to see the old North Church that I remembered from Long Fellow Ponds. We got on the big ship, we didn't see the ship we went out of the warehouses up a gang plank, there was a big jumble there where the First Sergeants were calling out the names to make sure that you got on the boat. This was the *USS West Point*, formerly the *SS America* luxury liner. We were crammed in to state rooms but they had like any troop ship, bunks anyplace they could put them.

I saw the big ballroom one time and it still had its decorations, it didn't look GI. We had boat drills along the way before we got to Liverpool, England. When we got in a band was out there playing. We got on the famous little British trains and went down south, almost all the way to London, to an area called Camp Barton Stacey. These were Quonset huts, they still had the bomb protection and they were grown over by grass, this was in 1944.

Fred B. Love Jr.
Infantryman 377th Infantry Regiment

My name is Fred B. Love Jr. I'll start my story with the ASTP. I was with the 76th division taking training at the border out west; the Company Commander called me in and asked me what my serial number was. I told him my serial number and he said: "You're supposed to report for ASTP," and I had no idea what he was talking about. I ended up in Blacksburg, VA and I took a bunch of tests and they determined that I was eligible to go to college so I ended up at Wigermere College. I went there for about nine months before they discontinued the program. I ended up going to Indian Town Gap to join the 95th division. Lieutenant Waiver talked to me and asked me if I was a Private and I told him yes, the next day I was a PFC, that was my first promotion. I had been in the service for 18 months or something like that. We took some mountain training there, some advanced training and bayonet training to prepare us to go overseas. We got on a ship that left out of Boston and sailed across to England and went in there and stayed for a little while.

Daniel F. McCarthy IV
Supply Sergeant 377th Infantry Regiment

My name is Dan McCarthy. I was inducted into the Army at Leavenworth, Kansas July 1st, 1942. From there I was shipped to

Camp Swift, Texas where the 95th Division was activated on July 15, 1942, and I became the supply sergeant for the 377th Infantry Regiment. On May 30th, 1943, we moved to the vicinity of Leesville, Louisiana for what we called the "Swamp Maneuvers". There was lots of water and snakes. As was the case in the Army, everything during the maneuvers had to be done in the dark of night so as supply sections we had to draw and distribute rations at night. One morning after we had worked all night, one of the men slid his legs down into his pup tent and discovered a snake had decided it liked the warmth of the bedroll in the tent. The next day he went into Leesville and bought a hammock and strung it up between two trees. The next morning when the soldier went to climb into the hammock, he found it was occupied by another snake. During the rest of maneuvers, the soldier decided to sleep on the cold, hard metal bed of a 2 x 4 truck.

On November 1st, 1943, the division transferred from the swamps in Louisiana to the sand dunes at Camp Coxcomb, California, where the temperature was 120 degrees during the day time and the sand got so cold at night, that we had to line our canvas cots with paper to keep from freezing. The sand was so cold that I kept a case of beer buried under my cot and it was the right drinking temperature for me to have a cold beer every morning at breakfast. It was tastier than the cold pancakes I could manage to get back to my tent from the mess tent.

In February 1944, we left the heat of the desert to make a 7-day train trip in a blinding snowstorm to Indiantown Gap, Pennsylvania. The trip took the "shortest" distance between California and Pennsylvania by going through Canada, thus arriving in Pennsylvania from the north over Niagara Falls. This train route took us through Southwestern Kansas making a distance of 25 miles within a one-day period. This was within a few miles of Larned, Kansas, where my parents resided at the time. Still I couldn't let them know I was in the vicinity. During the 7-day train ride, the time of over 100 daylight hours was spent playing Black

Jack. I won a total of $.25, which was an average of about $.02 an hour [Laughs].

While in Indiantown Gap we were sent to West Virginia for 2 weeks of mountain maneuvers. It rained so hard that we had to pile our cases of C-rations at least 2 high so they wouldn't float down the mountain. We had a detachment of pack mules assigned to our regiment. One night I had spread my bed roll in an opening in the trees along the trail going up the mountain. It so happened this opening was a few yards below the opening where the mules were bivouacked. I was asleep when one of the soldiers assigned to the mule detachment galloped up the trail on a horse and thinking he was at the opening where the mules were tethered, reigned the horse into the opening where I was sleeping. The horse stopped as there was a wall of trees ahead. He was standing with his front legs less than a foot beyond my head and his rear legs along my outstretched legs. This could have been the first casualty of scalping during World War II if the horse had been a foot shorter on his jump into the clearing in which I was bedded down.

On the trip back to Indian Town Gap, one of the drivers near the back of the convoy shifted his truck out of gear and could not get it back into gear. The truck gathered enough speed that the speedometer broke. The corporal was a good driver and controlled the truck as it passed the convoy without any mishap. It went through a stop sign at an intersecting highway before it finally rolled to a stop. The corporal was a private driving a truck the following day.

On July 26, 1944, the division moved to Camp Miles Standish, Massachusetts, where we made a 35-mile trip to our EPO for boarding the *USS West Point*, which sailed on August 9th, 1944, for Liverpool, England. We docked in England on August 17, 1944. The *West Point* was fast enough that it sailed by itself instead of sailing with the convoy which was awaiting to depart for England. When we were just south of Iceland, we received word that a pack of German subs was coming from the north to try to intercept us so we changed course down adjacent to the coast of Spain and up north to still be able to land at Liverpool. From there we boarded a train and sped across England to Camp Barton Stacy near Winchester, England.

Joseph W. Napier
Infantryman 377th Infantry Regiment

My name is Joseph Napier. I was born March 12, 1925 in Skidmore, Missouri. I worked on Bilby Ranch, Northwest of Skidmore, since I was 14 years old. I graduated from high school in 1943. Being that my birthday was the 12th of March I had to get a deferment because when I turned 18 you had to register, but they gave me a six-month deferment. After the six-month deferment I was called to go to Fort Leavenworth, Kansas to be inducted into the Army. When I got down to Fort Leavenworth they told me I had passed everything, but that I could go back home and get my affairs in order and come back later, which I did. Then the draft board did not call me for some time until finally I went down after the 1st of 1944 and asked them why they hadn't called me and they told me that they had a lot of draftees and that they didn't need me at that time. So I asked when the next ones were going to go and they told me Monday and I told them, "well, I want to go" and they sent me off on Monday. When I got down to the reception center in Kansas they told me I had to take the physical over because it had been more than 60 days, so I took it over and passed again. They told me to go home and get my affairs in order like they did before, but I said, "No, no I've already been through that, I want to go on." So they told me to go over to a barracks and wait. The next day I was sworn into the Army and issued uniforms.

That was in May 1944. They told me to read the bulletin board every day so I did and found out I was on kitchen police. I didn't know what kitchen police was, but I soon found out. It was to me, washing pots and pans. I got back late that night after having KP all day and went to bed. When I woke up I checked the bulletin board but my name wasn't on it so I was just around in the barracks all day until I checked the bulletin board the next day and my name was up there for KP again. The weekend came around then and I read on the bulletin board Saturday evening that I was on KP again and that I was also on guard. So I said to the sergeant that I couldn't be both and he said, "Well, you're on guard." The next day I was on guard at the main gate of Fort Leavenworth, Kansas. I didn't know what I was doing. Saluted anything that came along, didn't know one officer from another, or even if they were officers. People were coming to see their sons and daughters off, so we looked in the trunks of the cars and for cameras or suspicious characters, whoever they were. On Monday I read the board and I was on kitchen police again and I thought boy this was really something. I also noticed that I was on shipping orders so I went to the sergeant again. I told him that I was on both and he told me to go to the barracks and stay there, not to leave the barracks, so that's what I did. The next day they marched us across the river to Beverly, Kansas where we got on a train and road it for three to four days. We were zigzagging one way or another, we didn't know where we were going until we got into a station where the soil looked different and I asked a guy where we were and he said we were in Oklahoma. We got onto buses in this town after that and I asked another guy where we were going and he told me we were headed for this camp and that it was an infantry camp. I said, "Oh boy I'm in the infantry," I had wanted to go in the Air Force, but wound up in the infantry.

We got there and we had a formation and all fell out. We had an orientation and this and that and then this sergeant started bellowing down there, "You! You! You! and You! All have to have a haircut!" Well, I said, "I just got a haircut in Leavenworth I don't think I need one?" He said, "Oh yes you need a haircut soldier, move out." So I went to a barbershop there on the post and I noticed there were no mirrors in this barbershop. The barber was standing there and he said, "You look like a nice fellow, how do you like to have your hair cut?" I asked him to just trim it up a little and told him that I had just had a haircut a Leavenworth about six days ago. He said, "OK" and then went zip- zip and I didn't have any hair left. I had just gotten a GI haircut. So from there we did calisthenics, we did problems, we fired our rifles and drilled and did forced marches and ran a mile before breakfast, sometimes two. A lot of the times they would scream and holler at us to fall out in our Class A uniforms and our Class B uniforms, and we'd fall out in Class A uniforms and they'd say, "what's a matter with you guys I didn't say Class uniforms, I said Class B uniforms!" I could see what was going on, they were breaking us down to think that the Army way was the only way. So we finally got over the basics and if you were a good soldier, they picked three out of the company and I was fortunate enough to be one of them, they let us go to a rodeo. The fellows that put this rodeo on were local boys and they were good. They had some little pigs, one had a little dot on his nose and looked like Adolph Hitler, and that's what they called him, and they Tojo there too. Hey were selling the pigs for war bonds. There was this old Texan there, we were right near Taylor, Texas and Gladewater and the oil fields, and figured he must own a few oil wells. He had a big Stetson hat on and he said, "Well, if you boys can fight the war I'll buy the bonds!" So he give about $1,000 and another fellow bid against him so he bought Tojo. I figured they probably had plenty of cash considering I was only getting $50 a month.

We got a delay en-route to go home. I never got a furlough the entire time I was in the Army. So I went on the train that we went out on and started zig, zagging again. That's the way it was because they didn't want the troop movements tracked. I had top lift with the fellow that I trained with as we were headed for St. Louis, Missouri. We started talking about how we could make it home a few days earlier if we could just get off the train, so we got off at the next stop, Texarkana, Texas. We were in the train yard and went up to buy a ticket to Kansas City, Missouri, that's where I had to go to go home. So I went up to a ticket booth to buy a ticket and the guy behind me said, "soldier you don't buy your ticket here, you buy your ticket over there, this is for the colored folks only." That's when I realized that there was segregation in the South. I had never known that before. Well, I came home for four or five days and then headed back to Kansas City where Toplift was going to meet me. Well, something happened and he ended up not getting on his train so I got into St. Louis and from there they took us through Baltimore, Ohio from there. I didn't see Toplift until about one day later than I got there. He had somehow gotten on a different train. We were now at Fort Meade, Maryland where we got all new clothes. We went from there to Camp Shanks, New York. Andy Northcut had trained down in Texas too, but he was in a different company down there, but anyway we became friends and were talking when I mentioned that I would like to go to New York City if they would let us. He said he would like to go too so we got passes and we were u on the Empire State Building and Fifth Avenue and walked around and had a pretty good time, but we couldn't find the bus to go back to camp. So I asked a fellow there and he didn't even speak English, so I thought we were already in a foreign country. We finally found it and as we were waiting for the bus there was a restaurant there with banana cream pie. It was real tall and looked real good and I told Andy, "You know, we'll probably never see one of those pies again, I'm going to buy it and eat it." So we did. We got on the bus and went back to Camp Shanks and as we were walking down the street I started to get sick, I had been drinking a little beer on top of the pie and it didn't sit very well, in fact it all came back up on camp.

A couple of days went by until they marched us down to the shipyard. We got on a ship and late in the evening we sailed out of the harbor. I could see the Statue of Liberty out of the porthole and I told Andy we might never see that again. We went out to sea and the next morning when I got up and went up on deck everywhere I looked was a ship. Now those ships were zigzagging and zigzagging all the time. You could tell by the churn of the water behind them. About ten days later we got into England. It was very interesting, they had these submarine gates, they would open and pull them back, and then they'd shove us in.

Richard H. Schoen
Medic 377th Infantry Regiment

My name is Richard H. "Dick" Schoen. I was born August 10th, 1923, to Kathryn and Clifford Schoen of Toledo, Ohio. I was the third child of seven. Our family of seven went on to raise 67 grandchildren. My father Clifford A. Schoen was a machine gunner with the American Expeditionary Force in the First World War. My brother Jack was commissioned as a radar officer, my brother Jim was commissioned as a Seabee with the Navy and served in the Pacific during the Second World War. I attended Jesuit parochial school for my first eight years and then was sent to a Catholic high school for another four before enrolling in John Carroll University in Cleveland, Ohio, a Jesuit school for men. I was in my third semester of my sophomore year when the Japanese bombed Pearl Harbor. I remember coming home to the dormitory that night. The lights were out and it was quiet as a church mouse when I said, "What's going on? Where is everybody?" and all I heard was "Schoen SSSHHH!" and I said, "What's up?" They had just bombed Pearl Harbor. That was the first any of us had heard of the war. Being in school we were advised by the authorities at John Carroll that if we wanted to complete our degree work before we went into the service we should join the ERC, which was the Enlisted Reserve Corps. I followed this advice, hoping I could finish my degree before I was drafted, but it didn't turn out that way. The Enlisted Reserve Corps was disbanded and we all were drafted, not drafted, but instead we were called enlisted men because we had all enlisted in the ERC. I was taken in at Camp

Perry, Ohio for my induction. I can remember when they took my blood test, the syringe separated from the needle and the blood ran down my arm and I said, "Oh boy, I feel kind of wiped out" and then I went out cold. The next day I got my classification as a medic. Prior to that time if I smelled either or alcohol I would get faint, but there I was with a year of biology at John Carroll University so they put me in the Medical Corps.

From there I went up to Camp Grant, Illinois, in February. We lived in a 15x15 tent on a concrete slab with a potbellied stove, straw tick on cots. We slept with four men into a tent in full uniform because it was so cold up there at that time. When they said, "Fall Out!" we just jumped out of bed and fell out. I finished my medical basic and while I was finishing up the Army started the ASTP, the Army Specialized Training Program, so I volunteered and was qualified for it and was sent to Michigan State University at Lansing where they had courses in government, engineering and language. I chose engineering. I was up there for nine months. We lived like a fraternity in a fraternity house and everything, to include 3500 Co-Eds on campus. We would march to school and sing our songs as loud as we could, trying to out sing the air cadets on campus. On Saturday afternoons, we would have a dress parade and after that I would hitchhike home to Toledo. I thought I had the Army just where I wanted it! But that didn't turn out either. Just prior to the closing of the ASTP program the air cadets came through Michigan State looking for men who could qualify for pilot training so I went up to Kellogg Field in Michigan. I took a simple mental exam and passed so I was sent down to Miami Beach where I lived in the San Moritz Hotel. The government was paying $35 a day for that, right on the beach! That was something to write home about! While we were there I took the 64-physical, the mental exam again and a psychomotor exam and was qualified for the pilot training pre-flight program. But there again the Army stepped in. This was prior to the invasion so the government decided that anybody who was not in pre-flight at that time and had come from the ground forces had to go back to the ground forces. So they gave me another physical and I remember at the bottom of the physical it asked if I knew of any physical reason that I couldn't serve overseas duty and I had just passed the very difficult 64-physical so I said, "No, I can serve overseas duty."

So they put me on the train and I ended up in Indiantown Gap, Pennsylvania, a staging area for the 95th Infantry Division. They dropped me off at the dispensary and I thought that they were going to check my medical records, but no more so than that they assigned me to K Company, 3rd Battalion, 377th Infantry Regiment as a medical aid man. When I got there I wasn't too well accepted. I had come from college, from the ASTP and air cadet programs while these guys had been together for two years through Louisiana, the desert maneuvers, and were well-trained, good men. I just wasn't too well accepted there. It finally came to the point where they were talking about assault mountain climbing school at Seneca Rock, West Virginia, so I thought if I'd volunteer for that I might be a little more sociable with these guys, and I did. The only two guys in the whole battalion that volunteered for this were myself and Sergeant "Lefty" Sadjewski from Detroit, Michigan. So we went over from Indiantown Gap, Pennsylvania, and we were climbing a 980-foot exposer with pitons, and snap links, we took deliberate falls from 40-feet, we did tairolian traverses across ravines, we evacuated litters off the mountains, and you name it. The idea was that we were going to set the assault lines, they figured the division would be going through Yugoslavia, so we would set the assault lines and the troops could follow us in. After I finished the assault climbing training the whole division was sent up to West Virginia for mountain training. While we were on maneuvers my captain asked if I would like to go to medical administrative officers school and I said, "sure would." He said, "well, I put you in for that." So before the orders were accepted all the way back the Army decided to freeze the whole division, so I was stuck with the division. We sailed out of Boston on August

10th, my birthday, on the *USS West Point,* a big converted troop ship, and got into England.

William W. Taylor, Jr.
Infantryman 377th Infantry Regiment

My name is William W. Taylor, Jr. On December 7th, 1941 I was setting at home listening to the radio when I heard the bad news that the Japanese had attacked Pearl Harbor. I decided at that point that I should go and enlist. But I had a problem, in that my Mother and Father wouldn't sign for me. No matter how much I begged they wouldn't sign. Instead my Mother told me that, "They'll get you when they need you." So when I turned eighteen in January 1943 I registered and by April I was in the Army. I went down to Fort McClellan, Alabama for basic training. Basic training was an interesting thing, but I won't go into great detail on that. I joined the 95th in March of 1944. Now this was a bunch of guys that had been together for a long time. They had been together since the division was activated and here I was, kind of the new guy on the block. I wasn't too well received in many ways. I think that the guys wanted you to prove yourself in order to be accepted.

I went along for a while and played the game. They told me that we were going to West Virginia on maneuvers and that I would never make it. I didn't say anything and we went to the maneuvers up in the West Virginia Mountains. We finished the maneuvers by walking forever up a mountain with rucksacks. People got tired and I got to the point where if I sat down I figured I wouldn't get up again. At first I would sit down with that rucksack and roll over on my stomach to get up. I finally thought that I had better not even get down again. Going up the mountain the platoon leader said, "You better sit down, everyone is taking a break." I said, "No Sir, I can't do that." Then the platoon sergeant, "Big Bear" Van Cleaf said, "You better sit down Taylor" and I said, "No I can't do that." Then a squad leader said the same thing, but I just kept going because I knew I'd never get up again. I made it to the top of the mountain and the company commander said, "Where's your platoon" and I said, "Down the mountain Sir." He said, "Where's your squad leader" and so forth, but I was the first one up there.

When we got back to Indiantown Gap the platoon leader came to me and asked, "Taylor, are you a private or a PFC?" I said, "I'm a private Sir." I figured he was going to make me a PFC, but that night I got into a problem with a corporal. He was still harassing me, I won't go into all the details, but he made the mistake of swinging at me. I kind of knocked him out of his shoes that night. I had him on the floor, I thought there were only three of us that were on the second floor of the barracks, and then I was trying to get him to get up and go another round, or enjoy another round as I looked at it. When all of a sudden the door swung open and old "Big Bear" Van Cleaf stormed through and said, "What the hell is going on out here!" I didn't know he was in his room, but I tried to explain that I was trying to get this Yellow SOB to get up and fight. "Big Bear" Van Cleaf said, "Take him outside, you're making too much noise in here!" and he slammed the door and went back into his room. I thought, "There goes my PFC!" Well, I made PFC and they began to accept me then.

Willis E. Young
Infantryman 377th Infantry Regiment

I was in Company B of the 377th Infantry. I joined the Army in January 1944, they initially sent me home for a couple weeks then I went back the 1st of February. First thing they called a bunch of us for KP and I was the first name they called along with two more guys. The lieutenant that was calling off the names said, "Young you're in charge." I don't know if he thought that I was the only one who could read or not, I know one of them other guys couldn't. They put me in the officer's mess as a mess sergeant. The mess hall was a big long H-shaped building with all the troops from Fort

Sheridan eating there on the different sides. They put somebody in charge of each of the sides, and I had the officer's part in the center. About four or five days later I was in the mess hall cleaning it up, it must have been 9 o'clock in the morning, and the lieutenant came running in there and wanted to know what I was doing. I told him I signed the papers a couple days ago that said I was to stay at Fort Sheridan as a mess sergeant, "Yeah", he said "but you better read the shipping list today." Wouldn't you know it, I was the first name on it and the other two boys were on it too.

By noon we were on a train heading for Indiantown Gap, Pennsylvania to join the 95th Infantry Division, which was just moving there from the Nevada desert. I took my basic training with the 95th, in fact Company B gave me my basic raining. Basic training ended more or less as you progressed. They ended up letting us out of it in about four different groups. If you goofed up a little bit you went a couple weeks longer and if you goofed up more than that you went a few more weeks. After basic training they sent me to camouflage school for a week, I don't know what they thought I learned there except how to dig holes and put branches on them [Laughs]. When I got back nobody listened to me anyway when I tried to tell them something about camouflage? When I was at this school the last thing we had to do was dig a hole and camouflage it. There were two guys per company, except for Company B, I don't know why, but that meant I had to dig the hole myself. I dug the hole and throwed the dirt back behind a bush out of sight and then laid sticks over the hole with a bunch of leaves on it. Along came a one star general and his entire touring group that just went down the line in rank with a poor old lieutenant trailing behind. When they got to my hole the major started on me, "soldier you were supposed to dig a hole and camouflage it, where is it?" About that time the old general fell in it. He kind of sputtered and popped a little bit and then he forced a smile. Some of those officers, especially the junior ones, were real sober about it, they didn't laugh. The poor old general falls in a hole [Laughs].

Right now they wanted my name, rank and serial number. It's a good thing I didn't have any rank because I probably would have lost it. The lieutenant came up then and wanted to know what company I was from and everything else. I thought my God, I'm going to have to pay for his dirty pants. We got all done and filled up the holes and the general went on his way.

When we got back to camp they started to let groups of three off. Before I got half way to the barracks somebody stuck their head out of the orderly room and said, "the captain wants to see you right now!" I hurried up and put my duffle bag away and went to see what was the matter with the captain. I went in there and the first thing he wanted to know was if I had any money. I thought oh my God, now I have to pay for his clothes. I told him yes, I had some money, and then he asked a few more questions about what had gone on out there on the hill. I said you mean the general falling in a hole, and he said, "yes" and then he went to laughing. I figured it wasn't so serious then, before that I thought they might shoot a private next sunrise [Laughs]. He wanted to know if I had money for a trip home because the telephone call from the general suggested that I get a furlough home. He said, "when a one star general tells a captain that somebody should get a furlough you don't argue with him, so you have twenty minutes to catch the bus out of here."

From there we went down to Seneca Rock in West Virginia and learned how to rappel down a rope without breaking your neck. We were at Seneca Rock taking this training when we got word to head back to our camp. That was June the 6th when the invasion was going on in northern France. As soon as we got back to camp we had to get everything ready and it wasn't long until they sent us up to Taunton, Massachusetts to wait for a boat to come get us. On about the 9th of August we got on the boat and started about an eight-day trip to England. We ended up landing at Liverpool where we got on a train and went to London and then down to Camp Barton Stacy, just north of Winchester, England.

We did a little training there, mainly we walked up and down all the roads they could find for us until they decided to send us over to France.

As soon as we got to England my brother, who was in the Air Force as a crew chief on B-17 Bombers, came to see me. He knew that I was coming across because I was up as far as Taunton, Massachusetts, and usually when you're up that far you're not going to the Pacific through Boston Harbor. So he went down to the Eighth Air Force Headquarters and asked about where the 95th Division was in England. He went from a lieutenant, to a captain, to a major, to a colonel and finally they said come in here, this gentleman wants to see you. General Spatz, the commander, said, "what are you asking questions about the 95th Division for?" and he said, "I have a brother in the 95th, that's all, I figured he was coming here since they've been up by Boston." The General rubbed his chin and said, "When do you get your next leave?" They would fly a couple round trips and then they'd get a weekend off. He told him and the General said, "forget that rear echelon, next time you get your leave come see me", so he did. The General told him to go down to Camp Barton Stacy by Winchester but when he got down there some good soul Englishman thought he was a spy and sent him fifteen extra miles into Winchester. So he got to walk back another fifteen miles when he found out where the camp was [Laughs]. If that wouldn't have happened he would have beat us to the camp. We had just got our barracks bags in the barracks and hadn't even made up the bunks or anything else when he stuck his head in the door. Some lieutenant said I know where Young is so he finally made it down to our barracks.

He stayed there that night with us and went back to his base in the morning. He was not thrilled by infantry food, or the infantry for that matter. See they had it pretty good, they ate fresh bacon and fresh eggs, not the powdered eggs like we had. Army food was a lot better than some people gave them credit for, there were times I would have liked to have had some of that later on. I told some guys after the war that you should have gone and ate with the English or the Germans, either one if you didn't like the American food. They didn't eat very high on the hog, those old hard biscuits the English had, you could break your teeth on those things. The Germans pretty much lived on sour brautten, black bread and a little cheese. I don't know how an Army could operate like that but they did. Anyway, around Labor Day I got a pass to London, England and I met the biggest part of my brother's crew and then we headed back to camp. It was quite an interesting sight, but it was unbelievable the amount of damage that had been done in that town. Of course I guess there were plenty of German towns that looked just about like it. There were just blocks and blocks of nothing but rubble. It took a lot of guts for those people to keep going under those conditions, it really did.

Anthony N. Petraglia
Infantryman 378th Infantry Regiment

My name is Tony Petraglia. I joined the division right off of desert maneuvers in California. We later went to mountain maneuvers in West Virginia. We were down there quite a while and then back to the gap until we were finally shipped overseas. I was in high school when the war broke out, and I had enough credits so I got out of school, in those days they ran semesters by A and B, six months per semester. So I was in 12 B at the time after the war broke out and I had enough credits to graduate, so I graduated early, earlier than my class, in fact when my class graduated, I was overseas. I got my diploma in 12 B instead of 12 A. I had enough credits and that's when I went into the service. That was in February 1944. I took my basic training right from the 95th division training division. I took a 17 week basic but they covered it in eight weeks that's how well trained they were. So actually, I was trained by the 95th infantry division and in those days if you went into the service you were trained at different training camps, but I was trained straight from the division because we came off the desert maneuvers. What they did was form cadre, what they called a cadre outfit. They were trained men and they were the ones who put you through your training.

I remember this one time we were training to fire rifles, here Top Sergeant Milo, he was 16-year veteran at the time, a regular Army man. He was a big Hawaiian and he was going to bring me up to the firing range and train me how to fire a rifle. I'll never forget it, it was raining cats and dogs that morning and he told me, "Son", he said, "we're going up to the rifle range and I'm going to teach you how to hit bulls eyes." So we got up there and he asked me if I had ever fired a rifle, I had never fired a rifle in my life at the time. So, he got me up there and he said, "you do what I tell you and I'm going to teach you how to fire a rifle. You're just what I want cause you never fired a rifle." He said, "before we get off this range today, we're going to stay here until you hit bulls eyes, I'm going to have you hit bulls eyes before we leave and if you don't I'm going to kick your rear end all over this rifle range." "So you do what I tell you," he said. Boy he was tough. Everyone seemed to shun away from Sergeant Milo, but he was an excellent soldier, so he really trained me how to fire a rifle and sure enough I was hitting bulls eyes before I left that rifle range. I'm not bragging, but he taught me how to fire all the weapons and I qualified expert in everything I fired. He really taught me and he told me, he said, "You're the one I wanted because you had no bad habits in firing weapons and I got you right from scratch and that's the way I wanted to teach you".

They finally made me a sniper, I took sniper training and they issued me an .03 with the scope on it, an excellent, excellent rifle. The .03 is a World War I rifle and when but when they added the scope to it, it was wonderful. My rifle was brand new even though it actually was the kind they used in World War I. It was an excellent rifle, it never jammed on you, which an M1 would. An M1 rifle, if you would have it in the rain or if you'd got mud in the barrel accidentally and didn't clean it properly, which you had to do constantly, while it would jam on you. But you take an .03 and you can actually draw it down into the mud and fire it and it would fire itself clean. I never had it jam on me and you could hit anything, 500 yards, a hundred yards, within that scope. If you had it set within that scope you would hit it. An excellent rifle, if you knew how to fire.

Eugene M. Wroblewski
Infantryman 378th Infantry Regiment

My name is Gene Wroblewski. I was with G Company of the 2nd Battalion of 378th Infantry. I was born in Chicago and raised in Brooklyn, New York. I went to the Brooklyn Technical High School and just before graduation I was accepted at MIT (Massachusetts Institute of Technology). As a matter of fact I graduated From High School on a Thursday, and because of wartime accelerated - programming, I traveled to MIT on Monday to start classes. I finished six weeks of schooling with them before I was drafted. That was an advantage because as a "student in good standing," I was eligible to come back after the war. In high school I had passed what they called an A-12, or an Army Specialized Training Program course exam and that allowed me to take special engineering education when I would enter service. They sent a bunch of us, all with the same background, down to Fort Benning in Georgia to take Infantry Basic Training. We spent 13 weeks down there and then we were dispatched to the various colleges to start our engineering training.

I was sent to the University of Pittsburgh. Our barracks were on the thirteenth floor of a 35 story main building called "the Cathedral of Learning". We took elevators up and down to various classes and mess halls while in uniform and it was great. Once in the wintertime we were out throwing snowballs at each other. A newspaper photographer took a picture of us and the next day the headlines of a Pittsburgh paper read "These soldiers are throwing snowballs when fathers are being drafted. They could be throwing hand grenades instead!" Next thing we knew, and I'm sure it wasn't as a total result of the picture, we were disbanded and broken up after one term of engineering training and sent out to the various Army ground forces. I was sent to Indiantown Gap, where I joined the 95th Division. We heard that they were trying to improve the strength of the ground forces by adding one or two engineering students to each infantry squad. I doubt if this infiltration was that beneficial. Our serious infantry training including mountain maneuvers in West Virginia. We trained at Indiantown Gap for several months and were finally dispatched to our port of embarkation, Fort Miles Standish in Massachusetts. Our ship, the Santa Rosa, was a luxury liner converted to a troop ship. We traveled across the ocean unescorted in about seven or eight days. We had to be very careful not to show any lights at night. It was a grim sort of a thing. It was very crowded. Many of us slept packed in the same cabin or up on the deck as we sailed to Europe. We were constantly of the watch for submarines. We finally landed in Liverpool, England and were sent by train down to Winchester.

Frank Bever
Infantryman 379th Infantry Regiment

My name is Frank Bever and I'm originally from Wabash, Indiana. I was inducted into the service in June of 1942. I was working in a factory at that time but I was brought up on a farm. It was a completely new ball game when the Army said, "register" and I ended up being inducted. We went to our reception center in Indianapolis, Indiana, and eventually got on a train and headed west. We were not sure what our destination was to be, but it ended up being a new camp, Camp Swift in Texas. They were still in the process of building this particular camp when we got there.

There were a lot of sod details going on, pieces of lumber moved here and there and the barracks even had to have some paint done in order to complete the camp for the incoming soldiers.

We went through the regular routine of initial training at this particular camp in Texas. Close order drill and the whole ball of wax that is involved with green recruits was what was in store for us as we got there. The weather was extremely hot, however it wasn't much hotter than what I had been accustomed to in Indiana, but there were a lot of folks there that were from areas that were not near as hot. So instead of being receptive to this type of weather some of them were having a great amount of difficulty. They would take us out to different areas around Camp Swift and we would have to break our rifles down and be able to put them back together in "x" number of minutes. That was all difficult but then the training would get a little tougher and then a little tougher until we eventually had full field packs so that added insult to injury for a lot of folks. From that standpoint I was extremely gratified because I felt I was able to take a lot of these initial assignments a lot better than the kids who had been plucked off of the streets of the big cities like Chicago and a few others. With my farm background I had been subjected to a great deal of physical labor. Because of this I felt like I was a little better at contending with conditions as they were presented to us.

From Camp Swift we moved to Fort Sam Houston, Texas, for further training. That was a beautiful camp and it exists to this day to the best of my knowledge. There is a huge hospital there but we didn't stay in these great conditions very long. It was always a trip to Camp Bullis, the base camp for the Leon Springs Military Reservation, where we were subjected to the full field pack deal and rifle and rest of the equipment we were suppose to carry for about twenty-five miles. That was our first exposure to the long night-time movements. Camp Bullis is a plain little ordinary camp out in the middle of nowhere. Since we were infantry we were actually in Camp Cibolo, a smaller camp that was part of the reservation and the larger Camp Bullis. I can recall the retreat at about 10 o'clock each night. It would get pretty cool and we were in eight man tents listening to the morbid sound of that bugle blowing. The bugle meant that activities were to cease, you had better be quieting down, getting ready for your nights rest. That's one thing that really stood out in my mind from when we were out in this remote area. We would go back and forth three or four times in a course of a month from our main headquarters, which was in Fort Sam. From Fort Sam we received our first furlough. I think I had been in about a year by then. We got to go home for a week and then we reported back to Fort Sam and then we had to go to another camp in California.

It was another tent city down in the foothills of a huge mountain range in California. It was suppose to be somewhat of a mountain and desert training area. We never knew of course where we were eventually going to be sent, so we were thinking, "where in the world are we going to be going?" There was a lot of speculation about where the 95th would end up going during this period of mountain and desert training. It was also extremely hot during the day as I remember. The first night we got a rude surprise because of the difference in the temperature from day to night. About midnight the first night there everybody was up rustling around getting additional blankets and so forth to put on their cots so they wouldn't be so cold. It was an extreme variation in temperature at that maneuver area in California. We went through this, I'm not sure of all the dates here, but I would suppose that would be something like a three month period of time. Another thing that sticks in my mind is when we would go out in the open flat areas of California and in the distance you could see a great big mountain range. You would think to yourself that we should be over there in about two hours time, but we'd be on the move for maybe six or eight hours and it didn't appear that we were any closer to the mountain than we had been when we started out that morning. It was just an optical illusion.

When we had this part of the training schedule behind us we got word that we were to go to Camp Polk in Louisiana. That was just kind of a furtherance of our training. At that time they stressed the importance of doing without water for a great period of time down there. We thought that was kind of strange that they did that, but we figured there was a reason behind it. We went virtually for an entire day with one canteen of water. It was really hot and as you can imagine there was a lot of moaning and groaning from the guys as we went through the so called combat maneuvers at nighttime. During the night you had to be quite, with no lights or cigarette smoking or anything like that. We completed that kind of rough living period and then we got into the barracks for a short period of time. It seemed like we were constantly on the move to a different type of training or state in general.

Once we got through all that we ended up going to Indiantown Gap in Pennsylvania. Indiantown Gap is another beautiful camp north of Harrisburg. We then got the word that we were going to have more mountain maneuvers and that they would take place in West Virginia. We went to West Virginia where they had some pretty rough mountains. We spent a good deal of time learning to rappel off of the tops of these mountains with ropes and so forth. We learned how to kick properly and lower yourself to the lower areas from the tops of the mountains. That too was a beautiful area but it was very difficult terrain. I made an observation that about 4 or 5 o'clock every afternoon we got a heavy rain shower. Of course that didn't add to our convenience factor as we pulled out our ponchos and tried to put them on to keep dry at least a little bit. But invariably our feet would get wet and it was just the making of a rough night in the mountain area of West Virginia.

After about a month or so in West Virginia we went back to Indiantown Gap, our central headquarters. We got word after awhile that we were going to ship out. We weren't sure where, but then they started taking us northeast in the trucks and we ended up in Boston in August of 1944. We spent a short time in Boston before we found ourselves loading up onto a huge converted troop ship. I forget the name of the ship. Something that I was told just today, I had a little difficulty remembering the numbers on this segment, but they said there was around 12,000 of our 95th Infantry on that one ship. Some of the recollections that I had of the trip were our hammocks that were in the lower area of the ship and stacked four high. You were supposed to get a rest on those hammocks with three guys above you if you happened to be on the bottom. Water was difficult to come by too, no shower facilities on the ship. I can remember after getting to our destination in Liverpool that I was even dreaming of a nice warm shower. Unfortunately they were not available until we hit the mainland anyhow. It took us nine days to get across and as I said we landed in Liverpool.

Roger A. Bushee
Infantryman 379th Infantry Regiment

My name is Roger Bushee. I graduated from high school in Chicago in June of 1943. I graduated from Fanger High School. It was one of the many Chicago public schools and is located on the extreme south side of Chicago. In my senior year a lot of the fellows were enlisting. Some were sixteen, some seventeen, and they got permission to enlist. The Chicago high schools had a Reserve Officer Training Corps program and each school had their own ROTC unit with a regular Army man in charge of each. We had tactics classes and they had a gun range in the school, it was only a .22 rifle range, but at least kids got used to shooting a rifle if they had never done that before, and I had never done that before. They would have drill and question contests in front of regular Army people to see how much we had learned. We had uniforms with these white belts and we had to be inspected once a week. I don't remember what we washed them in, but whatever it was it made them white. Our shoes had to be polished and brass buttons had to be shined. There were students commanding, I was a lieutenant but didn't really think anything about it at the time. We didn't go out on maneuvers or anything, but anybody that went to the Chicago public schools got a little bit of basic training.

In December of 1943, I was eighteen years old. I was a student in the first semester of college and the draft board came and said that I had been drafted. I asked them to allow me to go to San Antonio to visit my older brother who is a year older than I am. He was in the Air Force in a pre-flight school of some kind there. When I returned from that I was inducted and sent to Indiantown Gap, Pennsylvania in February of 1944. So I was only eighteen for a couple of months. Part of my basic training was spent in the hospital because I got pneumonia, I guess because I wasn't used to the cold February weather in Pennsylvania. We went on maneuvers, and when we were on maneuvers in West Virginia on June the 6th, D-Day, we got the news about the landing in France. When we came back we prepared to go overseas. We went to Boston and took the boat over, landing in Liverpool. We left for Omaha beach around September 14th, I guess. We went across the Channel on an old wooden English boat. When we did get to France we were trucked, the trucks were waiting for us, and they took us to board the trains. After that we went into combat.

Eldon L. Knuth
Infantryman 379th Infantry Regiment

My name is Eldon Knuth. I was born and grew up in northeast Iowa. After finishing high school at the age of 18, I wanted to go to college but was aware that I might be drafted. So I took the initiative and talked to my draft board. They said that if I went to college they would draft me but quickly. I felt that I had a choice of either going to college, and hopefully someday finishing, or staying on the farm, in which case I might never get off the farm. I was Valedictorian of my high-school class, and really didn't want to stay on the farm. So I went to college and got really wrapped up in my studies. When they sent me the draft notice towards the end of the first term, it was really a shock; I had forgotten all about the draft by that time.

I reported for induction in August 1943. I was given the standard AGCT (Army General Classification Test) and did very well in it. I was given a choice of the Air Force or the Army Specialized Training Program, which is also known as "All-Safe-Til-Peace". I chose ASTP, seeing there an opportunity for college. I did my basic training at Fort Benning along with a lot of other young fellows who were headed for ASTP. I finished the basic training at the end of 1943 and reported to Carnegie Tech in January of 1944. We were about halfway through the first term when the Army decided that it needed more men for the lines and drew on the ASTP. Incidentally, I think that that is one of the more unfortunate things that happened in World War II; they selected out those with the highest AGCT scores, headed them for college, then pulled them out and put all of them on the front lines. If we had not aimed for ASTP, we would have been assigned to a mixture of duties, some of which included front-line service, some of which included other duties. From the standpoint of the use of human resources for the country I think that was very unfortunate. For some strange reason, when they announced that they were ending our portion of the ASTP program, the fellows cheered. I really don't understand that to this day. Perhaps they were ready for a break in routine. I was sent to Indiantown Gap with the 95th, did some more training there with the 95th, including mountain maneuvers in West Virginia.

In August of 1944, one year after I was inducted, we were sent overseas. After about one month in England, we were sent to France, where we had a bit more training in Normandy. In October, we were sent to the Moselle, near Corny, where we held a position for about a month. It was very quiet there, but a bit eerie. We knew that Corny was unoccupied, not even by civilians, but the church bells rang nevertheless. Some of the fellows went into Corny, helped themselves to French wine. I didn't.

Paul H. Madden, Jr.
Infantryman 379th Infantry Regiment

My name is Paul Madden, technically my name is Paul H. Madden, Jr. I currently live in Shreveport, Louisiana, but going back in time I was a member of Company A, 379th Regiment of the 95th Division. I initially went into military service in August of 1943 at the age of eighteen. I volunteered for induction and in September. I went on active duty and went to Fort Benning, Georgia where I took my basic training with the Army Specialized Training Program. Following completion of basic training in January of 1944 the majority of the two hundred boys that I had taken basic with went to Carnegie Tech in Pittsburgh, Pennsylvania. After about six weeks of school the ASTP program was cancelled and just about all of the ASTP members from Carnegie Tech and the University of Pittsburgh were put on a troop train and went to Indiantown Gap, Pennsylvania. I've understood since then that approximately four thousand ASTP members had gone into Indiantown Gap and about two thousand of these wound up in the 95th Division. I was assigned to Company A of the 379th Regiment in March of 1944 and became a member of the second squad of the third platoon. Most of the ASTP boys when they were assigned a squad were assigned to be either the first or second scout. We found out later that would be the lead of if anybody got shot. My group that went into Company A, I think we had a good group and after a little bit the older members of the company accepted us for something more than wiz kids, which they called us at first.

Later in June each regiment went down to West Virginia for a little mountain training up to a regimental maneuver. I recall that we were completing our regimental maneuver on June the 6th when we heard about the D-day landings at Omaha. Then in July the division was alerted for overseas shipment and we moved to Camp Miles Standish, below Boston out of Taunton, Massachusetts. Our Point of Embarkation was Boston. The ship that I happened to go over on was the *West Point,* which at one time had been the *SS America,* which was the largest American cruise liner at that time. I don't know that it actually ever made a cruise, I think it was finished about the time the war started and the Army took it over for transportation purposes. The 379th, which I happened to be a member of, was selected to be the MP's for the trip over so we boarded the ship about two days before we sailed. Fortunately we drew staterooms to live in, but the only catch to that was, if I remember correctly, I think there was about eighteen of us in a stateroom that was designed for two people. The trip over was uneventful. We didn't go by convoy because the *West Point* sailed fast enough that they figured they could out run a submarine. We landed at Liverpool and from there we trained to Winchester where my company stayed in a British camp called Barton Stacey, just outside of Winchester by about twelve miles.

Adolph Massa
Infantry Rifle Company First Sergeant 379th Infantry Regiment

My name is Adolph Massa, but my friends call me Al. I joined the military in May of 1937 and retired in 1965. I joined the 95th at Camp Swift, Texas in July of 1942 as a private. Prior to that time I was court-martialed and shipped to Camp Grant, from Monterey, California, to help open the reception center for the area around the Great Lake. When I joined the 95th Division I was suppose to go to recon or the 95th Scouts. Do to the fact that the barracks for the recon and the scouts at that time was not completed I was initially assigned to F Company of the 379th Regiment. After being in the company a few days, knowing all the different commands and so forth, Lieutenant Davis came up to me and asked, "Where did you get your prior military service, CMTC, ROTC or what?" I informed him that I had been in the service since 1937. He said, "Well, from now on you'll be the company guide." He also found out that I was supposed to be assigned to either the scouts or the reconnaissance troop and he said, "We'd like for you to stay in F Company." I told him it would be up to the F Company officers to have me transferred to F Company, which he did. So I became a member of F Company in approximately August of 1942.

Prior to being shipped to Camp Swift I was to be married. Well, due to the fact that I got court-martialed it kind of put a kimp in my marriage plans. My fiancé decided to come to Camp Swift so we could get married. So on September 18th of 1942, my fiancé came down and we got married at the post chapel. We then spent our honeymoon in Austin, Texas. Just prior to that our company commander Captain Kitinger had misread a directive from headquarters requesting that all personnel to fire on the first order of the range be submitted. Not understanding the directive completely he submitted all the cooks names. On the day that the men were supposed to be on the range Colonel Granager came to see Captain Kitinger and told him that half of the cooks were missing. The captain said that he could not send the others out because he had half of his company back and he needed cooks to cook for the balance of the company. Colonel Granager said, "You submitted those names, you get them out there even if you have to go in the kitchen to cook for the remainder of your men!" Captain Kitinger in the meantime asked Sergeant McCormick, "What are we going to do?" I overheard all this because I was in the next room in supply. I heard Sergeant McCormick say, "Oh, we have a mess sergeant and cook right here working with Sergeant Simons in supply." Captain Kitinger called me into the orderly room and asked if I had previous experience cooking and I informed him that I had. He asked me if I would mind going to the kitchen while the unit was out in the field and told me he would give me sufficient kitchen police help.

So, I did this for the next four days and upon completion of the four days I asked the captain for a three-day pass. He said, "Well, I think I owe one to you," so he submitted a three-day pass so I could get married. Colonel Granager refused the pass and informed Captain Kitinger that he was not allowed to give a three-day pass, only a one day. Captain Kitinger called me in and said, "I'm sorry Massa I can't give you a three-day pass, but I can give you three one-day passes, so you tear them up as they go by." Sergeant McCormick did have a vehicle and said, "Since you did us a favor I'm going to loan you my vehicle for your honeymoon." Therefore I was able to have a vehicle to travel to Austin, Texas for our honeymoon. I came back after my honeymoon and reported to the company. Sergeant McCormick says, "Massa you better read the bulletin board," and I said, "Yeah, I'm probably on every detail." When I looked on the bulletin board Captain Kitinger had promoted me to staff sergeant. I approached him and thanked him and he said, "Well, that's your wedding present." So I became a staff sergeant a few months after I entered the division.

John G. Little, Jr.
Artilleryman 547th Anti Aircraft Artillery

My name is John G. Little, Jr. I was born June 10, 1924, in Greenville, Alabama. I was the oldest child with three younger sisters. I graduated from high school in May 1942. While I was in high school I was in the band and boy scouts. I played the bugle and the trombone. That is how I became a bugler in my unit. D Battery, 547th AAA Battalion. After graduation I worked in a drug store behind the soda fountain. In the fall I attended the University of Alabama under the ROTC program. During this time the draft law was changed. Men twenty years and older were being drafted but it was changed to eighteen years and older. I got my draft notice before Christmas 1942. In late January 1943, three busloads of us from Greenville, Alabama went to Fort McClellan for our physicals. Most of us passed the physical. We had one week to go back home and tend to our business. On January 30, 1943, we were put on busses and driven to Fort McPherson in Atlanta, Georgia to be sworn into the Army. Several days later I was shipped out on a troop train to Camp Haan, California. Alabama and Georgia boys were joined with other draftees from North Carolina, Texas, California and the Midwest. Camp Haan was an anti-aircraft training center.

Upon arrival we were interviewed and since I could play the bugle I became the bugler and messenger. I spent most of my time at battery headquarters. I became very close to the battery commander, my first sergeant and the supply and mess sergeants. The battalion had four firing batteries and a headquarters battery and in each firing battery there were two platoons. Each platoon had four anti-aircraft gun sections. In each gun section there were two trucks, one pulled a 40-millimeter anti-aircraft weapon and the other truck pulled a trailer that had four 50-caliber machine guns. Our battalion trained for 18 months in Southern California before we went overseas to join the 95th Infantry Division in Normandy. Our anti-aircraft firing ranges were in Camp Irwin, now Fort Irwin, California. Our desert training was at Camp Ibis near Needles, California.

While at Camp Ibis we had a break to take a tactical motor march to the Grand Canyon, which was a great event. We were the only ones there because the civilians were on gas rationing. We stayed several days at an old CCC Camp. We really had a chance to explore the whole Grand Canyon area. Most of the enlisted men were from the south. Our officers were from the north. After that we returned to Camp Ibis, which was a tent camp. We built seven different tent camps. We also trained at Muroc; it was called Army Air Base then. Today it is called Sheppard's Air Force Base and that is where the astronauts land. While at desert training we trained

with the 90th and 81st Divisions. We should have known we were
going to an Army Infantry Division when we went overseas. That
is exactly what happened, we were assigned to the 95th Infantry
Division. The 95th Division had gone through the same desert
training we had gone through. It didn't happen very often but we
enjoyed going to Hollywood in Southern California.

On August 10, 1944, after returning from leave we boarded a
troop train at Camp Hann, California. A few men that had been
AWOL showed up on August 10, 1944 thinking they were going to
go to the brig but as it turned out we took them along anyway. We
carried a duffel bag and a pack on our back. I also carried a bugle
and a Sub Machine Gun called a grease gun. I never did fire a round
out of it in combat. I don't know what I'll tell my grandchildren
because I was just a water boy for an antiaircraft outfit supporting
the infantry. We traveled on the troop train to Camp Shanks, New
York. While at Camp Shanks I got to go to New York City twice. I
had a cousin that lived there and she showed a couple of us around
the city. We were alerted that all outside contact was to stop. We
didn't know where we were going but many people in New York
City told us the *Mauretania* was there and we would be going on
it. The *Mauretania* was a huge ship. It held 10,000 troops. We left
on August 23, 1944, at night. We left Camp Shanks in trucks, and
then took a ferry followed by a train ride to the pier. I will never
forget my buddy, David Nicholson, a battery clerk. We had to
carry a field desk up the gangplank and our Battalion Executive
Officer, Major Camel told us to hurry up. We were very small,
extremely tired and with the extra load we carrying, just couldn't
go any faster. We were so tired that we did not even see the Statue
of Liberty leaving port. We had two meals a day and hammocks
to sleep on. We slept on the floor.

Leon E. Langford
Ordnance 795th Ordnance
(Light Maintenance) Company

My name is Leon Langford. I'm going to relate some incidents from my Army life, particularly those that happened with the 95th Infantry Division. I was drafted into the Army from Kansas in April of 1943, having graduated from high school in June of 1942. I think that one reason that I had not been drafted into the Army earlier than that was because in our little town the chairman of the draft board was a good personal friend of my family. He knew our economic condition and the fact that my four older brothers and sisters had all married and left home and that I still had two sisters and a brother at home with my widowed mother and me. I think that he exercised some influence to delay the draft process as long as was possible. Also prior to that time I had taken a job working for a construction firm that was building a defense plant; it was an ammonium nitrate plant there in Cherokee County, Kansas. So that might have had a little to do with it as well, but in the final analysis, probably not. Anyway, I was drafted and proceeded to Fort Leavenworth in Kansas where I was inducted into what I had hoped to be the Marines. But they didn't want me for the Marines, so then my second choice was the Navy and they didn't want me for that either, so I wound up in the Army. They wouldn't even consider me for the Air Force because of my eyes, teeth or whatever? But anyway, I wound up at Aberdeen Proving Ground for basic training. Basic training was not particularly difficult, but it was different. After basic training I had applied to go to cadre school, which was also at Aberdeen.

I had gone through about half of cadre school until one day they came over from the company headquarters and said Langford report back to the company headquarters and pack up. You are shipping out. I didn't particularly want to go any place because I was having a good time wit my buddies in cadre school. So I asked why and where and all those sorts of questions but nobody had any answers. Even when I got back to the company headquarters they didn't have an answer. They just said that they had orders for me to ship out? In due time I joined a number of other young guys from Aberdeen Proving Ground and we got on a train that eventually wound up at VPI, which now is Virginia Tech in Blacksburg, Virginia. What had happened, I subsequently learned, was that I had made a good enough score on the aptitude test that they thought that I was college material. They were sending all the brilliant students, like me [Laughs], to various colleges and universities to become engineers. I think it was just a place to put us for a period of time, but anyway I eventually, after being at VPI for about thirty days, boarded a little tuner Ville trolley train and they took us up to Penn State in State College, Pennsylvania. At that point we became students in the engineering curriculum and life was tough [Laughs]. Our barracks were fraternity houses, the food was good and the studies were hard.

During the course of that period of time one of my buddies came back from down in State College and he said, "Hey Langford, you want to go to a dance?" I said, "Well not with you!" and he said, "No, no not with me, they have a place down there where they'll get dates for us with the co-eds." So I said, "Sure, O.K." He went back down to this office and told them that he had a buddy that would like to go to this dance and so arrangements were made for this blind date. To make a long story short my wife of fifty-seven years is that girl that I met on that blind date [smiles and looks at his wife]. We didn't get married right then or anything like that, but eventually we did. I was at Penn State for the Army Specialized Training Program, everyone calls that ASTP and if you talk to the old timers from the 95th they always refer to the ASTP guys that came in with their little suitcases and with their bath robes slung over their arms. It's very funny to hear them talk about how naïve we were going into the 95th Infantry Division at Indiantown Gap. I think that was early April of 1944.

Well, while we were at Indiantown Gap as members of the 95th we took additional training to try to catch up with the guys that had been in it for quite a long time. Eventually we shipped up to Camp Miles Standish. And to this day I still don't know where Camp Miles Standish was? I've tried to find out, my brother-in-law lived on Cape Cod and when we were up there to visit I would ask the natives where this camp was. Nobody up there to this day could tell me. Of course with your interview with Martin Lincoln who was in the 95th and lived in Boston, he said it was just a little south of Boston, not on the Cape, but someplace down there. Anyway, since I had taken basic training in Aberdeen, and was in ordnance, I wound up in the 795th Ordnance Light Maintenance Company, which was a unit of about no more than one hundred and fifty guys, and probably less than that.

We shipped out of Camp Miles Standish, or Boston, on August 9th, and as I recall we were on the *USS West Point*, which used to be the *USS America*. Part of the division had shipped out earlier on the 6th of August 1944, on a ship called the *Mariposa*. This poor little old country boy from Kansas had some misgivings. It was revealing, I've told my wife several times, August the 9th, which was just yesterday I recall standing on the deck of the *USS West Point* as it pulled out of Boston Harbor. Looking down over the side of the ship over the railing I saw all of these little fluorescent organisms, I don't know what they are, but to me be a "Flat Lander" from Kansas that was really something. That was just part of the new education that I was about to get as part of the 95th. I had some misgivings about being on that ship, as a lot of us did because they said we were going to go with out any escort. They said we could out run those submarines and I thought, "Yeah, we can out run the submarines, we're faster than they are, but what if they're lined up there waiting for us?" But that never happened, and we did make it over to Liverpool, England. I recall getting off of the ship, disembarking; it was blackout, dark of night as we marched off the ship, formed up and marched through the city up to the train station. All you could see was the girls and the guys lined up along the street, the ladies of the night, and it really was night. There were no lights at all.

It took an act of congress to make me a PFC [Laughs]. When we were at Camp Miles Standish congress passed an act that said all privates and all second lieutenants who had been in grade for I think a year were automatically made PFC's and first lieutenants. That's how I became a PFC! When I got into the 795th there were all "old" guys. Some of those guys were twenty-three, four or five. There were even some that were thirty and thirty-five because they were machinist in civilian life. They got drafted and they needed those kinds of skills. I think there was one guy that was thirty-nine or so, and he was not the commanding colonel either, he was just a regular machinist. All of the stripes and everything were gone, so we were just content to be little PFC's and do our job.

So our unit wound up at a camp down near Basingstoke, England. The camp's name was Camp Barton Stacey. It was rather spare, but it was no different from what thousands, or hundreds of thousands, of other guys had experienced there; the bunks were made out of wood, 2 x 4's or something, with straw in burlap bags. Not very comfortable, but we lasted for about a month. As I recall we didn't do much training there, it was more like a holding place. We were just getting everything ready to go across the Channel. Of course, that was well after the D-day invasion in June.

Martin H. Lincoln
Ordnance 795th Ordnance
(Light Maintenance) Company

My name is Martin Lincoln. I can tell you that I did come from a military background. There have been Lincolns in the service ever since the Revolutionary War. General Benjamin Lincoln was a distant relative and on my mother's side of the family some of her relatives were in the Civil War and then my uncle, who I'm named after and was a West Point graduate, was in World War I and was later stationed in Hawaii, by that time he was sixty years old, about General Patton's age, when World War II started. After the war began they flew him up to Boston and made him the Inspector General of the New England area. He was very unhappy about that. He wanted to go over to Europe and see some action but he got stuck in the Boston area for the rest of the war. He had had a regiment stationed out in Hawaii and he had been all around the world participating in various activities, but he had to sit out the war in Boston. My twin brother got into the flying cadets and ended up as a Lieutenant Colonel. My kid brother ended up in the marine air force, retiring a full Colonel after fighting in World War II and also Korea. He had quite a record, receiving quite a few Distinguished Flying Crosses and things like that. He was one of the one's that knocked out the bridges at the Yalu River in Korea to stop the Chinese from coming after the retreating American forces.

That's the military background of my family. I was the black sheep of my family, I was the only one that wasn't an officer, but we still get along. I was initially in the Marine Corps reserves. I won't go into detail, but I did have full military training, made expert with the .45 pistol and made sharp shooter with the rifle, I did better with the rifle in the Army, I made expert with the rifle in the Army. As it happened I was all set to go into the flying cadets, already to go from Boston to somewhere out around the Chicago area for further training but my aunt was sick. She got so upset at my leaving that I didn't go and ended up working for National Fireworks for fourteen months. Every few days they'd loose a good part of the labor force because they'd have an explosion somewhere in the plant that was in West Hanover, Massachusetts. They'd be working on the high explosives, there'd be an explosion and people wouldn't show up the next day after the explosion. I worked in a unit that specialized in handling tetryl powder. We had to use tetryl pellets. We weighed these pellets on a machine that operated when put the tetryl powder in the machine, close the door and then you'd pull a big handle on the machine and it would make the powder into pellets. That went on for some period of time until one day, we had a tendency to horse around every once in awhile, we set some booby traps for some of the other workers. We had the baskets up over the door with water rigged to splash all over somebody once they opened the door, and that was the time that the superintendent of the plant picked to make an inspection. He pulled the door open and got soaked with it [Laughs], he had everybody up on the carpet that time, but as a result I got removed form that section. Then they had me loading trucks and doing other things until they decided they wanted me working on another type of explosive with a bunch of females, so I was the only male working with fifty females for a while. That went on for sometime until one day somebody backed a truck up into load some ammunition and ran over some black powder that intern blew up and the whole duplex got destroyed and several people killed. Nothing in the paper, nothing was ever in the paper about any of these episodes, but half the force didn't come back the next day.

I continued working for them until finally the superintendent and his brother, they were from New Jersey, developed a trust in me so they put me in charge of a group of men moving things around the area. We had this old World War I machine that you'd load it with material and pull the big handle and all of this putty would come out like spaghetti. They'd use this putty to seal the ammunition boxes and so forth. They had developed a new machine so they called me in and told me to get a bunch of men to take the old machine down to the lower level where they could store it. They said to make sure that it got there in one piece so I got a truck and went up and tied it off to the end of the truck, it was a great big thing, and then we drove down to the lower level.

When we got there somebody said, "Hey Lincoln, Jim is on the phone and he wants to talk to you," so I went running over to talk to Jim and left the machine still tied on the truck. As I was talking to Jim, he was the assistant superintendent, the boys tried to save time by undoing the knots, but they didn't do it right and the machine fell down unto the pavement with a big crash and Jim said, "What was that!" and I said that I thought the machine had just fell off the back of the truck [Laughs]. He almost had a heart attack. He jumped in his Cadillac and came racing down and there was the machine in pieces on the ground. Jim fired every one of them on the spot and gave me the best possible move, two weeks unpaid leave. I thought that was great, I took a trip up thought he White Mountains and had a great time for two weeks.

Then I started turning yellow. My hands and face were yellow and I started getting rashes around my neck. I went to the company physician and he said you've been dogwood poisoned and that it would be ok. It kept getting worse, so I went to my own doctor in Tanton, Massachusetts. He said you've got tetryl poisoning and if you keep working there you're not going to last three or four months. So I thought I better get out of there, so I called them up the next day and told them I was all through. Then I got a letter from the union, I belonged to the AFLCIO munitions workers union, that they were suspending me because I hadn't paid my dues or something [Laughs]. We had a guy that had come down for a summer job and once he left he died. I had that in the back of my mind, but once I left there everything started to clear up, I wasn't yellow anymore. That's how I eventually got drafted into the Army. Then I ended up getting inducted down at Fort Devans, Massachusetts. The night before I left my sister and her girlfriend took me out and I had a few drinks and got in late. I had to get up early and run down to catch the train and the first thing they did was march us in and gave us an IQ test. I was in no condition for an IQ test. It was funny, I started taking the test and the guys on my left and right started peeking over to see what the answer was

going to be. There was no motion on either side of me, but when
I moved my pen they moved [Laughs], it was unbelievable. I never
did finish the test; I ended up in the 120's. I could have done better
but didn't finish it. I was reported to be heading down to Florida
for a job with the air force, but one weekend I went home to visit
my aunt, we could take a path right out the back end of Devans
and then I could hitchhike home. When I got back they said all the
guys that I was suppose to be with had already gone. So I ended
up in the 95th Division group and they decided to put me in the
infantry even though had already completed law school.

The minute I got back there they marched three other guys and
me into the infirmary. They gave us shots, new uniforms and then
marched us to company assembly where a major was in charge. He
told us that we were the four worst soldiers he had ever seen, we
had left the camp without a pass. The train was already ready to
head out to camp Swift so they lined the troops up to wait to board
the train and the MP's marched the four of us right to the head of
the line. One of the MP's was named Murphy, he was a friend of
mine that I knew from Boston, and he was laughing as he put me
right at the head of everything. Well, along came this major and
he said, "These four men are to have KP all the way down." We
weren't sure where the destination was, but what had happened
was that as soon as we got aboard the train I disappeared and they
didn't see me again until we got to Camp Swift [Laughs]. We had
a great time as we went up through Western Massachusetts then
through New York state and up into Canada and down through
Chicago. We had no idea where we were going until we ended up
down in Camp Swift in Texas.

I was in the 377th Infantry. I think it was Company C that
I was in for training. I worked there for a while and then they
established that I had been an ammunition specialist so I ended up
being assigned to the division ammunition section. That's how I
got in the ammunition section of the ordnance. The 95th Division
was a training division at that time. We were trained in every sort

of activity under the sun. We had all sorts of training in Louisiana, the Louisiana Maneuvers. From there we went out to the desert for desert training and went from the desert to Indiantown Gap and then to West Virginia for mountain training. We trained for two years I think. They had great plans for us but then they needed some bodies over in Europe in a hurry so we ended up being selected to go to Europe.

I was picked to go on the advanced party to Europe. I didn't know I was going to be on the advanced party, but a few days before that I was walking along in the city of Harrisburg. I was looking at some stuff in a display window and along comes a freshly made Second Lieutenant. I didn't even notice him but he yelled, "Hey soldier you didn't salute me!" He wanted my name, rank and serial number so he could report me to division headquarters. Well, I got back to the base and I was awaiting word from the division headquarters as to what my punishment was going to be. My punishment was no leave for a month but then along came the notice that I had been picked for the advanced party. The advanced party had a three-day furlough to say goodbye to their folks before we took off. We were also given the good conduct medal, so I got marched in front of the ordnance company and they pinned the good conduct medal on me. The company top sergeant said to me, "How does this happen Lincoln?" You can't leave the base for a month and they give you the good conduct medal [Laughs]?" So I ended up being sent to Camp Miles Standish in Tanton, Mass., which is located in North Tanton. It borders on my grandfathers land and there I was with the advanced party but I couldn't go home to say good-bye to the folks or anything. It was suppose to be a secret mission, so they wouldn't give us anymore leave. Well, I knew my way around Camp Miles Standish so I went through the woods and visited my aunt. She lived next door to my father so then I went over and visited him. I lived with an uncle and aunt up in Manchester, New Hampshire after my mother died so she was like a mother to me. I got back to the base and the next morning

we got on a train that went into Boston and got on board what I
think was the *West Point*, and started for Europe.

I think we docked in Liverpool, but on the way over we were
followed by German subs. I think they picked us up right after we
passed Halifax. You could see these fins sticking up out of the
water and one of the sailors said, "Don't worry, they'll never catch
us." I told him I wasn't worried, that I didn't think they would
catch us either, but they were trying. That German wolf pack
they had off of the East Coast was really something. I arrived in
Europe with the advanced party on about June 25th or 26th. They
took us to Winchester, England and we were boarded in with a
very exclusive boys school there. We took over the whole school
actually. We had a great time there. They picked different groups
that would have to go up to northern England or Scotland to pick
up ambulances and trucks and other ordnance to bring back to the
big Army base that they were getting ready.

It was on one of those tri[s that first came into contact with
a buzz bomb. I think it was Waterloo station. There were about
six of us in there when we heard the rumble. Somebody yelled,
"Buzz Bomb!" and a guy jumped out of the signal tower down
to the ground and broke his leg. When I saw him do that I dove
under a coal cart and got covered with dust. The buzz bomb flew
over the station and landed in an apartment building across the
street. It blew it to smithereens and shook up the whole area in
London. The six guys from the 95th Division weren't harmed and
we made it to another train and headed to Scotland to pick up
some ambulances. On the way back with the six ambulances we
got into an Army convoy coming through Liverpool or somewhere
heading south. This Englishman with a big mustache came along
and wedged in between me and the ambulance in front of me.
Well, all of a sudden the convoy stopped and I ran into the back
of this Englishman. He got out and he glared at me and picked his
muffler up off the street and put it in the back end of his car and
drove off. Boy, he was mad, but he shouldn't have wedged in there

so close [Laughs]. But anyway, we got the ambulances back safely to the Winchester area.

I forget when the division arrived, but I think it was sometime during the latter part of July. While I was there I got picked to drive General Faith around. He used to be the one in charge of the WACs until they sent him over to England to join the division. They needed somebody to drive him around so I got the job for a few days. He was a real nice guy to work for.

Harry T. Hessler
Clerk 95th Quartermaster Company

My name is Harry Hessler. I grew up in Buffalo, New York. In high school I knew that there was no money for me to go to college, but fortunately I was given a job with the New York Central Railroad. I worked for them until Pearl Harbor happened and then I knew that I would be drafted shortly. I was drafted and left the railroad for the Army, entering at Fort Niagara, New York near Niagara Falls. I went from there to Camp Lee, Virginia where I took basic training. From there I was sent to the University of Mississippi where I took office procedures and so forth. In the Army's innumerable fashion they sent us all up to Fort Meade as replacements for North Africa. My background of office work worked to my advantage. One night they came around while we were waiting and moved me to another barracks. I wound up working in division headquarters as a stenographer and all around assistant to the two generals, the commanding general, a brigadier general and to a colonel who was chief of staff. I was in that capacity at Fort Meade, Maryland for a little bit. It was pretty good duty because Washington and Baltimore were close by, but the opportunity came up to go into the ASTP program. I went to the chief of staff and asked him what his feelings were, should I do it or not since I was pretty well set there? He said, "well, do you intend on staying in the Army?" I said, "no, I really don't." And he said, "well, if you were going to stay in the Army I had wondered if you wanted to consider officer candidate school." I said, "no, I really don't want to stay in the Army." He said, "by all means then, go to the Army Specialized Training Program."

After a stint at Georgetown, to get caught up on some of the courses we needed, they sent us to the College of William and Mary down in Williamsburg, Virginia. We completed about 2/3 of the course there when they decided we should all leave, there were 500 of us there, and we all went up to Indiantown Gap as replacements. I understood later on that the whole ASTP program was to keep the colleges full. They were having a tough time because of the war. Of course the Army needed replacements since they were getting ready and they needed troops elsewhere so the course was broken off. So now I was in the 95th Infantry Division at Indiantown Gap, Pennsylvania.

II. Baptism by Fire

On October 19th, 1944, the 95th Infantry Division moved forward into France, taking up positions in the Moselle River bridgehead sector, east of Moselle and south of the famed fortified city Metz. Stepping from the pages of history, the Germans had reinforced French defensive positions from years long gone by. The multiple forts even included moats and drawbridges. The Americans were about to greatly empathize with their medieval counterparts. The XX Corps, as thousand had before, tested the Fortress Metz with a frontal assault in early October. The men of the 5th Infantry Division actually managed to breach the moats and enter the outskirts of the main fortifications on their second attempt. Unfortunately they came to realize that the intricate defensive system only began with the moat. Once inside the fortifications, they would be subjected to mutually supporting artillery fires, complex urban terrain and an enemy that was comfortable and coordinated in their modernized fortress. Just shy of two weeks into the attack the 5th Infantry Division was ordered to withdrawal to the bridgehead south of Metz.

The 95th Infantry Division would fight in support of the corps' mission to "encircle and destroy the garrison of the Metz fortified area, and to seize a bridgehead over the Saar River in the vicinity of Saarburg" from October to the end of January 1945. The corps would break the mission down into four lengthy phases and eventually redirect its efforts due to the Battle of the Bulge. Following the failed initial attacks and Allied supply problem, the

95th would receive its baptism by fire incrementally beginning in the staging area and gradually working its way toward Metz by first maintaining a bridgehead designed to keep the Germans off balance. The Victory Division relieved the 5th Division on October 20, 1944, and would operate there for the next ten days, completing the first phase of the corps attack. The division staff issued Field Order Number 1 on October 21, declaring that:

> The Division mission was to maintain the bridgehead east of the Moselle and to conduct active and vigorous patrolling to keep the enemy off balance. Each of the regiments was given the same mission within its assigned zone, and to each of them was attached one company from the 320th Medical Battalion and one company of the 735th Tank Battalion. The 95th Reconnaissance Troop was given the special mission of manning a series of observation posts on the extreme right flank of the Division. The 3rd Battalion, 377th Infantry, in Division Reserve, was to prepare three counterattack plans in coordination with Company D of the 735th Tank Battalion…The 320th Engineer Battalion was assigned normal engineer missions with priority given to the maintenance of roads east of the Moselle River.

> The 95th Division Artillery, with its attachments was to support with fire the Division effort and was to be prepared to repel a possible tank attack. Each of the regiments was given certain units in direct support…Field Order No. 1 ended with the general directive: "Battle positions will be held at all cost! All individuals and elements will be ruthless in destruction of all enemy attempts to penetrate battle positions. In this connection detailed plans for employing reserves, including us of tanks and maximum supporting fires, will be maintained by all units."[1]

William Lake
Anti-Tank Infantryman 377th Infantry Regiment

We did some road marches in England, anything that kept you moving. We stayed there about two-weeks before I was in the advanced party. We got on some kind of British seagoing vessel and crossed the channel and landed on Omaha beach. We went up the big walkway that they always show in movies and continued through the apple orchard where we set up bivouac and waited for the company to show up at the gate of the orchard. When our company showed up, we directed them in to park among the trees. Pup tents were the only shelter they had, there was no orderly room, only outside latrines, and we had large lister bags to hold water. The lister bags would swing in the breeze at night and every once in a while you would hear a gun shot go off when someone had seen a "German paratrooper." Of course the apples were falling too, occasionally contributing to the illusion. After a few road marches, they started this Red Ball Express where they took all our trucks and were gone a couple of weeks.

Fred B. Love Jr.
Infantryman 377th Infantry Regiment

The next thing we knew we were in Omaha Beach. But the war had moved on it wasn't at Omaha Beach when we went. Thankfully, I was so glad that it had moved on. We stayed around for a while and somehow came around the Red Bull Express hauling supplies trying to catch up with Patton. We moved from there I guess in October and we hit the front lines and we relieved the 5th Division. They said, "no retreat," now granted the 5th Division had earned it the hard way and we weren't supposed to give it up. So we moved in at night and my squad, I was PFC, I was in 3rd squad, we moved out to a small point of woods, just a few trees and there were some empty shells and shell craters around and the next morning it got day light and I looked over and there was a perfectly good GI shoe, it looked fairly new, and I thought why in the world would anyone leave a good shoe out in the open like that. I walked over and looked at it and it wasn't a shoe, it was a foot and I thought Boy, you're over for much. I knew then it was serious, but I didn't take it too awfully serious. We stayed around there for a few days and had a few funny experiences. One day there was a hog walking around there, a big pig, 100 pounds and Sergeant Bankrey I believe it was him that shot it. We cut pieces off of that hog, and Albert Tanner was my squad leader and Bart was my foxhole buddy. Everybody had a buddy, and Barter, which I knew for awhile, he was my closest buddy. Often times there was the staff sergeant, the squad leader, but the three of us buddied up. Barter and I did the foxhole and at night two would sleep and one would stay guard, so at lot of time Tanner would sleep in with Barter and me. We'd take turns, one man would be on guard and the other two would be in there, so we became pretty close. But old Bankrey shot that hog and Barter and Tanner and I took one of the hams and we put it on a stick and put it over a fire and started roasting that thing. We roasted it we thought well done, we started cutting in to that thing and it was by all means cooked. We sliced off the outside of the ham and got some slices of cooked pork, all we could eat. We passed it on to somebody else three or four times before it was all gone. We really enjoyed that. One morning they brought up breakfast to us, we didn't get a hot meal usually; we had K-rations and C-rations, K-rations mostly. We got a hot meal this morning and as we were standing there to get our food three artillery shells came in, German 88's, but it so happened they were all duds and they just hit around in the wood areas close to us. They would have killed us probably if they would have exploded, but they didn't. That was a fairly close call cause they could have exploded and destroyed us all.

I remember one night, we were sitting in the foxhole there and we were getting pretty tired we had been on the line for a while and artillery shells came in and just cut the woods down around us and I didn't know it until I woke up, I had slept through an artillery barrage. I couldn't believe it! I mean there were trees down everywhere and I didn't get scratched. Of course I was lying down in the hole, we just got so tired that when we did sleep we slept sound.

I believe it was the second night on the front lines, Albert Tanner came up to Barter and myself said, "let's go on patrol." We took off and walked towards the German lines, very cheerfully and we got way over there and a machine gun opened up and we got down out of the way of it and we found out where the Germans' were by that machine gun fire. We decided that was enough patrolling and we turned around and went back. We got back close to our old lines and there is a guy named Ferrier who got trigger-happy. He started shooting at us and every time we tried getting to the lines he started shooting at us. The only thing that saved us was where they had plowed the ground and there were low places in the ground. We lay down in that and that kept us from getting shot. Finally, Tanner said, "You boys stay here and I'll go see if I can get in." He crawled up there and yelled and finally got the guy's attention and they stopped the fire, but they had fired 17 times at us before we got it stopped, but we got back in safely. Barter and I went on several patrols after that but nobody ever shot at us coming back.

I am going to tell you about the best apple I ever ate in my life. We had been living on K-rations for about 2-3 weeks and we were starving to death. We were out there on patrol looking for prisoners and we walked under an apple tree. This was in the fall of the year, the apples were ripe and they had fallen off and were lying on the ground. We stumbled over them when we walked under it and I reached down to see what it was. It was a good big old apple, but it was dark so we couldn't see, no moonlight or anything, but I told Tanner, "Let's take time to eat an apple." So we sat down and ate that apple and let me tell you that was the best apple I ever had in my life! I have never had one before or since that tasted like that. We were so starved for fresh food that it was just delicious. What it had in them I don't know, we didn't look for bugs, we just ate them. I think we even ate the core too! We took a couple back to the guys on the line when we left.

Daniel F. McCarthy IV
Supply Sergeant 377ᵗʰ Infantry Regiment

From England, we departed from the port of Southampton and disembarked at Omaha Beach in Normandy, France, to bivouac in the hedgerows near Norrey le Sec, France. After a short time of bivouac in the hedgerows we took off for the war by truck convoy. We were excited to be able to see Paris but the Army had the streets lined with MP's and speeded up the convoy to 50 mph and then called a rest halt as soon as we reached the eastern city limits.   I never was able to get leave to visit Paris while we were in France. On our trip toward Metz we set up a supply station in what had been a Kraut POW camp. The room we were in had a potbelly stove and a pile of coal in one corner with the end of a box visible in the middle of the coal. My assistant and I moved the coal and uncovered two cases of champagne. Neither of us claimed to be a connoisseur of champagne, but we started drinking it, beginning with the bottles that had the oldest date on the label [Laughs]. We finished off seven bottles each, smashing the ten remaining bottles against the coal. A short time later, an officer from division quartermaster stopped and requested that we prepare a requisition for some item that division thought our regiment needed. Neither my assistant nor I were in any condition to type anything, so the officer typed the requisition and I signed it.

Joseph W. Napier
Infantryman 377th Infantry Regiment

We got off the ship and went to a staging area they called it. We stayed there in a big warehouse for a few days until they marched us down to board a Limey ship. It was a cattle boat as far as I was concerned; it sure smelled like one anyway. They gave us bread and jelly and tea to drink twice a day and that's all we had. We were out in the English Channel, the channel was real rough and some of the guys were sick. I didn't know what was going to happen and there were lots of rumors. One rumor was that submarines had sunk part of the 66th Division, but there was no way to verify any of that. Another rumor came that we were going to land in France the next day. Well, we were out there and I couldn't sleep much, I got to thinking about what might happen so I went out on deck, we weren't suppose to go out on deck after dark, but I did. I was watching the Navy ships out there, they were talking back and forth by lights. The next morning a landing craft came up beside our ship and we went down these ropes into the landing craft. It was quite an experience. It was real tricky, about the time you thought you were ready the boat would go up and the landing craft would go down and it was real easy for someone to get hurt. I made it down into the landing craft and we circled over and over until our turn came and we went in toward the coast. When it was our turn he really opened the motor up and we were moving. When we hit the beach the door dropped open and they were screaming at us to get out. I stepped in a shell hole or something and under I went, rifle, pack and all. Evidently my pack floated me back up, but I was sopping wet, sweating a cold sweat and scared to death. About that time an airplane came down the beach and I thought it was one of ours but it wasn't. He was letting us know who he was. They were shooting at him as he came on down but evidently they must have hit him because he was trailing a puff of smoke as he flew over me.

We finally got up off of Omaha Beach and into the hedgerows. They had an area there for us to get into. I met a little French kid there, he was probably ten years old, and he said to me, "Yank, go home." When I heard him say that I thought he had heard that from some grown ups, he didn't come up with that on his own. We did tear up a few homes there, but after all we were trying to liberate them, but of course the little boy didn't realize what he was saying and was just repeating what he had heard at home. We were there maybe a day or two until they marched us to a train station there in this little village for my first experience with 40 and 8's; in World War I they called them forty men or eight horses. They had four wheels on these boxcars and every time you'd hit a seam in the track it would bump and bump. So we got on there, forty of us, or maybe more than that, very uncomfortable our feet were over one another's, no place to urinate you just opened the door and let her fly. We road along stopping and going for a day or two and then one night we pulled into a field with hedgerows and I could see flashing in the sky at night. They moved us up with some trucks and I noticed the flashing was a little bit more and the next night you could hear the artillery, "Boomb," so I figured we were getting pretty close. The next day a red headed fellow came down to the building where we were, Andy and Me and Toplift and some other guys, and said, "You guys sew these patches on your arm you're in the 95th Infantry Division, part of George S. Patton's Army." That was about the 12th of October.

Richard H. Schoen
Medic 377th Infantry Regiment

We were in England for three months, or something like that before we went over. We were shipped over to Omaha Beach and stayed in the hedgerows for about three weeks while they ran the "red ball express." We We got there about 40-days after the invasion, but on the way in some of the medics found a 55-gallon drum that somebody thought was alcohol. We picked it up and carried it with us and it was pure alcohol. At that time, that lasted all the way in from the end of the beach and until the end of the war I imagine. The price of the orange juice went way up since we had a drum of 180-proof alcohol. We didn't abuse it, but we used it. We were then sent into combat just short of Metz and I was an infantry aid-man with K Company.

We were moved up to the lines just outside of Metz. That's where I had my very first casualty. It was a guy from a rifle company, at night you could see the shell fire out in the distance since we really hadn't been committed yet, but he didn't think he wanted to go any further so he put an armor piercing bullet in his rifle and shot himself through the ankle. He knew if he used a regular bullet it would shatter his ankle, but the AP bullet looked like he had just taken a drill to it. It went right straight through and I had to take him into the battalion aid station. In all the excitement, we couldn't the coleman lantern started and we were holding flashlights until they got the lights started. Here was Captain Herberson, our surgeon, is lecturing all these technicians I have with me, "this is the fibula, this is the tibia, this is the nerve ending" and I said to myself, "Oh my God!" Here I am a surgeon technician, if I can't hold onto this light here I'm not worth a damn! It never bothered me after that. That son of a gun, my first casualty, he got to go home and we didn't.

Right before we went into Metz we were reviewed by General Patton. Of course us aid-men had a medical brassard on our helmet front, back and rear, on our shoulders, on our back and our chest. He said, "You guys look like a bunch of Christmas trees, do you know where you are? You're at Metz, this is SS territory, get those G.D. things off!" So some of us did. I remember getting into Metz Fort and these other forts. These forts were so thick that an 88 would just bounce off of them. In one fort we found 40-pound sausages, 100-pound cheeses and I came across some Portuguese sardines. I hadn't eaten too good prior to that time and I stuffed myself with Portuguese sardines and they were great! I was with the group when they captured General Kittel at Metz. The first two or three nights we hit Metz we took prisoners that we brought back and interrogated. These prisoners were told by their German officers that the 95th was a composite of the 5th Division on our right and the 90th Division on our left. That wasn't true. We were a brand new division that was committed when they were sent back for R and R.

We were in combat there and I can remember going through a grove of trees and Captain Pinckney, the K Company commander, was killed there. We were hit with 40mm overhead bursts. You can't hide from overhead burst. We were all lying there when Sergeant Peterson said, "we can all lay here and die or we can get the hell out of here!" With that he took off and everybody took off after him [Laughs]! If we would have stayed there would have all been killed, you just can't get away from overhead burst. For that Peterson was given a field commission.

William W. Taylor, Jr.
Infantryman 377th Infantry Regiment

When we were at the Gap they came around and said they wanted people to join a scouting outfit, combat scouts they called it. So I said, "Well, yeah I'll do that." They took my name down along with two or three other people from the company. We didn't think anything more about it until we got to France. We were there putting up our pup tent and trying to live a little bit when they sent for me. They took us out for some training in this scouting business. Just took us right out of the company for training. At some point we moved up on the line along the Seille river I believe. We went up with one of the companies that was up there. Well, this scout and I had it made. We were living in this French château down behind the lines.

I only went up to the lines after it got dark. We would go up to the lines and go out in front and mess around, and chase Germans or one thing or another. Sometimes it was difficult to get back in. Your own troops are there and they see people moving. They're itchy anyway, so you think you might get shot any night trying to come home. We went out every night, come back in the morning before daylight and go back to our château and climb up in the barn they had there and sleep in the hay. It was a pretty good deal. We figured, if you get killed out here it's your own fault. If you goof you might get killed, but if you don't goof you won't. That worked out for a while and then they moved to another position. One day they said we were going to jump off tonight at 9 o'clock. Well they had E and F companies and the lieutenant took a bunch of us down from the scouts behind F Company. We had a mission to go out and secure a road junction when F Company moved out in order to keep the Germans from using it. They had put a big artillery preparation in and the way they told it, it was going to be pretty easy. Well, I've never seen so much artillery in my life coming back the other way! F Company had a problem trying to get out of their holes and move forward. They got shot up pretty bad that night and we never did go out to the road junction. We were kind of trapped there behind the company.

Willis E. Young
Infantryman 377th Infantry Regiment

We got on an old rusty boat that they called the Lingby Castle, it was anything but a castle [Laughs]. Their fresh meat run loose on the deck, they had goats and sheep on the deck. When we got over there, as usual, we were the first ones off the boat. Only 39 of us got off that day because it got so rough that the water tore the cargo hatch off the side of the boat and the captain wouldn't let anymore off that night. The other guys had to stay on there and eat that good mutton for two more days [Laughs]. They were ready to fight by the time they got into shore. We went from there down into the apple orchards, probably twenty miles south of Omaha beach is where we went in. The Americans had already made their break through and gone east because this was early in September. We went down into the apple orchards and pitched our pup tents and waited until everybody from the division got in. At that time Patton's Army got into a little trouble and needed supplies so they took all the guys who had a government drivers license and ran the Red Ball Express for about a week to get a couple round trips in hauling supplies east. When we went over we had a guy that had been in World War I. He said, "I didn't get any medals in World War I so I'm going to get some in World War II." By the time we got over there he had to be forty-four years old. We were all just kids, and wouldn't you know it, he was one of the first casualties. He got his medal, a purple heart, posthumously. From there we got on the "40 and 8's", forty men or eight horses they said. Of course the horses had been there ahead of us.

Anyway they hauled us up to just behind the front to the area of Nancy, France. Nancy was down in the wine-growing region and that's where we first went on line the evening of the 12th of October 1944. Along about 7 o'clock the next morning my platoon sergeant came to me and told me he had a guy for me to take to the first aid station. He wanted me to be sure that nothing happened to him, he didn't say anything about me. I told him I didn't have any idea where it was, but he said to "just go right straight west, it's a mile west of here you can't miss it". I started back there with him but he could hardly walk and it wasn't like we had a road map or anything. We were back about a quarter mile behind the rest of our guys and all of a sudden people are shooting at us. We thought we were supposed to be in friendly territory but we weren't. There were four Germans lined up like a firing squad standing down at the bottom of the hill shooting at us. So I put my bayonet on his rifle and I grabbed a hold of that with my left hand and then laid my rifle right down on my hand. I was probably a hundred feet above these guys and they were shooting at me, they weren't very nice guys. So I went right down the line since they were all lined up, standing almost shoulder to shoulder and I went bang, bang, bang, bang, about like that and they were all laying down. General Patton said you should put at least two bullets in them because you had a better chance of disposing of them that way so I went back and gave them each another one. I was looking around to see if there was anyone else and about that time there was somebody crawling out of a foxhole behind them. Whether that was the officer or noncom I don't know, but he was standing up and before he got straightened clear up I let him have it. It looked to me like he had a rifle with a scope on it and I didn't want him taking a shot at me. The Germans would count your rounds and since I kept one in the chamber and eight in the clip that gave me nine rounds instead of eight like everybody else normally carried. I don't know if he was counting but I got him too. I was fortunate to get the five of them, they only left four holes in my jacket but they didn't leave any in my hide.

After that we went on pretty uneventful but when we got over to the first aid station I found out what was wrong with this guy and I felt like making him number six. All that was a matter with him was that he had his leggings so God dang tight that he had cut off all the circulation in his legs. To think I risked my hide for him doing something like that [Laughs]. I found out later after the war that I had been put in for the bronze star medal and the combat infantry badge because of that incident. I never told anybody about it, but I guess Bill Elder, the guy I took to the first aid station, told some of the guys when we got back. It wasn't until 1953 that I started getting my medals all of a sudden in the mail.

Then everything went on pretty peaceful for the next four or five days until the company commander came to me one day and looked me right in the eye and says, "I want you and one other guy to get in that jeep up there with that driver and go with him." "The rest of the guys are going to walk," he said, "we gotta walk thirty miles, we're going to start in the morning." So then Bill Elder and I went with the jeep driver but we didn't know what we were getting into. We went up to northwest of Metz and we were going to relieve Company B in some other battalion. The infantry company had their headquarters in a big old castle, sitting out on top of a hill. In the basement was their headquarters so I went down there and was introduced to the commanding officer and the rest of the officers and some of their noncoms. They said, "you boys are going to go with us tonight and we're going to show you out where we've got an observation post over there in the Maginot Line and you're going to have to take your men each night over to it." I think I made nine trips over to that box and back. We found it every night, it's a good thing we did because the Germans had the rest of them. My buddy brought up the tail end to see that nobody tried to go back. You had a few of them that kind of wanted to, but he was a pretty good size boy. After the other company was off the line for about a week and then when they came back on the first thing the captain said when he came in the room was, "my God Young, you're still alive" and I said "yeah, why?" He said, "I never had anybody make it over three days." So I guess I was using my supply of luck up early, but it was just one of those things that had to be done.

Anthony N. Petraglia
Infantryman 378th Infantry Regiment

The 95th had just come off desert maneuvers and we went up to Indiantown Gap and that's where we went on through the mountain maneuvers and overseas, after we left from Camp Miles Standish. They shipped us out in the middle of the night and all the barracks up at Miles Standish were black I remember that. These barracks were completely painted black and built underneath a cluster of trees so you couldn't see them from the air. They were all camouflaged. When they shipped us out they sent us out at night on trains I remember the shades were all pulled, everything was a hundred percent security then. Nobody knew we were even leaving. , The Port of Embarkation was from Boston, where we left on the SS Mariposa, a ship called the Mariposa. After England we landed at Omaha beach, and then we moved quite a ways in after the beach. We went through St. Lô, I remember going through St. Lô. Now dates and exact locations I have problems remembering, but there were many incidents, quite a few incidents stand out in my mind, which I'll never forget.

There was one incident, when we were going through this open field, this actually happened before Metz, where me and this fellow from South Carolina were pinned down in this field, he was a full blooded Cherokee Indian, his name was Henson. I saw a concrete embankment, a concrete structure, so I yelled over to him and we tried to make it up to this concrete structure, we dove into the embankment and it was a pigpen. I remember Frank Siegen, a fellow from Chicago that trained with us, also an excellent soldier. He was to my right flank and I remember him getting hit dead center as we were crossing this field. I also remember Colonel Maroon, he was behind me, he might have been behind me maybe ten to fifteen yards, or ten fifteen feet rather. He got hit immediately behind me but I couldn't get to him cause' we had to move up into this pigpen to get this sniper out of there. I remember this sniper as we got him. Anyway, Colonel Maroon got hit pretty bad and another sergeant got hit also at the same time. I remember the three of them getting hit, Frank Siegen was to my right flank and Simer was behind me and Colonel Maroon was behind him and they all got hit at the same time. Incidentally Frank Siegel was killed instantly, but Colonel Maroon pulled through and Simer also recovered and came back to the outfit afterwards. Henson and I were fortunate to make it up to the pigpen.

As we made our way through there I looked around the corner and there was a sniper on top of this barn. I could see him looking out a window but we were unable to actually fire at him from the position we were in, so we had to fire from our left side and we took turns one at a time firing at him. The firing stopped and I yelled to Henson that we should try to make our way over to the barn. When we got over to the barn, I could see we got the sniper; he was hanging out that window with his tongue hanging from his mouth. We finally got him! When we went into the barn we saw three of our GI's in there from either the 377th or 379th regiment, I'm from company G 378. All three GI's were wounded real bad, so I asked how they were being treated and they said they hadn't been given any food or medical treatment. We had captured either three or four Germans I can't remember, but we brought them outside and I had them up against the wall. We were going to take care of them out there, but then we were stopped because they wanted to interrogate them. So I said well, we'll interrogate them down there behind the lines, so we sent them to the back of the line. The 2nd lieutenant still wanted to interrogate them, but I said they'll interrogate them back there, so we sent them back and they were taken care of. We got medical treatment for our three guys, they were crying like babies when we found them, they were really hurt bad. That's one thing that stands out in my mind.

Eugene M. Wroblewski
Infantryman 378th Infantry Regiment

We were in Winchester, England for several weeks. Training was a daily routine but we did get a 24-hour pass to London. Finally about two months after D-Day we were sent from Southampton in a ship connected by cable to a barrage balloon above it. The trip across the English Channel took three days. We slept in hammocks. It was quite an experience, but very few people got seasick. At this point we went on to, I believe, Omaha beach. We landed several months after the invasion but the remnants and the hulls of ships and many, many facets of the war were still there. Tanks were broken down and in tank traps; graves sites were starting to show up on the hillsides. We were sent into the French apple country and we pitched our tents underneath the big hedgerows. There was a call for drivers for the Red Ball Express. This was a special truck convoy system organized to bring fuel to General Patton's fast moving tank forces. He was in danger of outrunning his fuel and other military needs. I was not a driver. I was a Brooklyn kid who took a subway wherever I had to go. I had never learned to drive so I was left back beneath the hedgerows with other non-drivers. After several weeks, all the guys came back from their driving experiences and we were put into "40 and 8" (capacity 40 men or 8 horses) box cars to ride across France, through Paris and Versailles. We felt like military hobos. We ended up in a staging area. We asked some truck drivers where we were and what we were doing here. One of them replied: "You is in General Patton's Third Army". Our hearts sank. We knew we were going into battle now and were going to face combat reality. So, [pause] the chronology of everything is a little bit hazy at this point after fifty years, maybe sixty years [Laughs], so I can only talk about things that occur to me as we go along.

I can remember hearing the first sounds of battle. We could hear gunfire, shots way out in the distance and as we marched, we had to do a lot of marching, the noise of the artillery became louder and louder. The next thing we knew we were in it. One of the things that I learned very early was to recognize the direction of flight of a bullet passing nearby. Since a bullet creates a partial vacuum as it flies through the air it makes a "pop" as it passes by. If you look in the direction of that sound you will be fooled because a split second later you will hear a second report. That is the one that will tell you where the bullet is really coming from. This is one of the hardest things to teach a new combat infantryman. In battle, when I look back, I can remember lots of mud, lots of marching, lots of riding in trucks from one place to another and seeing the devastation, seeing the blown out buildings and I can remember in particular the livestock that would get killed. Shrapnel would hit a cow, as an example, and after a few days it would blow up like a great big balloon. The odor was awful, and its legs would protrude in all directions. During the night as we were fighting we could hear their calves wondering around, bellowing, or mooing or whatever it is. We also saw dead humans for the first time.

Frank Bever
Infantryman 379th Infantry Regiment

I can remember the train that they put us on to take us down through England toward Cheltenham, which is closer and closer to the area where we would go across the Channel into France. That was a kind of a nice excursion down through there, but the old trains that they put us on were something else. We ended up down at camp Barton Stacey near Cheltenham, England. We were there a week or two I suppose then we went on across the Channel into Omaha beach. That's one of the beaches where D-day had taken place three months prior to our getting there. Incidentally, while we were in West Virginia we got word of D-day and that was cause for a little elation because at least the 95th was not going to be involved in the D-day invasion of mainland Europe. So by the time we got to Cheltenham it was almost D+3 months, reassuring us that we would not be involved in the dangerous invasion process that took many, many a life. We finally ended up on Omaha beach as I indicated and then we were put into open areas, they were apple orchards really. We had our own pup tents so two of us would be in the tent. We were there for I suppose a week or ten days anyhow with nothing special to do. I liked to play sports then and they had volleyball nets up, so we played an awful lot of volleyball to keep half way in shape and also to pass the time of the day while we were in this tent area awaiting orders. We would get a lot of volleyball playing in, especially in the afternoons.

As time went by we moved a little closer and a little closer to the combat zone. We eventually moved up further to the battle lines and we replaced the 5th Division on the Moselle River in France. I can recall how huge the foxhole was there. It was a nice foxhole that the 5th Division boys built. Me and my buddy from Milwaukee, Wisconsin, were in the same hole and we took a heck of a lot of fire from the enemy as we stayed there for probably about a week or something like that. Old Ed Riley, my buddy in the next foxhole would get up in the morning and say, "boy, we got everything thrown at us last night but the kitchen sink, and I'm not so sure that I didn't hear it one time!" That was a safe area at least, because we didn't know at that time what combat was really about.

Roger A. Bushee
Infantryman 379th Infantry Regiment

I don't remember the time frame on that, but we did relieve the 5th Division, at least that's what we were told. When we did relive the 5th Division we either used their foxholes or dug our own. The lines were more or less set up since we did relieve them so they could go back and rest. Up to now we had only been under war like conditions I guess. There were buzz bombs when we were in England, there were some home air raids going on and when we got to France we did experience the 88's that came over and dropped in on us. There was some machine gun fire and of course guns and rifles and German patrols. This was how we were indoctrinated in to combat. One of the first things we did was have a company patrol. Why, I don't know? We went out and we were dispersed and the company commander called for artillery fire to locate where we were, to make sure the coordinates were fine. Well, the artillery fire landed right in the company and of course it injured and wounded and killed some guys. In those conditions human error like that just is not needed. For an eighteen-year-old raw recruit combat man I was really scared. It's tough for a new kid to come under these conditions.

Another incident that I would like to mention was one day we heard that there was going to be hot food brought up to us. We had been using K-rations and we could see as we were looking down across the bridge. This jeep was coming and it had a trailer, a thermos type trailer that kept food hot, and I can remember taking turns coming down from our crest once they got in position. We didn't all leave at once, I waited until my partner went down to eat, then when he came back I went down to eat. Well I started walking down, and something told me to run, so I ran down the rest of the way and as soon as I got to the bottom there were some phosphorus shells dropping down on the path that I was just walking. I had just made it because I ran. Well, that made me feel like somebody was watching over me. Needless to say I went back a different route when I went back up [Laughs]! I probably would have been killed I suppose if I hadn't decided to run down.

Eldon L. Knuth
Infantryman 379th Infantry Regiment

Early in November, we moved into a holding position west of Metz. While moving into position, down a ravine, I saw off to one side a German soldier that apparently had been killed several days before. I liberated his pocket watch, which I still have. When I reported that there was a dead German soldier in the ravine, I was told that since I had found him (and probably because I had taken his watch) I was to bury him and bring back half of his dog tag. I went back and took half of his dog tag. The German dog tags are different than the American tags in that they are one piece, which can be broken into two. You turn one-half in and one-half stays with the body. His name was Kepler; I remember that because in Iowa, where I grew up, we had a neighbor with that name. But rather than bury him, I piled rocks and dirt on top of him. In the process of piling rocks on him, I noticed that there was wire running from a tree to his belt, and there was a hand grenade fastened to his belt. If I had moved the body, it probably would have set off the hand grenade. Close call number one.

We were in holding position for about two weeks. I was pretty cautious -- didn't expose myself to the enemy anymore than I had to. I stayed in my foxhole a lot. One day about half a dozen fellows from our outfit were drying and warming themselves around a fire when a round came in. I heard later that it was a short round fired by our own troops using a captured weapon. It killed a couple of my buddies and injured several of them. It shook me up in the foxhole, but I survived with nothing more than a scare. Close call number two.

Paul H. Madden, Jr.
Infantryman 379th Infantry Regiment

I'm not sure, but we probably stayed in Barton Stacey about eight or nine weeks and then boarded in South Hampton to cross the channel and then landed at Omaha. When I was on a trip to Europe I had the occasion to visit Omaha on June the 5th of 2002, I found the spot about where our company had landed, come across the breach and gone up the hill. Of course we actually landed one hundred days after D-day. After we got set up in the apple orchards in the hedgerow areas they took all of the division trucks and a good number of men for drivers and assistant drivers to work on the Red Ball Express. In September Patton started to run short of supplies because the advancement was so rapid across France. So they were taking every available truck and as divisions came ashore they would take their trucks to haul supplies to the forward depots areas. These trucks ran on a twenty-four hour basis. I didn't get on that detail, but I can remember one of the men that was on it, he had an assistant driver that really didn't know how to drive a truck so he wound up driving both shifts. After they released the division trucks they moved the trucks up under their own power, as most of the personnel boarded trains in the Normandy area, and I think it took about four or five days before we got to forward positions. When we were originally moving we had been assigned to the Ninth Army, but sometime during the move they switched the 95th to the Third Army and we wound up in the Metz vicinity.

Our first line experience was in October, I forget the exact date, but the 379th moved across the Moselle River into a beachhead that the 5th Division had secured in September. We relieved one of the regiments in the 5th Division on the east side of the Moselle. We were there for a few weeks then the 5th Division came back and relieved us and we moved back to the west side of the Moselle.

Adolph Massa
Infantry Rifle Company First Sergeant 379th Infantry Regiment

I became the platoon sergeant of first platoon and remained the platoon sergeant as we went over to England and onto France. We crossed the Moselle River where we occupied for about three weeks prior to November the 14th. On November the 11th Company F was sent out at night on a mission to knock out a couple of pillboxes that were to oppose us on the 14th during the initial assault. That night it got so dark we were unable to see where we were going or able to pick out our objective. Captain Carter called for one round of artillery that we knew was zeroed in on one of the pillboxes in order to give us a direction. The round came in and we were already positioned exactly where we wanted to be. One lieutenant, Ame Spoker, was not aware of what was taking place so he called on the radio to me and asked what that was all about. I told him that the round showed us where the pillbox was. He said, "I didn't see it I'm going to call for another round." I informed he that he couldn't due to the fact that we were advancing closer to the pillbox. Lieutenant Ame Spoker was in charge of a three-man demolition squad, which was to blow open the doors of the pillboxes if we couldn't get in.

The lieutenant called for the other round before I could bring my platoon to a halt and withdrawal them to the rear a little bit where it was safer. The round landed right in my platoon area killing three of my men immediately and threw me in the air about twenty feet, tearing off my helmet and wounding about four other personnel. Because of this tragedy we had to call off the mission and withdrawal. We couldn't leave the area immediately because we had this one guy named Campbell that wouldn't leave without his buddy. We had to scrounge around looking for his buddy and when we finally found him he had one leg blowed off. We withdrew back to our lines but we couldn't find the area where we came out because it was so dark. We had to request the balance of the company that stayed back, which had placed machine guns at the openings where we had picked up the minefields, to fire tracer bullets so we could come in through that area without tripping any of the mines that we had set out. We were allowed to go back to the rest area for approximately two days and then we went back up to our initial positions.

John G. Little, Jr.
Artilleryman 547th Anti Aircraft Artillery

On August 26, 1944, we heard that Paris had been liberated just before we were to dock at England. We figured the war would be over before we got into it. We thought we would stay in England for a while but we didn't stay there very long. On August 31, 1944, we were in Liverpool, England unloading our equipment, it took a long time we didn't finish unloading until September 1, 1944. We traveled by truck a short distance to train at a place called Blackshaw Moor near Leek and Stoke-on-Trent, which was the large city in the area. We were there about a week and we drew all of our heavy equipment, anti-aircraft guns and trucks. September 22, 1944, we drove to Southampton. We were restricted, stayed in tents and lived on C-Rations for three days. This was a British camp and I was put on a honey pot detail. The honey pots were in the latrines. To clean them the pots were loaded onto two wheeled carts and then disposed of.

On September 29, 1944, we arrived on Utah Beach. I was on a supply transport with Merchant Marines and we pulled up to a Navy barge to unload our equipment onto the barge. The first sergeant told me it was my turn to go over the side down to the barge. I told him I did not know how to do it. He asked me where I was in the desert training exercise on learning how to disembark off a ship climbing down a rope net. I told him I must have been on a detail digging a hole. He told me it was easy. Just climb down backwards and when the barge comes up just step off. When I got to the bottom a Navy man helped me step off. While we were on the barge we got fresh eggs and bacon, the Navy eats good. We unloaded under bright lights. The war was a long way from there and we had air superiority.

We joined the 95th Infantry Division in Normandy. During our campaign with the 95th we only shot down a few planes due to the excellent air superiority. On October 15, 1944, we departed with the 95th Infantry Division to the Third Army, commanded by General Patton. I was on an advance party going to a bivouac area in the Metz area when I saw General Twaddle for the first time at a road junction. Water trailers were very scarce; we had to haul water in 5-gallon water cans. We saw several water trailers on the beach at Normandy and they belonged to the Army Air Force. We sent men back to get a water trailer. When they got there the guards guarding the trailers asked them what they were doing there and they said, "we are here for our water trailers." The guards said, "OK, they are over there. Go get them." Thanks to them we had five water trailers in the battalion.

Leon E. Langford
Ordnance 795th Ordnance
(Light Maintenance) Company

I don't remember the exact day that we sailed, but our unit sailed out of Weymouth, England. As Martin Lincoln will tell you, we were on LST's, and man they had a meal for us that was out of this world. I recall there were about four or five of us that got right up in the very bow of that ship and ate our dinner and watched the other guys line up along the railing along the sides and hurl their dinner over the sides into the English Channel [Laughs]. Another thing that was very interesting to me was that when we looked at the other ships in that convoy, it was rather rough that day, the LST's would raise up until you could see about 2/3 of the keel on the ship; only the aft section, or the back part, would be in contact with the water and then the front section would slam back down. Those guys were just hurling all over the place as we went across.

We landed at Omaha beach at night, of course it was well after D-day and I was thankful for that. As a matter of fact they had some lights on the beach as we landed. From there we got on trucks and traveled up that steep hillside and eventually wound up in the apple orchards of Normandy, where we stayed in our pup tents, well, I was in there for about six weeks. That was another experience. We had gone through all of this training as to how you use a pup tent, you know my half of the shelter would be joined with yours, just buttoned really. I don't know what they have now, but you would button the two pieces together and then two guys with your duffle bags and everything else that you owned would be inside of that tent. Well, I was in the tent with a good friend of mine and as it turned out throughout our experience over there, George Wisusik (Although he later changed his name to Winters) who was from around Saint Clair Shores, I think up around Detroit, Michigan. I'm 6'2", of course I was a lot skinner then, but George was also about 6' 2" and by the time we got in that pup tent with our duffle bags and all of our gear, we filled it up [Laughs]. As I recall it was not very good weather. I think it even snowed a couple of times toward the end of the time that we were there. You know, If you touched bottom of the underside of the pup tent the water comes right through, which it did several times. Regardless, we shipped out from the apple orchards, well some of our units I should say were involved with the Red Ball Express. Since we had a section in the maintenance company that was automotive, a good many of those guys went up to, Chartre I think it was- it was near Paris anyway. They spent some time up there working on trucks, maintaining trucks in order to keep the Red Ball Express going back and forth from the beaches to the front. Patton had broken out and we were assigned to Patton's Army. He had broken out through St. Lô, of course he was going like a house on fire and ran out of gas, so that's why the Red Ball Express existed I guess.

Let's see, where do we go from there? Oh! Joyful, Joyful! After about six weeks in the apple orchard, every time I think of those apple orchards I think about those guys who landed on D-day a few weeks subsequent. I have thanked God many times that I did not have to fight through those things because it would have been absolutely disastrous. It provided all kinds of cover for defensive positions and defensive actions, all you have to do is read the history books, you know what happened. But anyway, we eventually received orders to go up to the front, which provided another interesting experience. I don't know how many of us, we did not go up on trucks, we went up on the 40 and 8 rail cars. I had heard that there was some kind of a society that was begun in World War I called the 40 and 8, but I had no idea what it was or how you became a member of it [Laughs]. Regardless of that we rode those little French trains for either four days and five nights, or four nights and five days, I don't recall. All I know is that it was a long time. I'm 6' 2" and there were I guess forty guys, forty guys or eight horses, that's what those trains would take. I remember sitting on my duffle bag with my feet scrunched up underneath me for several nights. You were just as uncomfortable as you could be. There was a lot of us that did that because there just wasn't room to lie down. Those who managed to lie down first were reasonably comfortable, as comfortable as you can be on a boxcar like that. On the last night before we were going to disembark off of that train I said, "To hell with it! I'm going to stretch out!" So I stuck my feet in some guy's face and I stretched out. He was about my height so he ate my boots and I ate his boots on the very last night.

Oh, I recall we went past Paris and I think we went past the gardens of Versailles. I'm not sure but we went past some beautiful, beautiful gardens. Also, the food on that train wasn't too hot. I understood that the train commander or somebody had decided that they would make a few bucks off of our rations so they sold them to somebody on the black market. About all we had to eat was some of that canned cheese in the gallon cans and some hard crackers. One day the train stopped. Those little French trains had signals, when you heard two little "toot! toots!" you'd better not be off of the train because they left. Well, we stopped one time in the countryside and right next to where the train doors were was a huge big field of carrots. Well, you know what happened to that carrot field. Here was this French farmer out there running around crazy, raising cane in French. I pictured what was happening to those carrots like something in a Bugs Bunny movie- "plup! plup!" carrots coming up, but anyway we had some fresh vegetables that one day. Another thing that happened on that train was when we got up to a little town just west of Metz, where eventually we went into the line, I think the town's name was Bar-Le-Duc. Anyway, the order came down from the train commander that you guys had been on this train for a few days, it's time you shaved and cleaned up a little bit. So, we got off of the train. It was stopped in the yard where there were a lot of other railroad tracks, trains and boxcars. So we all got out and set up our little mirrors and got our helmets out and were trying to shave and clean up in the cold water. About the time we were half to 2/3 of the way done you heard, "toot! toot!" and the train was ready to take off. There was a lot of throwing stuff in the boxcar doors and running and jumping on the boxcars. Behind us on the other side there was a whole trainload of German prisoners going the other way and they were just laughing like crazy. Here we were going up to do battle and they were all done. I don't know where they might have wound up but I'm sure some of them got back to the states.

Martin H. Lincoln
Ordnance 795th Ordnance
(Light Maintenance) Company

Anyway, we had some special training there in England until finally the day came when we were ordered to go across the Channel. I was on an LST-- I guess it was an LST? It was pitching and rocking so nobody but the sailors and I could eat. We had a nice meal while all the other guys were throwing up until we landed on Omaha. We ended up being bivouacked along the coast there and that's when we were doing the Red Ball Express. Driving the trucks up to the French to take care of Patton's troops, then driving them back. Ultimately we started to move forward. I was in the division ammunition section, which was tiled the division ordnance.

The ordnance officer, Lieutenant Colonel Shawhan, headed this set up. It was pronounced Shawn even though it was spelled like Shaw-han, but you couldn't say Shaw-han. If you ever said that he'd blow your head off. I think his first name was Owen. He used t be interested in the 95th Division Association. I think he attended a lot of the meetings and so forth. Anyway, he was a real tough cookie that was about as old as Patton and tried to be as tough, but [Laughs]. Then under Shawhan was Major Waller. He was a former football player from Ohio Sate or somewhere. He was a real nice guy. Then there was Lieutenant Rawlston and Captain Wentz was in charge of the ordnance company itself. Shawhan had his ordnance office and it had Major Waller and Lieutenant Rawlston in there and Captain Robinson. Robinson was in charge of the division ammunition section where we were all supposed to be specialists on ammunition. We had about six people that would be bivouacked away from the company so that units could contact us when they wanted different types of ammunition. If the artillery wanted something they'd just come order it and we'd get I from the ammunition dumps and stuff like that.

Harry T. Hessler
Clerk 95th Quartermaster Company

I was put in the advanced party to go over to England. We went over to England on a boat out of Boston. In England we picked up vehicles for the division. There were 69 enlisted men and I forget how many officers, but any way when the rest of the division came over we went back to our original companies. I was in the Quartermaster Company, now a truck driver [Laughs]. From there we went over to the mainland and were put into the "red ball express" because they needed supplies more than they needed troops at that point. We ran back and forth from the coast up as far as the division was located at that time. After they got caught up we went back to the normal truck duties, hauling supplies and troops primarily.

Fortress Metz

The division received the order on October 30th to hand the Pagny bridgehead back to the 5th Division and proceed north to relieve the 90th Division on the Metz perimeter. The transition was complete by November 2, 1944. From their new position the Victory Division could see the formidable defenses of Metz. There was a river and three small mountains, with vicious valleys providing a natural perimeter around the city. This terrible terrain was only worsened by the fact that Metz "had served as a garrison and fortress throughout its long history, the natural defenses had been improved by the best military minds of the successive powers that had controlled the city, from Imperial Rome to Nazi Germany." Initially the division's mission was only to hold the front and execute a feint at Uckange and Maizieres-les-Metz. In support of this mission the division line was arrayed with the 377th Infantry Regiment in the north, 378th Infantry in the center and then the 379th Infantry, less 1st and 3rd Battalions who were located in a separate assembly area. Operations consisted of little more planning, patrolling and waiting until November 7th.

As a result of the delayed actions of the 90th Division the Victory Division received a change of mission a few days later. The 95th was now directed to establish a bridgehead at Thionville and upgrade the feint on Uckange to a full-scale attack designed to link up with the bridgehead. From there, the Victory Division, instead of waiting in reserve, would spearhead the attack on Metz from just east of Moselle. The preparatory portion of the operation took place from November 8-14th. The 377th Infantry was assigned the first two operations; a limited objective attack on the Maizieres Pocket, and the establishment of the bridgehead at Uckange, code-named operation Casanova. The third operation would go to the 2nd Battalion, 378th Infantry that had been designated the division reserve. Because the flooded Moselle River had prevented the 90th Division from establishing a suitable armor bridgehead the 2nd Battalion was rushed foreword to an alternate site at Thionville where the high banks had contained the overflowing river. Thionville had not been chosen as the primary site because it was well within the fields of fire of Forts Yutz and d'Illange on its east bank. Nevertheless, it was the only suitable crossing that remained due to the flooding and the 2nd Battalion was ordered to bridge and eventually cross in the face of heavy fire from the over watching forts.

While the Americans were maneuvering to adjust to current conditions the Germans were doing the same. Unfortunately for the German defenders there was a serious debate as to weather or not to fight and withdrawal from Metz and the outlying forts or to strengthen the garrison and further reinforce the defense in an attempt to fight forward at the outlying forts, then withdrawal to the main fortress area and continue to fight even after the city was encircled. Further compounding the problem of German indecision, which still raged as of November 12th, was the shuffling of troops and command. Of the two German divisions present one was an upgraded administrative and mobilization division that was scheduled to be replaced by a combat division commanded by Lieutenant General Kittel. While the general made it to Metz in enough time to hastily prepare and eventually witness the fall of the city, his division only managed to emplace a few piecemeal elements. Nevertheless, General Kittel had earned the reputation of an urban warfare expert from early battles in Polish and Russian cities. His area of expertise was further defined as a specialist of the tactical retreat. It was for this reason that the general had been rushed to Metz, but even with his vast experience there was just not enough time remaining to prepare for the American attack. The general took command on November 10th, and by November 12th it was clear that no additional support was available. Based on his isolated situation he issued this defensive order:

Commander of Fortress Metz   Command Post 14 Nov 1944

a. I have taken over the defense of Fortress Metz as of noon, November 14, 1944.

b. The witnesses of a thousand-year-old borderland fight are watching the soldiers now engaged in battle. It is my duty, as well as that of all officers, to hold Fortress Metz even at the risk of our lives. I expect all soldiers to prove their worthiness in the battle, in memory of their ancestors who fought on the battle-fields of Metz in 1870 and in 1914.

c. The battle efficiency of the troops here is varied. The evils of meager training, unwise commitment, misdirected care and softness are left mostly by the reserves. Reserves are not here to neutralize breakthroughs resulting from carelessness, neglected reconnaissance and lack of liaison.

d. The counterthrust with reserves is too often used and wastes forces unnecessarily which might be better employed elsewhere. I demand, therefore, and this applies especially to unit commanders in the front line, greater alertness on the part of all outpost, constant visual reconnaissance, reconnaissance by small units in front of the main line of resistance and constant liaison with the units on both flanks. Every commander, from platoon leader upward, has to have a small reserve. A commander without reserve may be compared to an empty letterbox, which is of no use. As soon as the last reserves have been committed, the commander loses his initiative.

e. The seriousness of the situation compels me to announce the following: Commanders and units losing men as prisoners or as deserters will be reported. The families of the deserters will suffer the consequences of desertion. It is intolerable to receive reports from the artillery that groups of soldiers abandon their weapons without a fight in order to surrender to the enemy or to disappear altogether.

f. If I discover any soldiers loafing in Metz, I shall have them shot on the spot. Deserters and those who allow themselves to be captured must expect to be fired on as enemy by our own artillery.

g. It is forbidden for any unit or supply installation in Metz and its surroundings to issue anything to soldiers, no matter how long these soldiers have been away from their unit. Couriers, signal personnel, etc. will have written permits. So-called "self-supplying" will cease immediately. All soldiers in Metz will be attached to some unit within 24 hours.

h. The welfare of our fighting troops must be improved. It is the duty of commanders to see that soldiers have at least two warm drinks a day and that handling of food and consumption of alcohol is supervised.

i. It is possible that enemy tanks or troops will breakthrough the outskirts of the city. The troops are to be instructed about the following:

j. During the day, machine guns and the bulk of the troops will occupy the second and third floors of corner buildings. The house entrance must be protected by two guards.

k. The corner house will be manned by no less than a squad.

l. At night, the troops will be on the ground floor.

m. To hang around the street corners and then disappear at the first sign of enemy fire is forbidden. Every street must give the appearance of emptiness and ambush.

n. The opening of fire in streets id effective only if the enemy cannot find cover.

o. Instead of extending in depth, the defense must be linear and should be echeloned in height up to the roofs on street corners and individual streets.

p. Panzerfaust troops must be on the ground floor. Window open! Ambush!

q. Running about in the streets is forbidden. It is necessary when occupying a house, to establish a messenger and supply route not under enemy fire, through the courtyard and garden (by wall break-throughs, etc.).

r. Local fighting quickly exhausts the energy of troops. Therefore, everything must be done to stop the enemy outside the towns. Penetrating tanks have to be taken care of with Panzerfausts.

s. My battle experiences around and in large towns: Rumors take on gigantic proportions. All blabberers, rumor mongers, deliberate liars, commanders who invent false reports in order to shirk their duty, ghost seers, and the usual clowns have to be reprimanded for their stupidity by cold blooded people. For example, on November 14,1944, the rumor circulated that enemy tanks would be in the city within 10 minutes. Rather than immediately arresting that type of rumormonger, people annoyed me with questions as to the truth of the report. Every commander must maintain the point of view: "Where I am there exists no rumors but only facts. What my own eyes have not seen is 99 per cent swindle."

/s/ Kittel

Generalleutnant

Distribution: Down to platoon leaders.[2]

By November 14th engineers had completed a bridge at Thionville and the 2nd Battalion, 378th Infantry had begun its attack on Fort d'Illange. Without this valuable fort the Germans would no longer be able to place observed fires on the newly established bridge designed to pass the 10th Armored Division. Based on the division's gains as a whole, Major General Twaddle requested to change the original corps plan to allow the 95th to attack the next day instead of waiting for the 5th and 90th Divisions to encircle Metz. His plan called for the two separate battalions, the 1st Battalion, 377th Infantry and 2nd Battalion, 378th Infantry, to form Task Force Bacon. The task force was given the mission of attacking from east of the Moselle on November 15th. The 377th Infantry (minus) was to be the main effort and ordered to attack and seize south with the suburb of Woippy as their limit of advance on November 15th. The 378th Infantry (minus) was a supporting effort designated to attack the northern group of western fortifications and aid in the advance of the 377th Infantry. The 379th Infantry was also a supporting effort, ordered to continue the attack to the south of the western fortifications that began on November 14th. By ordering the 379th to attack a day prior, the division staff had hoped that they would be perceived as the main effort, and thereby draw defenders from prepared positions in response. The four isolated attacks were designed to support the 379th Infantry and eventually come together for a massed final assault.

Charles R. Fowler
Artillery Officer and Infantry Rifle Platoon Leader 377th Infantry Regiment

After Omaha beach we went to the hedgerow area on Normandy. Patton had run out of gas so they took people that could drive trucks, and some that weren't very good drivers, to deliver gas to the front lines. When that was finished we joined the 5th and the 90th Divisions in order to try and conquer Metz, which they had already failed to do. When we went there we moved in on the Moselle River. I was in the 1st Battalion under Lieutenant Colonel Decker. The decision was that 1st Battalion would cross the Moselle River as a feint and then pull back. But as it happened we were successful in capturing two little towns so the higher command left them there. Well, the Germans counter-attacked with tanks and flamethrowers and captured some people and run some out in the woods. Most of the 1st Battalion was cut off. It was raining a lot and the river was flooded and very wide. Back in the little town where the battalion headquarters was we kept getting artillery direct hits on the headquarters even though we moved every night. We would move and still get direct hits. Colonel Gaillard ordered the evacuation of the town. When we searched the town we found that the French Free Fighter that was supposed to be helping us was actually a German officer. He had a radio in a church steeple directing fire in on us. We sent him back to a prisoner of war camp, but the camp wouldn't take him because he had been cleared as a French Free Fighter. About that time Colonel Gaillard came there and immediately called back, but they never did get the German.

We had a lot of wounded. One boatload of wounded came back across the Moselle River, it was flooded about three hundred yards wide by then. Just as it got to the bank a German 88 shot and hit the boat. They all went down into the river but two, the two that were handling the boats. I was then put in charge of all the vehicles. We were supposed to go fifteen miles down the river to Thionville to join the 2nd Battalion. We moved out at night in total darkness and made it there by daylight. It took about two or three days across the river for the 2nd Battalion to get the Germans out and get to the 1st Battalion. From there we moved on into Metz.

As we got on into Metz we captured a fort and a bunch of Germans. It was getting dark so I went back to talk to the battalion commander to see if we were going to hold up there while we took the ninety prisoners back to the rear or if we were going to go on forward. I was walking back and then all of a sudden the fort blowed up. People were just running from the area. You couldn't get anyone to go in and get the wounded. I remember picking up one soldier that had both legs blowed off at the knee and his arm was all torn up, and he kept yelling, "Oh my legs!" We carried them on blankets and put them on jeeps to evacuate them.

William Lake
Anti-Tank Infantryman 377th Infantry Regiment

We motored across France all the way to the 3rd Army area near Metz. The line companies all went in the 40 and 8 boxcars and it's bad enough to listen to those stories, let alone to experience them. We got to Verdun, and few people knew that Verdun had been in the First World War. We were told not to move around anymore than we had to because there was a possibility there were unexploded shells that were covered up a little bit. We got up to Metz and got in to a holding action. The Mosselle River was in its highest flood state since Julius Caesar's time or some God-awful expanse of time like that. We had an outpost in a hotel where we stayed on the second floor. We put some booby traps on the steps because the Germans, they snuck around like anybody else. Then when we finally started the first offensive, we went up to fire direct support across the river, just doing our part. The line companies were down there and the boats didn't show up, they showed up at the wrong place. The plan was kind of screwed up. They got across the river and immediately got cut off while the 90th Division was making a bigger assault across just north of there.

We packed up and started going south to attack Metz from the west coming down from the north. We went in this town Whoippy, and it made a believer out of you. Yes, Lord, they were out crying, praying and shouting. The dead horses were the thing that was most upsetting for me. Tanks were zooming around there and jeeps were carrying litter patients. I don't know if we stayed overnight there or not, but the next day we went down to Metz proper and we crossed over a little piece of water and then a larger piece of water, that I think was the Mosselle. They had some kind of low-water bridge or ford made of concrete that the farmers put in streams that are not in high water. There was a big ordinance building there and by then the people were getting back on the streets and these Free French Fighter people, I don't know where they had been hiding, but they came out with their little arm bands, shaking their fists at the prisoners. We stayed over night and sometime the next day we went up to Bousandale, to the east. That whole area is beautiful in the summer, but in November, well it was like wintertime any place, dark at 4 o'clock and temperatures falling like a rock as you were trying to find some structure to sleep in.

We ate 10-in-1 rations, and sometimes K-rations. 10-in-1 you could have a little Primus cooking stove and utensils, and we got cans that were like in the grocery store, canned corn and pork and beans. We looked all over for potatoes and onions, but there were none to be found, they took everything when they left. We didn't see any civilians at all. This is where the German border was and they defended their homeland and they knew it. They fought like tigers there, the same thing we would have done if it had been reversed. We would have done everything we could to defend our own. They had this big tank trap east of St. Barbara and we fought in there for four days. There was this stupid little town on a hog back, it was only maybe 8 or 900 feet long, but at the far end was a double back s-turn switch back with three German tanks there and you couldn't get a shot at them. We had tank destroyers there but they couldn't get them in position. So they were going to try to do it with the Bazooka.

My squad leader, Sergeant Rex Garsline, he was married and had a couple of kids but he had been an expert infantryman in the states. He could have stayed in the states but he went over and he came back and got a volunteer, a guy named Manny Schlagel, (he had a huge nose) to go with him. Sergeant Garsline was with the 7th division, which was where the cadre was from that built our division. They went and the first thing I knew there was an extra heavy barrage of mortars. These mortars walked down the street, they don't come as a barrage, they come boom, boom, boom! It turned out Sergeant Garsline lost one of his legs, below the knee I believe, and Schalgel got hit in the stomach. I talked to Schlegel after the war and he said he was on a Jeep and some more artillery was coming in and they parked the Jeep and ran in the building and left him out there. He said to himself, "I'm not going to die, I'm going to try to stay alive" and he got himself off the Jeep and inside the building and he made it. He married his nurse in England. He had a job when I met him after the war in San Francisco at a Haps Brewery, he couldn't have had a better job because he liked to drink.

During the same barrage, one of the fragments went down the hallway where our squad was and hit another man in our squad in the spine. And oh boy, it was true confession time, he was screaming and wailing and made confessions to the Lord and I'm sure it was sincere. He got evacuated out but three men just within a few minutes got our attention. Somebody finally got down there with a bazooka and knocked one of the tanks out and the other one got in gear and took off. Oh, no, no, no, they had pulled us back, I guess the next day and they concentrated artillery on that place from several different areas and the tactical Air Force came in with B-47's and dive bombed and that's when we broke through.

Fred B. Love Jr.
Infantryman 377th Infantry Regiment

We moved from there to the other side of Metz, we had a pretty serious scrimmage there, it was nine o'clock at night and we did some fighting. A lot of our guys were getting shot at but our particular squad didn't, I don't think we lost a man. We went in from the slag pile, all the 95th would know about the slag pile. There were dead German's all around the front of it, and they killed all those German's and there was a bunch of them lying there. The night before the engineers had gone out there and cleared the strip of about ten feet wide and put markers around the mine fields and we walked through there and you could look on either side and see those Bouncing Betty's, three little wires sticking up. We didn't know if they'd missed one. Barter and I were platoon scouts and we moved out about at least 100 yards ahead of the company and we were going along there just fine and suddenly something zipped through the grass, bullets were flying and popping around us. They sent a tank out there to go with us and he started out and the tank hit a mine and blew the tracks open. I remember looking back there and those guys were scrambling to get out of that tank, so we went without any armor with us and we advanced to Woippy, France. It was three or four miles, quite a ways to move in combat. When we came up there close to the barn there was a ditch there and I walked up to the ditch and there was a German lying there with his rifle ready to shoot us. He didn't get off the first shot, I fired first and after about three shots we went on and he stayed there. There was a barn close by and old Barter said, "Well, there may be somebody up in there, a sniper or something," so he ignited that barn and it started burning. As it turned out it was a blessing because that night they used a part of that barn for an aid station to treat the guys that got shot. There was a lot of our men that got shot while we were advancing.

We got into Woippy and there was a sniper there and wiped out almost one whole squad, Sergeant Herbades squad. That night Sergeant Herbades took a nap before they got wiped out, the next day that sniper shot them. He was standing there and he heard some horses coming, he thought there were Germans riding those horses up there. He yelled, "Halt!" and the horses didn't halt so we halted them and killed both of them, two big draft horses. There were quite a few Germans lying around in there that we had killed; what we did was we took hand grenades and threw them in to basements of houses and the people that moved in later said they found a lot of dead Germans taking refuge in basements that we eliminated with hand grenades.

We got to the little town of Woippy, the first town our company took. We pretty well cut the town to pieces, it was a small town; we were pretty gun happy by that time and we followed the tanks there, the tanks went with us as we were taking Woippy. I remember this one time a German soldier stepped up to a window and this tanker saw him and he fired his, I guess it was about a 70 mm gun, he fired it and instead of having delayed action, it was armor piercing and exploded when it hit that glass and three of our men just dropped, essentially, they were just walking along there. So he killed three of our own men by firing into that window. He got the German, but we could have gotten him without him shooting a main gun round. Later that tanker, he was going down this street and we wanted to turn to the right, kind of angle off and there was no way we could get him, we got out front and we waved we didn't know he had a telephone in the back. We waved and motioned and everything and he didn't go and the last we saw of him he went down the street by himself in the tank and we went down this other street. We moved in some houses along the edge of Woippy and the Germans decided they wanted to wipe us out and for about two hours they shelled that town and we took some casualties, kind of scary experience. But then later when they quit firing we moved out to the open and we could sit out there and look across there and there was a German. He walked out there to an apple tree I guess and he picked an apple and he was standing there eating and you could see him putting it up to his mouth and taking it back down, only must have been 300 yards from us and we started shooting at him and the silly guy just stood there. We fired several times at him but we never did get him and he turned and walked away. We never killed that German.

As we started to go into Metz, they had this new construction, a big old building that they were building, it looked like some kind of an apartment building. We went into that apartment building, it was all open, it wasn't anywhere near completed. We were going to stay there over night and just as it got dark and Bart and I were standing in the hallway and a German stepped in the door. Bart was closest to him and the German had a rifle and Bart reached over and grabbed that rifle and they wrestled for the rifle and Bart took it away from him. He turned to leave but he didn't get more than three steps and Bart shot him. He lied outside the building and moaned a time or two and Tanner said: "Well, we can't leave him up here." So we shot him again and the German didn't moan anymore. We fixed him. This sounds kind of brutal but soldiers are brutal. We got even more brutal. It got to where it was all too common when a man pulled the trigger. That night, after Barter had shot that man, it kind of shook him up a little bit, he had to wrestle with it and he stepped in a hole in the floor and scraped his leg real bad and he couldn't walk real good.

Later that night when orders came down to go on a patrol in a boat, there was a railroad bridge that had been mined but it was still intact. The Colonel sent word down that any of us that survived taking the mines off that railroad bridge would get a silver star. We weren't much interested in silver stars, we were much more interested in living. We picked up that old boat and there is a bunch of us, I don't remember how many, but there were several, Bart, Tanner and myself I remember and others as we carried that boat behind enemy lines. We heard the Germans in the buildings on both sides in Metz. We got to about a couple of hundred yards away from that bridge and all of a sudden there was an explosion you wouldn't believe. We sat there for a little bit and the railroad bridge was being attacked. We clapped, it wouldn't have been good if we had been attacked but we were sitting there and woosh, woosh, woosh, a big piece of steel fell down about twenty feet from us, if it would have hit us it would have killed us. We barely clapped quietly because we had our own lives, we were very happy we didn't get a silver star because that was a pretty dangerous situation.

Well, we moved on up, we had to fight our way in; we had to take to street fighting and lost a few people. We finally got to the river, the Moselle River ran through Metz, we got up to the river and they put us in boats. They had an engineer with each boat, there were ten to twelve or, maybe even 14-people in the canvas covered boats. We were in a canal and were shielded from where the enemy was across the river. The Germans laid an artillery barrage on the other side of the river, a real heavy barrage, but they just quit all of a sudden. It was two hours before we moved out and we were in this canal and rode those boats out in the river. As we came out in the river, I was in the second boat and we had smoke pots we were going to put out as we crossed the river, they were anchor pots that you pull on the river and they smoke. We crossed the river and set out the smoke pots and we got about half way across and the bullets started to fly, it was pretty harsh to lie right there exposed. I saw the Germans in fox holes shooting at us, so I stood up and I started shooting at them, they were only a couple of hundred feet away so you could hit the target it was that close. I saw guys rising up in the foxholes and Lieutenant Waiver said: "Love, cut that out, they'll know we're here." Well, being a GI, I very crudely told him I thought they knew we were here all day, and he said: "Well, give them hell!" So I continued shooting and Lieutenant Waiver had given orders to Tanner that if he needed to promote somebody he would give me a promotion.

When we got across the river Lieutenant Waiver was dead, he had been killed in the boat and old Sergeant Van Cleaf was shot. So Albert Tanner took over as the platoon sergeant and I took assistant squad leader with John Clark as squad leader. I went from Private to Sergeant in one little short boat ride. In that trip crossing, I lost ten people that I knew well enough to all their wives and families back home to pass the word along. It was a very trying time. When we got across the river though, we established a breakthrough there. I had heard about a Bazooka somewhere before we started to cross and a kid named Kealan had the ammo for it. We saw a house down there about a couple hundred yards away so I thought I'd try the Bazooka on that house. I shot the Bazooka at the house, that was the only time I fired a Bazooka in combat and that thing blew back something in my face and burnt my face, it was all bloody and I was so mad I felt like wrapping that Bazooka around the tree. But I laid it down by the tree and we piled the ammunition through. After we had enough there we moved on out to a stone fence going up towards town.

Most of the company went on the one side but our squad went on the outside of the fence. It was open and there was a house and an open area. We went up to the house and there was a hole blown in the wall and the squad went through the hole and I brought up the rear as assistant squad leader. Barter went through the fence and I heard, "Hey, Bart come here! Let's check this house!" Well, "house" and "rouse" in German sounded a lot alike and there were some Germans hiding in a cellar there that came out and I said, "Hands up." So they dropped their arms and rifles and had their hands up and I pointed to this wall and they went over and they stood by this wall. Eight of them came out before Barter got there, to say that I was scared was an understatement! But I didn't let them know that, I was too much of a hard head at that age. I was getting kind of mean by that time. I had been in combat long enough and I was getting a little mean. Anyway, we lined up those eight Germans there and I said, "Is that all?" and one of them said "Das ist alles," that's all. I fired down in that cellar just to be sure and somebody down there screamed in German, "Nicht schisten!" don't shoot, so I quit shooting and out come three more. By that time several guys had gotten there they had heard us shooting and came back. They had heard us holler to the Germans. We lined those eleven Germans up and I said, "is that all!" They said it's all so I took a hand grenade and threw down in that cellar and nobody else came out so that was all I guess. I told a couple of guys to take the Germans to the river and hold them until somebody could take care of them for me. We had orders when we started to cross the river not to take prisoners because we didn't have anywhere to put them, but I had been raised to be a gentle person and I didn't see a need to kill somebody unless it was necessary and that wasn't necessary. I could have shot them down I could have killed every one of them or they might have fought back and got me. But it worked out best to take them prisoners I thought, it was Lieutenant Waiver who gave the order and he was dead anyway.

That night when I saw my dead buddies, they had laid them out there in a row, and somebody carried them up there and put them in this building and I saw them and from then on I was just about as mean as you can get. I was a seasoned soldier by that time. The next day though the warehouse had been hit and we had control of the territory. There were French people in that warehouse, they carried out clothing but I didn't get any of the stuff, it belonged to the Germans. A shell had hit this building and it had lot of ammo and artillery shells lying everywhere. There were two horses there and they were tied up and Joe and I went up there and untied them and I guess they were hungry. We untied them and started walking off and here came these horses and they both came walking towards me. These were German horses and I didn't know what the Germans had taught them, I got a little hysterical when they were just walking right at me, so I raised up my rifle and aimed at a vital spot and I said, "If they come any closer they are dead!" Joe said, "Oh, they are not going to hurt you," so I didn't shoot them. That was the battle of the horses. We fought the battle of Metz and had several pretty bloody days. About the third day after that the squad leader John Clark got hurt and I made squad leader. I went from PFC to squad leader by the time we secured Metz. That's when we got our nickname the Iron men of Metz from the German General, he said, "You men must be made of iron to take this city." I found out later that's what they called us. We didn't feel like we were iron men, we were just soldiers doing our job.

Joseph W. Napier
Infantryman 377th Infantry Regiment

We moved on up into some barracks that the Germans were building there in France. They weren't finished, no windows or anything so at night it was cold and chilly and rainy off and on all night. The next morning we went up, I think it was near Wappy, France. We walked down the street and into some other buildings and stayed there for a few hours and then we went up the Moselle River and took some boats and crossed the Moselle. As we got into Metz, France we were walking down the street a sniper fired at us and of course being new we didn't know exactly what was going on, but Andy and Northcut and I headed for a building. We got inside the building and there was this red headed guy from E Company already there. After a little bit we went out of this building but we didn't draw any more fire from the sniper. After that I went on up to join E Company. There I met Alvin Tiner, which was the platoon sergeant of the 3rd platoon. Toplift went into the 1st platoon and Andy and I were together in the 3rd platoon. Alvin Tiner asked me where I was from and I told him Skidmore, Missouri and he said he was from Randolph Highway. That wasn't too far from where I lived. He put me on a telephone, a sound power phone, and I sat there all night listening to it. The next morning Fred Love and I got together, he was a buck sergeant, and went to going around and looking in some buildings. We got into a warehouse that was full of German flags and their other supplies: ammunition, Mouser rifles, and so on. We went on and pulled all the bolts out of the rifles and threw them in the canal so they couldn't use them again. When we were doing that, being an old farm boy, I saw some horses that were tied up. They had probably been there for four or five days without water or feed so I untied the horses and turned tem loose. Of course being a horse they thought we were their buddies or something and kept following us around. I told Fred that the one horse liked him and he said he was going to shoot it, he thought it was going to stomp him [Laughs] but I told him the horse wasn't going to hurt him, that he was just hungry and thirsty and wanted some food and water. After that we run them off and than ran down the street clompity-clomp and the next thing I knew I saw a GI riding one of them.

The next morning we shoved off and were in fighting again and I was in this house, I think it was about the 15th of October, with a lieutenant by the name of Bowman who had taken the company over about a day before. Anyway, I was off in another room and I heard "Bang!" and a sniper had shot him right between the eyes and killed him. We went on fighting from house to house until the 22nd of October when they declared it a "Free City." We declared it free but they were still fighting in there. We had to seal them in some of those forts they had. I was back there in December and they were still held up in some of those forts. It's hard to tell how long they held out. Anyway, we went out of there one night. We took a road out of Metz and as we walked out of town there was this convoy of German soldiers, horses, artillery, horse drawn artillery and a mess wagon. Everything had been upset because the Air Force had bombed them. We walked by that for hours and of course the smell was terrible as you can imagine, who knows how long they had been there.

Richard H. Schoen
Medic 377th Infantry Regiment

We left after taking Metz and I was somewhere between Boulay, France and Saarlautern, Germany along the Siegfried Line, maybe near Maizieres-les-Metz I guess. I can remember the slag pile. Before that we got into a brewery and stayed there a couple days. But eventually we got into Maizieres, to a steel mill that had the slag pile. If you've ever heard an 88 or a mortar bounce off a steel plant it is just like thunder. We had casualties up there with K Company. We asked for a litter squad to bring these guys off. They didn't know where in the hell they were going or how to get up there so I came off the slag pile and would pick up the litter squad and lead them back out, four squad men and myself. Dick Peticourt was the last man in line, and on our right was an M-42. The guy could have killed us all [Emotional Pause], but he didn't. I guess he saw our medical brassards? Anyway, he shot about knee level and hit Peticourt, the last man, in the leg. So now we had to take Peticourt back and I needed to get another squad. My parents used to go visit Dick Peticourt regularly when he was back in the hospital in Kentucky. Unfortunately, he was so badly wounded he got on drugs and died from that. We took that slag pile twice. You can't dig in on a slag pile. We just took it and lost it and took it and lost it until finally we could keep it.

There were other times like that. One time I had a guy that fell on a landmine. He was conscious, but almost totally destroyed and he said, "hey soldier, kill me, I don't want to go back." [Emotional Pause] I had nightmares that I had done it [Emotional Pause] but I didn't do it! We got him back but I don't think he survived. He didn't want to go home that way and I can't blame him either. Patton had started what we called marching fire. We would leave a position and just walk across a field a fire from the hip. We had all the ammo in the world. The Germans wouldn't dare come out of their holes, we would walk right over top of them, but you had to get through all the indirect fire and minefields before you could do that.

I was wounded with mortar fire. When I was hit I thought I had wet my pants, but it was blood. It ran down my leg. I didn't know I was hit, but I was scared as hell, I mean really scared! I was a medic, and to talk about wounds, it seemed to me that we saw more casualties with shrapnel than with small arms fire. It just seemed like that when we got inside the 88's, got through the minefields, got through the mortars and by the time we got into small arms range they were coming out with their hands up. But it was extremely difficult getting there though. Most of my casualties were from shrapnel. You know they say there are no atheist in the foxhole and it's true. When you're out there and you're under fire, whether it be small arms fire or whatever it is, there is only one guy you can turn to. The guy next to you is going to be a casualty too, your mom and dad and brothers aren't there, there is only one place to go and I went to God. Whether it got me through or not I don't know, but it sure made a better Christian out of me. I was wounded November 26th, 1944 between Boulay and Saarlautern I think.

I was a medic so I evacuated myself and took another man with me. I bypassed the aid station and got on a jeep and went straight back to the collecting company where they laid me on a stretcher. I had been lying in open ditches with sewage so they just took a knife and cut my clothes off from toe to head. They picked me up and put me on another stretcher and said, "Schoen, count to three," and I said, " one, two" and never got to three because of the sodium penethol. I was out cold. I was sent into Paris when I was wounded, in a hospital there, and just a few days later the break through came in. They were so concerned about the Germans making it all the way to Paris that they evacuated all of us over to England and I spent 6 months hospitalization in England. I remember that plane. There were 13 stretchers on a DC3 and I heard this beautiful music. It was Wagner's Triston estan de love music when the Triston crescendo builds up and collapses over. That was the feeling that I had, that I was escaping this thing.

While I was there my dad was so concerned that I had died or was dying that he tried to join the Merchant Marines and come over and see me [Emotional Pause]. Instead, my cousin Father Charlie Sullivan, a Jesuit Priest, said to my father, "Cliff I'm going over there and the first thing I'm going to do is see Dick." And he did. He immediately found me in the hospital, and he said, "Dick, you didn't stop talking for three hours!" [Emotional Pause] It's good to see family you know! One of my best buddies from home, Jim Saddler, was wounded the same day I was, different division though. But our folks got together and knew where we were and helped us meet in Edenborough, Scotland. Here comes Jim all hunched over and limping along and there I was hunched over and limping towards him, it was some site. We had our pictures taken in our kilts and all, but I can't find that pictures!

William W. Taylor, Jr.
Infantryman 377th Infantry Regiment

The next day things got moving forward and we went on towards Metz. We're moving along and at this point we're not getting too many missions. We were moving too fast for us to go out, so they put us on details and things. They had us pick up replacements, gather up and escort prisoners, and things like that. This went on awhile and I guess I considered myself lucky to be in the scouts at that point. One day they just dissolved the scouts and the three of us that had made it went back to the company. I became a squad leader, and in fact the other two guys became squad leaders too, one in the third platoon and one in the second platoon. We moved on for some time until one night I was sitting in a house and I had a man that knew he was going to die. Sometimes you see people like that. He sat and talked to me for hours. He showed me pictures of his wife and kids and I knew that that man knew he was going to die. Some people, in war you'll see them.

Willis E. Young
Infantryman 377th Infantry Regiment

We were relieved there and they pulled us back. We alternated several times relieving different companies so they could get cleaned up and rest a few days before they went back on the line. On the 7th of November Company C went across late in the evening, they crossed the Moselle River and dug in on the bank and on the morning of the 8th Company B went over. We went through them and went on up and took the hill up above. I was the second man across, the first boy didn't make it. Mr. Busbee from Alabama drowned in the Moselle River. He got tangled up in a barbed wire fence and the old river kept a rising and they couldn't get to him. Of course the damn Germans wouldn't quite shooting at him. That was where we ended up in our so-called lost battalion because the Germans blowed up a big dam on a lake and flooded the whole Moselle River valley and then we had a week of rain. The heaviest rain they had in a hundred years and between the two they shut off the supply of food and ammunition to us and all we could get was what they flew over and dropped out of Piper airplanes. We were glad to see those little rascals come. We spent till the 14th of November in this here trap.

Metz was one of the most heavily defended cities in Europe, yet it was never bombed during World War II because there was a lot of poison gas stored there. They had these great big forts, but I was captured about two days before the Americans got into these big forts. According to General Patton we were supposed to make a feint and catch some prisoners for him to interview. Well we got across the river and we had just started up the hill when the radio crackled, "you're doing fine men, hold at all cost." Well then five minutes later the radio and the radioman got shot and the company commander had ordered that if they had not heard from us by a certain time to lay the artillery in on the top of the hill. By that time we were at the top of the hill and they laid it in on us. We had about eight boys wounded, I don't think anybody was killed, but some of them were pretty badly wounded because of his stupidity. You don't say if you don't hear from me to fire artillery! Our officers never seemed to lead while I was there. I was usually in the lead, I was a scout, but if we were going some place they would say, "this is where we're going, you take the lead." It wasn't anything like you see pictures of these civil war generals out there in front, we didn't have any general with us, we didn't have any sergeants with us! They were back behind, bringing up the rear I guess, seeing nobody fell out [Laughs]. General Patton did put out the order after I was wounded that all officers and noncoms will lead from the front and not the back.

The day before I was captured I got into a hand grenade competition with one of the meanest looking suckers you ever saw. He was looking over the railroad tracks at me and I tossed one to him and as soon as I throwed it I new I had made a mistake because I didn't hold it long enough. Pretty soon it came right back. The next one I pulled the pin down in the hole then reached up like I got it and throwed it. He grabbed a hold of it and got it just back to his ear when, BANG! Then I could hear a lot of scurrying around like people were coming to his aid so I threw a couple grenades on each side of him. Three guys took off running, but by that time my rifle was too far away from me where I couldn't reach it. In a little bit they came and set up a machine gun in the brush on the side of me and took a few shots at me and hit me right in the stomach. Knocked me right on my back, clear off my feet. That made me mad, so I stuck a couple down that guys neck. I either hit the machine gun or else his helmet because it hit metal before it exploded. Then I put another one over there and there wasn't any more nonsense. A bullet hit my pistol belt and ruined everything on the right hand side of it. It actually set my belt on fire from the powder, I wasn't long getting that rascal off. It was just like a mule kicked you. A bullet will stop you in your tracks. The Lord was with me though. That was war I guess. You can't say well, I'm not going to shoot them because they'll kill you if they get a chance. If you're there you better defend yourself because you're not going to be there long if you don't.

What had ended up was that the Germans had set up a machine gun in front of our first aid station and captured the first aid station. I was in the aid station for trench foot. We were in the water see, we couldn't dig our foxholes as deep as we wanted to because of the water, our foxholes were only about waist deep. It rained all week and the Germans had blowed up a dam just after we got across. As we were making this feint the engineers were suppose to build a bridge three or four miles to the north of us but the engineers couldn't reach across the flooded river. They had to wait pretty near a week for enough bridge to come up and then they assembled it under fire. They did a heck of a job getting it up, it was under bad conditions, raining and the Germans shooting at them. After they got it up they started down towards us, but they had all these forts and pillboxes, it's pretty hard to throw a hand grenade in an 18" pillbox with a little slit without getting right up to it.

In the meantime, our company commander surrendered about thirty-five officers and noncoms that was in the house attached to the first aid station. So about a total of seventy guys out of the company were captured. By the time B and C Companies got into Metz they were pretty much wiped out between the captured, killed and wounded. There couldn't have been more than thirty-five guys left in my company and there couldn't have been many more than that in C Company either. When they got into the edge of Metz the Germans had planted mines or something down along the railroad track and anyway everything blowed up and it killed a bunch of guys. The thing about the infantry, some of these outfits that went in at Omaha beach had turned over their supply of men at least three times. If you look to see who died in World War II the majority of them were privates, PFC's and sergeants, the ground troops. There were officers killed too, I'm not saying there wasn't, a second lieutenant was not a long life job in the infantry, but on the big numbers it was mainly privates.

From the aid station I was taken in a German ambulance to a German Army hospital in Melzig, or something to that extent. It was west of Saint Wendle about eight miles. That was a regular German Army hospital and I was there about three days before I was evacuated because the American Army was getting too close. They put us on a hospital train with all these amputees. They had anywhere from three limbs missing to one. We got as far as Saint Wendle where there was an air raid going on so they pulled us in by the depot to protect the train because there was an anti-aircraft gun right there by it. Unfortunately, somebody forgot to tell this B-51 pilot not to go down there and blow that thing out of the hole, so he did. I ended up with a hunk of shrapnel in my knee, and when the dust and the smoke settled me and the one other American that was in the car were the only ones that were still in the bunks. All the Germans were lying in a pile on the floor. That was quite a mess trying to get all the guys with fresh amputees back in their bunks. Anyway, they finally got everybody back in a bunk somewhere and we went down the road and I ended up in the hospital at Stalag 5-A in Ludwigsberg for about three weeks. There were thirteen of us in the hospital. On about the second day in there by golly we were getting more attention from the nurses than the doctors appreciated because we were the first prisoners of war that had ever been in that hospital. That second morning the nurses brought in some apple strudel and of course we had the strudel ate before the doctor showed up, but somebody told him about it and he almost had a stroke. That ended our apple strudel, we didn't get anymore [Laughs]. One day a German doctor came in and said, "you've got gangrene we have to take your foot off sign these papers". I said, "when it rots off at the knee you can take it off at the ankle." He said a few choice words in German then told the guards something and they picked me up and took me outside and threw me in a snow bank. That probably saved my feet, because they looked bad, they were only broke open in about fifteen places. I really think the walking around in the snow for three weeks saved them. They were just too quick to amputate as far as I was concerned.

Anthony N. Petraglia
Infantryman 378th Infantry Regiment

So as we moved into France and we were getting up into Metz, which was one of the most fortified cities in the world, it was never, I found out later on, conquered since sometime in 400 B.C., we had a lot of pretty fierce fighting in there. We finally liberated Metz and captured a German General and he nicknamed us "the Iron Men of Metz" and that's where we got the name. That stuck with the division all the way through to this day. We moved along in through France and there were quite a few other incidents. Another close buddy of mine, his name is Smokey Lowe, he was from the Smokey Junction, Tennessee. I remember when he came into the service, he was unable to read or write; his first pair of shoes were actually his Army shoes, he had never worn a pair of shoes. He was really from the hills. He was a very, very close buddy of mine. We were close, he was about twice as tall as me and he was really, really a great guy.

I remember this one incident overseas. We were once again pinned down and he was about four feet away from me, and there were two snipers up in a tree. This was just as we were approaching the forest. We were in an open field, and the two snipers started firing at us so we hit the ground and I told Smokey to "Play dead!" I remember this one sniper firing at me from a tree. I had my head turned facing down to the left and this one fired at me and just missed my head. I could see where the bullet had embedded in the ground. That's when I told Smokey to "Play dead!" We must have been lying there for about five or ten minutes and finally they found out we were out there and sent a tank out. The tank blew them out of the trees. I spotted a big farm house quite a distance away so I said to Smokey, let's see if we can make it down to that farm house, because we didn't know if there were any more snipers around. We were fortunate to make it down there to this farm house and as we made our way into this house I saw this door that was leading down to the basement. Smokey had big feet so I told him "Break that door down!" The door was locked and he thrust it with his foot and we threw a couple of grenades down into the basement and then we heard yelling and screaming. Finally I think there was about thirty Germans that came out of that basement. So we grabbed them, sent them back and took them prisoners. Then Smokey and I joined the rest of the men and went on.

I do remember crossing the Moselle River. When we crossed it, it was about two or three in the morning. It was pitch dark and the river at the time of the year when we were crossing it was very, very swift. We had to cross about two miles upstream because they had gun emplacements directly on the other side of the river from our other crossing point. We were going to cross in pontoon boats, which took about twelve men in each boat. I remember this one fellow John Campenella from Brooklyn, New York, and he was right to my side. We were going to go in the first pontoon, to try to make the crossing, but there was room in the second so they wanted us in the second boat. But then they found out there was more room in the third boat, so what we did was even everybody out so there were less than twelve men in every boat. So Campy and I went in the third boat. The first one started off, it was pitch dark and he started off and got about half ways across when all at once fire opened up and they got hit. They went down and the second boat took off and they got hit at the same time. In the mean time we took off and we made it across. In the first two, I can't tell you exactly how many men we lost, but I know we lost quite a few. We were actually unable to get at them because we had the ammo on us in our packs and we couldn't even see them that's how dark it was. We finally made our way across and fought our way up onto the bank and they were right there waiting for us. We were lucky enough that some of us made it up on the bank. They finally retreated back part ways, but not too far and in the meantime we made our way up the bank. We left one or two men back to guard the pontoon boats in case we had to make it back to retreat. We dug in and went to get the men that we left back at the boats. A stroke had gotten to them and killed them.

I remember Patton wanted to bring some tanks across for us, but we couldn't go any further for they were really at us. We were partially dug in but we couldn't make a move because they knew we were coming. Patton wanted a pontoon bridge built so they could bring supplies and tanks across. I remember this as plain as day, the engineers came up and tried to put up a pontoon bridge. As they came half way across the Germans had them zeroed, just waiting for them, and blew them right off the bridge. So they had to start off with another one. They blew them off four times, it took four attempts to build this bridge. They were unable to build the bridge and all these men were getting killed at the same time. So finally Patton brought in the Eighth Air Force and they started strafing and bombing continuously and then the engineers finally put the bridge up under Air Force protection. Then Patton finally got the supplies across and that's when we really moved in on them and got them off the bank. We just kept moving in and they just kept retreating. I guess we lost a lot of men on that bridge, it's pretty sad because those engineers knew that they'd get half way across and they would zero in on them, yet they kept attempting to build that bridge and they finally got it across.

Eugene M. Wroblewski
Infantryman 378th Infantry Regiment

Now we started into the battle. It's very nice for a tactician to look at maps and say "this is the way the battle should be fought" but from the stand point of a foot soldier you only know that you're near Metz, for example, but you don't know what part of it you're in because you're not privy to maps. You're just doing your job, depending on your training and moving in whatever direction the officers indicate. You just try to hold your own and do the best you can. Many times there would be fire directed at you. With mortar fire, you could see them falling one in front of you and one behind you and you realize the next one is going to be right in the middle and you better get out of there fast. Or sometimes you'll actually get into a nest of machine gunners. The German machine guns have a very distinctive paper ripping kind of a sound as opposed to the staccato of the American machine guns. You can distinguish the sounds of war that way to give you clues for survival. Also, the Germans were kind of crafty in the fact that they would fire tracer bullets over your heads and you would think that it was perfectly safe to advance and at the same time they would have another machine gun that was mowing you down at belly level. You had to be very aware of that. I can remember going across open fields and being pinned down by machine gun fire and wondering how the heck I'm going to get out of this one. We carried a little folding shovel in our backpacks and I'd try to take it out of my backpack while on my stomach and attempt to dig a hole right near me. The hole created by the first scoop filled up with water. Quickly I realized that that's no way to get out of this battle [Laughs]. I can remember figuring out which way I should face while pinned down by machine gun fire in the open.

Should I actually face with my head toward the machine gunners, or should I put my body across? I figured well, maybe if I get hit in the leg I won't have to go through this battle anymore. That's the way I did [Laughs], I didn't get hit at that time so it worked out.

In one battle, I can also remember that our regiment was the first of the three in a kind of a spear point. Our battalion was in lead. Our company happened to be the first company and ours was the first platoon. We were actually moving by foot across this large flat area, at a tremendous clip and as we went over a hill we saw the Germans soldiers down in a town in front of us. We fired at them. The Germans started to disappear out of the town in all different directions. When we looked back for further directions from our leaders we found that no one was behind us, not even our own troops. We couldn't go into the town because the Germans started to come back into town and were preparing to fire directly at us with their artillery. Despite our tactical advantage, we had to move back. There was a big lack of communication there. We were all gung ho to capture that particular town but it never happened.

We dug an awful lot of foxholes. Sometimes we'd do it with a ¼ pound block of TNT. Mostly it was by the shovel full. Or, sometimes we would use the foxholes of previous occupants. We'd set up a series of foxholes if we were going to stay in that particular position for a long period of time. To protect ourselves at night, we would set up wires, strung out to trees with hand grenades tied to them. If we found that there was a suspicious sound we'd pull the pin on the hand grenade and it would blow up at the tree. We also tied little tin cans on horizontal wires and if anybody was trying to sneak through our territory we could hear them go through. One of the problems was that if we had three people in a triple foxhole, one of us would be on guard duty at any time of the night and then two hours later somebody else would go on duty in rotation. We would have one wrist watch which we passed down from one soldier to the next. The only trouble was that when the watch showed six o'clock in the morning and it still wasn't light, we realized that whoever was on guard duty before us was moving the watch ahead. They might have been on guard duty for an hour and they actually moved it up an extra hour so that dawn didn't come sometimes until nine o'clock in the morning [Laughs].

The title of this piece is the *Iron Men of Metz*, but it's hard for us to remember how "iron" we were. I do remember that when we were supposed to go across a swollen river at Thionville one night, in the big attack, I developed the flu. I was shivering with hot and cold flashes. I was sent me back to the hospital where I recuperated for three days. When I came back I found out that most of my outfit had gone across the river and that a lot of them had been wiped out. From that stand point I was very, very lucky. By the time I was wounded, many months later, I would be the fifth from last of the original 180 men in my company to be killed, wounded or captured.

Frank Bever
Infantryman 379th Infantry Regiment

We eventually went across the Moselle River and it was not really under any special fire at that time. Perhaps I'm getting a little ahead of myself here because we went into Metz, France, before this. The first morning of our jump off going into Metz, now this seems to vary between fellows, but in my particular experience I can remember a big open area. We were part way across this open area under pretty heavy fire and one of my buddies that I had been with for a great number of days, Ron Bleaker from New Jersey, took a hit and then I helped get him in a big shell hole that was there and dressed his wound the best I could with what I had available on my belt. By the time I had gotten that done the rest of the company had pushed through that area and I wasn't too sure which way to try to go out of there. I was more familiar with where we had come from so I went back to the more secure area.

As I said the rest of my friends had already pushed through. That was one thing that probably saved me from serious injury later on, well that particular day anyhow.

Roger A. Bushee
Infantryman 379th Infantry Regiment

Once when we were pinned down, a pillbox had us pinned down, of course we were still raw and green and didn't know the signs of pillboxes because they had them camouflaged pretty good. So we were pinned down and there was another pillbox off to the side that opened up with a machine gun, and it was just scattering the dirt. This stream of bullets was coming right to me and I just kind flinched and closed my eyes expecting to get hit in the legs but it stopped. Well, I didn't stay there, I got up and ran and jumped in a crater from a bomb. It was a small, probably a five hundred pound bomb that an Air Force P-47 had dropped earlier. Anyway, I jumped in this crater and then when we were able to move we did move and went back to our foxholes. These are just some incidents that I remember.

Early one morning we were moving out. Of course the weather in Europe in November is rainy and cold. It was dark when we started moving and I slipped and twisted my knee, actually I fell on my knee. I was able to get back up on my feet, and of course you don't want to fall out because you're a tough, stubborn guy. I limped along and I walked as long as I could. Later in the afternoon I just had to go to the aid station because my knee was hurting so bad. When I got to the aid station they said that they needed some litter bearers because the Germans were shooting at the medics. There were guys out there that needed to be brought in but the medics were afraid to go out. I put a red cross on my helmet and dropped my ammunition belt and hand grenades and told them that I could maybe work one side of a litter but that I was really having problems just walking myself. There were three of us, two at the head and one at the foot. They knew where to go so they led and I limped along while they were shooting at us. I don't know if they were just trying to harass us or what because they were missing us. I could see why the medics were afraid to go out though. We got back and I told them at the aid station that I just couldn't walk anymore because my leg hurt me so much.

They had to cut my pants off in order to get to my knee because it had swollen so much by then. I waited until all the serious wounded were evacuated and then they took care of me and I went back to an aid station and then another and anther until I finally wound up in a hospital in England. They wanted to operate on my knee but I told them that I would rather let it try to let it heal itself. Finally, it did heal good enough. When I was able to walk they released me and I rejoined my unit. I can't remember where they were then but I think I was probably in the hospital longer than I was in combat.

Eldon L. Knuth
Infantryman 379th Infantry Regiment

Early on the morning of the 14th of November we jumped off for the assault on Metz. The artillery fire in preparation for that was the most intense artillery fire I had ever experienced. But I'm not sure it did much to the enemy. The advance was pretty chaotic as I saw it. I had a general sense of the direction to our objective but had no map and knew relatively little about the terrain. During the advance I came upon several 95th soldiers who were trying to get a German soldier out of a foxhole. They were ordering him in English to get up and put his hands up, but he didn't understand. Our men couldn't handle German – the German couldn't handle English. I can handle German, but before I could help with communications, they shot him in the back. For quite a few years after I was discharged, if anybody had asked me if I ever saw anybody get shot at close range, I would have said no. I blanked it out of my mind. Years later it came back.

I got separated from my squad, but then came upon one of our sergeants – Sergeant Bill Gallagher. Bill and I agreed that we would do what we could to use our mortar against the enemy. I had the barrel and several rounds, but didn't have either the base plate or the sighting mechanism. Somebody else from the squad had these. We were a five-man mortar squad so we divided up the various components. Bill picked the target and I did the best I could to use my experience to land near the target. Bill would watch to see where it landed and what was needed in order to adjust for a better hit. We fired several rounds and then a German shot him from long range in the stomach. I suppose that the German had a choice of aiming at Gallagher or at me. Close call number three.

Bill took his sulfa pills with water before he remembered that when you're hit in the stomach you're not supposed to take water. I bandaged him as best I could. Then he wanted me to go on, so I told him I would find a medic for him. I put the bayonet on the end of his rifle and stuck the rifle in the ground so that the medic could find him. I found a medic; he said that after the fighting had quieted down, the medics would collect the wounded.

Then I went on in the general direction where I understood we were supposed to hold at the end of the day. It was a bit beyond Fort Jeanne d'Arc. I circled around Fort Jeanne d'Arc to the left-hand side, that is to the north side, and there found quite a few of the rest of the battalion, mostly company F. We dug in there, not far from a stonewall on the edge of the hill on which the fort was located. One of the other fellows for some reason didn't get around to digging his foxhole. When it got dark he didn't have a foxhole, so I told him he could share mine. That is the most uncomfortable night I have ever spent. We didn't have room to turn around and spent all night in one position. During the night, horses ran wild in the area. We could hear a motorcycle and horses and wagon on a road down below us. I was in constant fear that the Germans would counterattack. It was not until the next day that we realized fully the seriousness of our position. Our troops to the right and to the left of us had not reached their objectives and the German front line had been reestablished. We were trapped behind the German front line!

Two days later, on the 16th of November, Concetto Femino and I needed to relieve ourselves. Being somewhat tidy and maybe a bit modest we jumped the stonewall east of us to relieve ourselves. Femino got shot in the stomach by a sniper and I jumped back over the wall. Close call number four. I fired my carbine in the direction of the sniper, but it was largely just to scare him. We had a young German prisoner of war, in his late teens, with us at that time. I had interviewed him briefly a day or so before. We had him help bring Femino back over the wall. There were doubts if this was really allowed by the Geneva Convention, but Femino needed help. We also had the POW dig a hole near the wall where Femino could rest more comfortably and more safely. But Femino died the next day.

Incidentally, the 95th veterans were invited to help celebrate the 50th and 55th Anniversaries of the liberation of Metz. My wife and I went and were treated like royalty. During the 50th Anniversary I went back to the area around Jeanne d'Arc and found the foxhole that I had dug in 1944. I also found the foxhole that was dug for Femino. On the 55th I went back up to the area to visit the foxholes again and put a small plaque on the wall near where Femino died. On the occasion of the 60th Anniversary I plan to go back and see if the plaque is still there.

Back to November 1944. We spent five days there behind the German lines from the 14th to the 19th, in constant fear that the Germans would attempt to eliminate us. All I had to eat during that time were some rations, which essentially were just chocolate bars. We were wet and cold. Small liaison planes dropped some supplies and blankets, but I don't remember seeing any of the blankets. The only supplies I saw was the box of machine gun ammunition that landed close to me, almost hitting me. Then on the 19th the 95th Division troops were able to advance and free us; we all advanced together down towards Metz. On the way, we met troops with rations in their packs. One GI offered me a tin of ham and eggs – the best-tasting cold ham and eggs I had ever eaten! We held up at the Caserne in Moulin-les-Metz. The Caserne had been used recently by the Germans, but I don't recall seeing any as we went in.

Although my feet were bothering me, I nevertheless scouted around a bit in the buildings. Then I heard that they had set up an aid station so I went there to have them look at my feet. They took one look at my feet, announced that I had trench foot and put me on an ambulance. The ambulance took a road that was apparently in the direction from which we had just come. On the way I looked out the window and at one of the intersections I saw a machine gun. The machine gunner was still sitting at the machine gun but his head was missing. I don't recall if he was American or German. We spent that night in a tent -- an Aid and Collection Station set up by the 32nd Medical Battalion. (I have a complete day-by-day log of which hospitals and aid stations I passed through.) On Thanksgiving Day I arrived by plane at the General Hospital in Newbury, England. We got there rather late in the day but they still had American Thanksgiving dinners left for us. About that time the Battle of the Bulge was going on so I was afraid that I was going to be sent back to fight in the Battle of the Bulge. But my feet did not respond quickly. I learned only later that trench foot leaves permanent damage and is not something that can be cured quickly.

Paul H. Madden, Jr.
Infantryman 379th Infantry Regiment

The 379th began its actual combat on the 14th of November. The assignment of the 1st Battalion was to take four forts in the

Maginot Line. A and B Company were in the initial attack, I was in A Company. B Company was to take the two forts to the north, one was St Hubert and the other was Jussy Nord, which was kind of a connected fort. A Company was to take Jussy Sud and Bois de la Dame. Our route took us across what we later found out was the Metz ravine, which was mentioned in the Franco-Prussian War in the 1870's. As we came to the top of the ravine facing the forts our second platoon was assigned to attack Fort Jussy Sud and they moved out across a field firing. Suddenly, there was a bunch yelling from the fort. It turned out B Company had already occupied Jussy Sud and Jussy Nord thinking they had occupied the two northern forts. After we established that Jussy Sud was already occupied we swung to the south towards Bois de la Dame. We were unsuccessful there because the Germans were in a subterranean building, I imagine that building was about four floors and the top half of the last floor was all you could see from the surface because it was built in a great hole in the ground. There was nothing we could do. The biggest thing we had was a bazooka. The bazooka was no good against the forts that the Air Force had bombed previously without any effect.

When we started getting shelled the company commander pulled us back and we occupied Jussy Sud and B Company moved into Jussy Nord. By the end of the day we discovered that the Germans had moved back into the Metz ravine and we were surrounded. The second day C Company, and L Company from 3rd Battalion were suppose to relieve us or at least try to come in and re-establish contact. L Company was unsuccessful but C Company got through. Unfortunately after they got through the Germans went back in the ravine, so we were no better off than we were. For the initial attack we had been issued three K-rations, which we carried. Of course by the evening of the first day very few people had not eaten all of their K-rations. So we were there surrounded with no food or re-supply of ammunition. We had no medical assets other than the company medic and we had a number of wounded to include our platoon leader who had been hit pretty bad. We were in those forts for four days, from the 14th to the 18th of November. The liaison plane from the artillery dropped D-rations to us, of course we had to recover them at night because the Germans could cover the field where they dropped them. If you're not familiar with the D-ration chocolate bars I think they contained about six squares of chocolate and were made by the Hershey Company in Pennsylvania. After they recovered the bars and counted the people they decided that everybody could have one square of a D-bar. I think about the third day they did drop some K-rations so we had a real ration. On the 18th we moved out in an attack forward, instead of going back through the ravine. The artillery fired preparatory to our leaving the fort. It was an excellent demonstration of artillery fire because after they had fired for a few minutes their fire moved forward as we came out of the fort and as we progressed behind the barrage the artillery started firing to both sides of us as well as the front. As we got further away from the fort they started to fire in back of us, so we were literally within a box of artillery fire. As we moved across that field there was no opposition so the artillery ceased fire to save ammunition. We went into the little town of Jussy and later Ste. Ruffine. I believe it was in Ruffine where we spent the next couple of nights until we relieved a unit of the 378th around Fort Plappeville, its one of the Forts around Metz.

We lost a platoon leader at that spot. They decided our platoon was to relieve a platoon of the 378th that was dug-in in foxholes and could only move at night. They said there had been no firing from the forts during the day and that it would be all right to go out there. I, being the platoon runner at that time, was with the platoon leader and the platoon guide, along with a guy from the 378th. The four of us were going out to these foxholes to coordinate the change over during the nighttime when all of a sudden the Germans started to fire. The platoon leader was killed and the other three of us got back safely into the woods. That was the second platoon leader that I had been with that was hit. The first one was wounded and the second killed. Later on that day the Regimental Chaplain of the 379th arranged a truce with the German commander of Fort Plappeville to pick up our dead. We knew there was one body out there, we assumed was from the 378th when they made their initial attack. I think the chaplain and I believe four or five of us took two stretchers and went out into the field. As we walked out we could see the Germans standing on top of Plappeville Fortress. We went out to pick up the bodies and I happened to notice that there was a M-1 Carbine that the paratroopers carried with a collapsible stock and pistol grip laying on the ground. I thought that would be a good item to have as platoon runner, so I told the fellows that I was going to pick up that gun, and they said, "don't do it, the Germans will shoot." So I told them to ease the stretcher down and as we eased the body on I eased the carbine on the opposite side. When we were done we carried the two bodies back and later on that day I was cleaning this carbine when Captain Ladden, the Company A commander, came by and asked me what I was doing. I told him that I was cleaning my carbine. He said, "well, as soon as you get it clean turn it in to the supply sergeant." So I didn't get the carbine. I always wanted to ask the captain if he happened to have a collapsible carbine [Laughs].

Adolph Massa
Infantry Rifle Company First Sergeant
379th Infantry Regiment

On the 14th of November at 5 o'clock in the morning we jumped off for Metz. I took off with my platoon. We had an area to cross, an open field that looked to be about a quarter of a mile, but it probably wasn't. Anyway, it looked like a long way. I barely got across with five or six men. The rest of them were knocked out. I lost my radioman, and as I got across this black top road

I was all alone looking at the face of a pillbox about forty yards in front of me. I thought I had better get moving and just as I lifted myself up on my hands and toes a round went of from the pillbox. It grazed my face and caught me in the ankle, knocking me back onto the ground. Just prior to looking at the pillbox I also saw a German foxhole about thirty feet to my left. There was a barbed wire entanglement there, and to this day I don't know if I went over or under the barbwire entanglement, but I did land headfirst in the foxhole. It was full of water and I had a difficult time righting myself because it had cement walls especially built for the protection of that pillbox. By the time I got around to get myself facing up in the foxhole I had lost all my ammunition. Later on it was starting to snow as I was trying to get a tourniquet on my wound. At the same time two Germans came out of the pillbox and they started to pick up ammunition that was lying there. I fired two rounds and knocked them both out of commission. Although neither one of them went down, they both staggered back into the pillbox.

Captain Carter was on the opposite side of the black top road, which I did not know at the time. He yelled, "Massa, don't shoot at them anymore. I'm wounded too and they'll come out tonight and shoot us." I told him that I didn't know about that, and then I found out that there was five other guys from my platoon over there. Sergeant Uldrich, Corporal Knoll, Private McQuarter and the Captain. I asked them to lay a field of fire on the pillbox parapets. When they did I was able to get out of the foxhole and back across the black top road to the same side they were. We laid there for approximately an hour and a half while the Germans in the pillbox tried to pick us off. Luckily the crown of the road was too high and the bullets ricochet over us. After about an hour I told Captain Carter that I was going to try to get back to our original lines or I would freeze because I was sopping wet and it was snowing. He said that he didn't think we could, but I informed him that three or four days prior to the eleventh I went on a patrol and there was a line of trees with a small creek in it. I told him that if we could work our way along the road to it we could crawl back through the crick to our own lines. We would probably have concealment but not complete cover. So I decided to go and the captain said he wasn't going, but when the rest of the guys said they were going with me the captain said, "Well, I guess I'll come along too." I proceeded to the lead the way as we crawled back through the line of brush and trees to the creek. We were eventually able to crawl back through the water to our own lines.

We were evacuated by the medics to a field hospital that was in a schoolhouse. That was my experience of the battle of Metz. When I got hit there was only about seven guys left in my platoon. Three of them got captured, I don't know what happened to the other four. One of them that was captured was killed by one of our own aircraft that strafed the airplane that was evacuating him out of Metz.

John G. Little, Jr.
Artilleryman 547th Anti Aircraft Artillery

When we arrived at Metz we relieved the 5th Division. We went to the mess truck and the 5th Division Mess Sergeant asked our Mess Sergeant what were we doing with a water trailer? He said well it is on TO&E (Table of Organization and Equipment). The 5th Division sergeant said, "TO&E hell! Where did you steal it?" That water trailer saved me a lot of work. I still had to handle 5-gallon cans but not near as many. One other note I would like to make at this time is that just before we left California we knew that one blanket and a shelter half wasn't going to be very warm in the winter time. Two soldiers made a tent out of two shelter halfs and slept together. Our battalion arranged to buy sleeping bags, similar to a Boy Scout sleeping bag, that were tan colored and cost about 8 or 9 dollars each. That ended up being the best investment I ever made! We had to learn to pack it in our duffle

bag, roll it up real tight because and enlisted man was only allowed
to have his duffle bag and pack. I will never forget that bedroll
in the wintertime in France on rainy nights. I would think about
those poor infantrymen of the 95th Infantry out in the cold. They
didn't have a bedroll. The modern Army today has a lot of good
stuff but we sure didn't have it back in those days.

A lot of my specific information and dates come from a book
by the 547th AAA Battalion published in the summer of 1945 in
Germany. The name of the book is *Mission Accomplished,* dedicated
to the nine men that died from the battalion. Two of the men were
from Battery D, my battery. We didn't have a lot of causalities like
the infantry did but we knew these people for so long that is was
very bad when someone was killed. I think we had about thirty-
five wounded in the battalion. The first part of the book tells
about the training in California. The second part is overseas and
lets each of the five different batteries tell its own story. This book
includes a map of Europe showing the route we took throughout
the war.

We left on October 15, 1944, on our way to the Lorraine
and Metz area. It took several days to get where we were going. I
remember going through Paris in trucks. We had plenty of trucks.
Going through Paris was something else! The streets were lined
with people with bottles of wine and champagne. We were throwing
out chocolate bars and cigarettes. October 19, 1944, we were at a
village called Mardigny and then we moved along a day at a time
through Montois. In early November, we were moving around to
little villages, Amneville that was a village about twenty kilometers
from Metz. On November 17,1944, we crossed the Moselle River
near Metz at a place called Uckenge and then moved twelve miles
to Rugy. On November 18, 1944, we were moving to Argansy.
All of the villages were bombed out and in total ruins. We were
in Metz on Thanksgiving Day. We didn't have our Thanksgiving
Dinner until several days after that because we didn't have time to
stop to prepare the meal.

In the End...

The American attack split the German forces into two groups. With the eventual capture of the city the outlying forts were forced to fight isolated, individual fights with an almost predetermined outcome. They were instructed to hold until the end, but because of the terrible predicaments of the unsupported positions the Americans would not have to assault them directly. The state of these latter fortifications is represented in this captured report from one of General Kittel's field commanders just four days before he surrendered:

Von Stoessel
December 2, 1944
Colonel
to the LXXXII Corps

On 17 November I received the order from the commander to move to Fort Mannstein (Fort St. Quentin), to gather there all troops I could reach and to defend the fort to the last cartridge and to the last piece of bread. When I arrived there at 1800, Lt. Col. Richter, commanding officer of the 1010 Regiment, was getting ready to move to Fort Kronprinz (Fort Driant). I remained with my staff of about 25 men, and with a detachment of engineers, also about 25 men strong, I occupied the four gates of the fort. I had at my disposal the Fortress Engineer Battalion 55 and the 2nd Battalion of the 1010 Regiment, which arrived the morning of November 18, together with a small number of stragglers from other units. According to my order, one company of Fortress Engineer Battalion 55 was given to Colonel Vogel, the commanding officer of Fort Alvensleben (Fort Plappeville). Furthermore I supplied

Fort Alvensleben with food and ammunition. From November 18 on, we were encircled. The night before, the enemy was only one kilometer away from us, but remained inactive. A few tanks stood for some time in front of the gates of Forts Mannstein and Alvensleben.

The garrison amounted to about 650 men. The supply of ammunition was scarce. Mines and wire were completely missing. Of heavy weapons there were and still are only two heavy infantry howitzers and two 80-millimeter mortars for which there is no ammunition. There was food for about 10 days, and an additional supply for eight days was carried by the troops. The main scarcity is in bread, potatoes, salt and coffee.

Due to the lack of heavy weapons we could do very little to fight the enemy. He keeps himself out of the range of small infantry weapons, and in this is favored by the terrain. We succeeded, on November 19, in putting out of action a bridge crossing of the Moselle by our machine gun and destroying the personnel of a pneumatic boat. The pontoon bridge across the Moselle northeast of the city was taken under fire by our infantry howitzer. From our fort, we directed the fire of fortress guns of Fort Jeanne d'Arc and Fort Driant on a few targets. This was a difficult task due to the incomplete supply of radio and radio equipment. In the course of time, all targets which showed up in a distance of 2,500 meters were attacked by machine gun and also by rifle fire, especially motor vehicles. Thereupon the enemy became very cautious. The pontoon bridge was taken under fire at a distance of 3,500 meters.

Every day patrols were sent out to the surrounding villages. At the present, we try to supply Fort Alvensleben with food and to get in personal contact with Fort Jeanne d'Arc. But it seems that the enemy has our radio code, because all attempts have failed so far...

The morale of the troops is good. Due to the mentioned lack of so many important things, however, the value of the encircled troops cannot be shown. I myself intend to send out two patrols with the order to get through to their own troops. I am giving this report to these patrols, also a list of identifications of all soldiers on Fort Mannstein, with the request to inform their relatives accordingly.

To Greater Germany and the Fuehrer
Sieg Heil!
v. Stoessel[3]

General Kittel, the overall German commander of Metz, was captured on the operating table due to wounds sustained in the battle. Although he refused to surrender the city, he did state during his later interrogation that he was impressed, in contrast to the Russians he had previously faced, by the diverse and subtle American strategy and tactics used at Metz. The attack and subsequent seizer of Metz was a resounding success. From their first large scale combat action the soldiers of the 95th had earned a new name. "The Iron Men of Metz" was a nickname that described the fortitude of the division and still remains a cherished remembrance of the hard fought battle of Fortress Metz. The main assault was from 14-17 November, but the city did not fall completely until the 22nd. Attackers had not successfully taken Metz for the past 1,500 years. By the time the fortress complex was secured the German 462nd Division and 73rd Regiment of the 19th Division had been eliminated from the war. The Victory Division had captured 65 smaller towns, 19 forts, numerous strongpoints and pillboxes, killed or wounded approximately 4,000 enemy troops and captured another 6,000. Initially a decentralized effort, the division conducted a consolidated attack during the second phase of the operation to complete the seizure of the city. The operation was not conducted without a great deal of pain and sacrifice on the part of the Iron Men. Conditions were less than tolerable, from the direct fire battle to the terrain and weather the seizer of Metz was paid for in sweat and blood. Upon completion of the actions the division commander commended his men in a message of praise that was issued to the soldiers. Later, in a letter to General Twaddle, the Third Army commander General Patton praised the Iron Men for their courage and efficiency at Metz when he wrote:

> The achievement of your division and attached units…in successfully completing the assigned mission in connection with the reduction and capture of the strongly fortified city of Metz by the Third U.S. Army was outstanding, both in the combat skill of individual units committed and the control and sound tactical judgment displayed by commanders of all echelons.
>
> The fourteen days of continuous attack against a strong and aggressive enemy, along a 26-mile front, drove irresistibly to the heart of the city of Metz where contact was made with American forces advancing from the south. In the course of this attack you successfully (1) made four assault crossings of the Moselle River at its high flood stage, (2) penetrated the line of defending forts, reducing those necessary to accomplish the mission, and (3) greatly contributed to the destruction of an entire reinforced German division. Against these fortifications which had never before in modern times fallen by assault, in terrain favorable to the enemy, and under almost intolerable weather conditions of rain, flood, and bitter cold, your officers and men met a most searching combat test which required not only individual courage, skill, endurance, and determination, but also sound tactical judgment coupled with an insatiable desire to close with the enemy.

Boy it was Cold

This achievement has added luster to the glorious history of American arms, for which you and all the officers and enlisted personnel of your division and attached units, are highly commended.[4]

The Saar

The division had been bloodied at Metz, and as a result of their condition General Twaddle requested four days to rest and reorganize his men. Thanksgiving in Metz would have been nice, but higher-level commanders and planners had a different idea in mind. They saw Metz as little more than a speed bump enroute to Frankfurt, and instead, on November 21, 1944, directed the division to swap positions with the 5th Division and await follow-on orders to continue the attack. The Iron Men carried out their movement orders over the next several days, while the XX Corps prepared and then issued the new plan of attack on the 24th of November. In continuation of the offense, the 95th was ordered to push northeast to the Saar River, seize crossing sites and expand a bridgehead in order to pass the 90th Division. To accomplish the assigned mission the division ordered two of the regiments to move out abreast with their attachments, the 377th on the left and the 378th on the right, and the 379th to follow in reserve.

The division moved out on the 25th of November, encountering little resistance initially, but finding the damaged infrastructure, terrain and weather stacked against them. The 95th was headed from the German Nied River enroute to the Maginot Line, where enemy resistance would be added to the existing obstacles. During the movement the division was hampered by enemy contact that resulted from a gap on the right side due to another corps, the XII, deviating slightly from its axis of advance. The division also found out on 26 November that they would be responsible for another five miles of front because of another change to the XX Corps plan. Enemy resistance incrementally increased along the march, and by the 29th the 95th had reached the Saar plain and was experiencing some of the worst fighting it would see at any time during the war. Ten counterattacks were thrown against the division line on the 29th, only to be repelled by the Iron Men. After the counterattacks had been defeated the division was faced with fighting a tough urban battle in complex terrain for the avenues of approach leading to the Saar River. While the majority of the division was fighting in close quarters urban combat, the 1st Battalion, 379th Infantry conducted a daring, surprise night attack late on December 2nd, and captured the main bridge across the Saar from the far side, the east, with a company simultaneously securing the near side from the west. Even in the face of fierce counterattacks, supported by numerous artillery barrages, the division was still able to hold the valuable bridge, completely securing it by the night of the 3rd.

Charles R. Fowler
Artillery Officer and Infantry Rifle Platoon Leader
377th Infantry Regiment

When we finished in Metz we started towards the Saar River. There was resistance beside the Saar in a town called St. Barbara. C Company had gone in there but the Germans counter-attacked with three tanks and pushed them out of town and captured some of them. I was in charge of the two remaining anti-tank guns. A shell hand landed one night and destroyed the third gun and its truck. About dark we were pulling the two guns with jeeps because the Germans had destroyed the bridges and the only temporary bridges we had could only handle a jeep. Colonel Decker sent me into town because Captain Savage the C Company commander was wounded and needed help fighting the tanks. As I went forward stragglers told me that the Germans already had the town and that we wouldn't be able to get in. So I went back to tell Colonel Decker, he was from Georgia, and the colonel said, "What are you doing back here?" I told him I wanted to get you up on the latest information that the Germans now have the town. He said with his southern drawl, "Fowler, go get'em!" [Laughs]

So we left again to go into town. By then it was pitch dark you couldn't see anything. I left one gun and jeep outside of the town and as I approached the town I didn't know where the C Company commander was or anything. There was one street that come down a ridge with a house on fire on the left side of it. The house was on the edge of town as we came in. So I got out in the road to see what I could see. I was silhouetted and all of a sudden, Bbbbrrrrppp, Bbbbrrrrppp, a machine gun opened up! Just beyond the fire in the dark there was a tank set in and then Wham! The cannon fired. We had bazookas with us so we ran into the house that was on the right. There happened to be some soldiers in there. I don't know who they were, but they were up on the second floor. The tank pulled down the road and I remember firing at the tank with a bazooka and he pulled back. It quieted down a little after that. The Germans were still shooting into the house and throwing grenades, they killed one guy with a grenade, but the tank wasn't after us then. About 3 or 4 o'clock in the morning we heard a moaning sound so we crawled out and found that when the cannon had fired there was a boy sitting on the jeep and it had knocked his foot off. He had rolled over in the ditch and used his belt as a tourniquet so he wouldn't bleed to death. After we heard him moaning and got to him we loaded him and a few others on the jeep and pushed the jeep out of machine gun range of the tank. I sent the sergeant back with the wounded and to get more bazooka ammunition. When he got back he said that I was crazy and that I was going to get him killed and refused to come back.

I don't know whether they court-martialed him or not, but by the next morning I looked out the back window and there was a German soldier crawling up to the house. I fired at him two or three times and he quit crawling. I later discovered that I only shot him in the leg. He gave himself up later on when our troops started moving. At the break of day a 90mm Tank Destroyer gun of ours shot into the German tank and burnt him up. Then that 90mm gun went on down the street, there was a little bend in the street, and just as he stuck his nose around the bend a German tank shot into him and burnt him up. I had been walking right along side of it and I didn't have time to react it went up so fast. In order to get rid of the German tank the sergeant in charge of the tank destroyer that burnt up went into a house there on the bend and was shooting at the German tank, now about a hundred yards away. It was a rock house and we were standing in the doorway with the wall towards the tank so he could shoot at the house but he couldn't get to us because of this wall. After a little bit the tank pulled out. As he pulled out a mortar shell landed in the street and killed the guy that was right next to me. He hollered, "Oh, my leg!" But when I laid him down I found that a piece of shrapnel had gone into his back and it was just a matter of a few minutes until he was dead. When the German tank pulled back we proceeded on down the street searching as we went. I discovered some German soldiers down in a ditch. I don't know why they weren't active, but they were sitting down in this ditch just talking. So I pulled a grenade and throwed it in the middle of them and they all gave up. It had happened so fast that I had already pulled the pin on a second grenade. I had this second grenade and I didn't want to throw it at them so I threw it down the hill and another German came out! We marched those Germans back. They had to carry one of them as wounded from the grenade.

Fred B. Love Jr.
Infantryman 377th Infantry Regiment

We moved out and started out east of Metz, headed toward the German border. There were several scrimmages and delaying actions as we pushed on. We got to the city of Boulee, or the town of Boulee, and one morning we were going to take some pillboxes. They were Magnums and we knew that. I got four new replacements, just fresh into combat and I didn't even write their names down as we started out that morning. My squad was getting butchered as we moved toward the pillboxes. I yelled, "get in that low ditch!" The ditch had six inches of water in it and it was close to freezing but we got down in that water and it felt pretty good to get out of those bullets. I kept looking, I raised my head up to see if those Germans were shooting at us and I put my head down quickly and moved to another place. Every time I'd put my head back down, three bullets hit the bank, right where my head had been. I did that two or three times until I'd had enough. I told the guys to crawl back down and get into that ditch and we crawled back down in the ditch until we got back to the company. When I go there the Company Commander sat there all hurdled up, and we told him, we used nicknames instead of Captain, "Piggy, what do you want to do with my squad?" He said, "I don't know what to tell you to do." He was scared to death; he was sitting there shaking. I said, "What I am going to do is take my squad up in those woods and work around and try to return to the destination." We had a point we were supposed to get to up in the woods, so I took all the guys I could, it was eight or ten, they weren't all my men.

We went up in the woods and the Germans saw us walking there and they just shelled those woods, you wouldn't believe it, but we never did lose a man there. We got all the way up to a big old ditch in the woods and I counted my squad. I had four men out of 16 that I had started with that day. I had lost twelve men there in three hours time. That was the roughest day I ever saw in combat. I was sitting up there and these new guys, there were some new guys that had never been in combat before, and I sat up on this bank and the Germans started shelling us. I said that shell is going to hit over there and I could hear them, you could tell by the sound where they were going to hit. Pretty soon there was one where there was the sound and then it just quit, and I said, "hit the dirt!"

John LittleChauny, France, 1945
Little

Paul Madden on pass
from the hospital April 1945
Madden

Louis O. Vogt 1944
Vogt

Gene Wroblewski 1945
Wroblewski

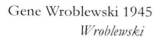

Tony Petraglia
Petraglia

Richard E. Hunton
Hunton

The Commanding General
Major General Harry L. Twaddle
Victory

Rolf Greunwald
Hunton

Frank Bever
Neuss, Germany, March 1945
Bever

1st Squad, 2nd Platoon, Co. A, 228th Battalion, Camp Blanding, Florida

Richard Hunton during basic training in Camp Blanding, Florida
Hunton

Company Street during desert maneuvers Camp Coxcomb,
California December 1943
Bever

Frank Bever Camp Coxcomb
California, January 1944
Bever

Assault
Climbing with the 377th IN
Seneca Rock, West Virginia
Fowler

Engineer Bridge
Schoen

Dick Schoen climbing with an instructor
on the top of the north face
Schoen

Schoen and Sadjewski
having a bite to eat
Schoen

Mountain maneuvers end with a 25-mile forced march
with 80-pound packs

Schoen

Indiantown Gap Aid Station   *Schoen*

Gene Wroblewski and his Mother
Camp Miles Standish, Massachusetts, 1944
Wroblewski

Willie and Ralph Young London, England, September 1944
Young

A Co, 379th IN Officers
(Top left to right) Robert Hughes, Jim Hart, Ralph Bonavist
(Bottom left to right) John LaCrosse, Max Stambach, Willard Bloom
Madden

(Above) Anti-Tank Gun Crew HQ Company, 2nd BN, 377th IN
Metz, France, 17 November 1944
(Below) The 95th Infantry Division moves into Metz, France
95th D (IT)

Regimental Scout
A 19-year old William Taylor
Vic. Champy, France, October 1944
Taylor

A "40 & 8" railcar
Hunton

The "Cow Picture" A Co, 379th IN
Driving to Saarlautern early December 1944
Madden

C co 377th IN Soldiers near Fraulautern
Edward Stepanik (Medic Above, 2nd from left) was later awarded
the Distinguished Service Cross

Fowler

Urban movement (Above)
(Below) Lieutenant General Patton in Saarlautern

Victory

Paul Madden and his
"borrowed Grease Gun"
Saarlautern, January 1945
Madden

Destroyed German ME 109
Near Felsberg, January 1945
Little

(L to R) Daniel F. McCarthy IV, Ben Shank and William Reisman
in Germany

McCarthy

"Friends for Life"
Joseph Napier (Left) and William Taylor (Right) pose for photos
in Millen, Belgium

William Taylor and part of his squad in
Millen, Belgium, February 1945

Taylor

"A picture is worth a
thousand words"
Victory

Marching prisoners
from their barracks
in Soest
Victory

Medics treat a wounded soldier in Dortmund, Germany

Victory

Infantrymen from the 378th take cover behind a wall in
Dortmund, Germany, April 1945

95ᵗʰ D (IT)

Artillerymen near Neuss, Germany
The 95th Infantry fired 250,000 artillery rounds
during their 145 days of combat

Victory

Richard E. Hunton
On furlough from the
hospital March 1945
Hunton

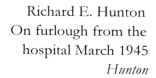

Remnants of the Hamm train yard (Above),
(Below) Russian "Displaced Persons" celebrate May Day
with the help of an American Color Guard in Hamm, Germany
Victory

Paul Madden (top right) near Bockum, Germany, early summer 1945
(Paul still has this flag that he originally acquired near St. Ruffine,
November 1944)

Madden

95th Infantry Division train wreck en route to Camp Old Gold

Taylor

Chow line in Le Harve, France, June 1945

Bever

Joyce Vogt's 21st Birthday in Hattiesburg Mississippi,
September 23rd, 1945

Vogt

I got just about down and it went off and man, it felt like I had been run over by a steamroller. That blast hit me and I guess it had hit the back of the trunk or something too that must have caused the shrapnel to go a different way, cause I got this one little piece of shrapnel in my back and that was it. I pulled up my shirt and I was bleeding there from right beside my backbone, of course I would have been taken to the hospital if I would have wanted to go, but I was pretty macho, or at least I thought I was. I was a kid, just 21 years old, a man among men. We stayed up there all night and I got this medic to put some sulfur powder and a band-aid on it, or we didn't have band-aids, we had tape and gauze. The next day we had some armor reinforcements, artillery and we moved out, through the Maginot Line without any more casualties. I got more replacements so I had twelve men again. They brought in fresh warm bodies to replace those who we had lost. We moved on up and we took some little towns and had a few little minor scrimmages and moved in to Germany.

We got in to the edge of Germany and we went in to a small town there, kind of a fun experience, we went in to this German house, Bart and I, to check it out and check if there were any German soldiers in there. The German people would follow us around and we asked if there were any "Soldaten?" "Nein, nein" was always the answer. One of them went over to the cabinet to pull out a big old bottle of something and he said, "Schnapps, gut!" We thought it might be poisoned for us, we wouldn't drink it, we weren't too good for it, we just didn't want to take any chances and even if it wasn't poisoned, we wanted to have our heads as clear as possible. That night we stayed in a little thin old wooden building. I don't know why we stayed there, we would have been better off on the ground because as the Germans would fire the bullets went through the walls like paper, but it so happened, the Germans didn't shoot at us that night. The next morning we jumped off early, just after daylight and we were walking along. Everything was peaceful as we formed a scrimmage line. We were going to do marching fire, so we took our rifles and fired as we walked and anything that moved we shot at it. It was drizzling rain as we walked and all of a sudden a German machinegun opened up. Rain was the normal situation, it was always raining, it seemed like almost half the time we were there it was raining and cold. The steam started to come up and we knew where that machine gun was. Of course they had flash less powder, you couldn't see where they were, but when the steam started to come up from the barrel, we concentrated our fire on it. When we got up to the gun there was a little boy who looked like he could have been ten or twelve years old and a man manning that machine gun. Of course they were both dead, we wiped them both out.

We were walking along later and I had my squad on the side of the woods and the main company was going through the woods and we were kind of on the side and there came two Germans walking and talking to each other carrying buckets. I have no idea what they had in those buckets, but they had no idea we were there I don't know why because we had been shooting? I yelled, "Get those Germans!" I used GI language on them and we opened up. All of us were shooting at them and they ran about a hundred yards into the woods and we didn't even scratch them. I don't know why we couldn't hit them, because we were pretty good marksmen by that time. We came to a long ditch the Germans had dug, a tank trap, and we crossed that thing before we came to a big old barn. Off to the left of the barn there was a machine gun nest and they started firing at us. We opened fire, concentrated fire on them, I directed my squad and the other squad there and as we were firing at them they got up and started to leave. Turner, the Platoon leader, told us to come around the other way, follow him, as the Germans turned and went back in. In the mean time we shot and hit one of the Germans, I am not sure what we hit, but he was holding his hand on his hip and taking steps about ten feet long running in a zigzag pattern. He went across those fields. At least one of them got back and manned that machine gun and started firing at us. That's when Joe, a bullet hit his rifle and his face as he let out a yell. I turned and looked he had blood all over his face. He put his hand on his face and saw the blood and thought his face was blown to pieces I guess. His hand was all bloody, those parting shell fragments had hit his hand and face. About that time there was a big Bam! and it felt as if my right arm had been torn off. I thought it was gone, I couldn't feel it, I looked down and my hand was still there. A bullet had made a black streak all the way across my shirt and jacket to my arm and if I had been two inches further ahead I would have needed open-heart surgery that day to remove a bullet. But it went in my arm, parallel with my arm and it hit a nerve. It didn't cut the nerve, but it damaged the nerve in my arm and cut a slot in the bone. I looked down there and it didn't bleed and I was thinking, "did it just numb my arm, bounce right off me and not wound me?" I couldn't use my arm and then I looked down and I saw a bullet hole in the seam of the jacket, it had gone right through there and I looked in the back side and there was a hole there too and I knew I had to get treatment. I wasn't so macho then.

There was a German out there, I guess he was a medic, because he was treating some guys and Barter was lying out there in the field, he got shot seriously in the back and I couldn't do anything for him, I mean I was incapacitated. I took that German prisoner I stuck a German pistol in his face and I told him where I wanted to go. I wanted to go in to town to the aid station, but that ditch was as deep as a room and there was no way I could get across. So Napier and that German prisoner somehow got me across that ditch with one hand. It was raining, muddy and slick but we finally got across there. I made the German, he was all smiles and helpful, hold my rifle before we got across. He was content to be a prisoner. Joe got me back to the aid station and they treated me and when they loaded me in the ambulance to take me back to the hospital, that German prisoner was standing there with some others and he was all smiles and he nodded at me as I walked by but I didn't say anything to him, I wasn't too happy with German's about that time. I came to the hospital and there was nothing wrong with my legs but they had me on restriction in this ambulance. This old Sergeant, this big old black fellow, and another guy started to carry me in. I said, "I can walk in" and he said: "You walk when the Captain says you're gonna walk! Right now you're gonna ride!" So I rode in and they did surgery on my arm and got it bandaged up and everything. I didn't know what they did, when I fell asleep it was daylight and when I woke up it was dark and I was in a tent. I didn't know where I was but I lay there until the morning.

Daniel F. McCarthy IV
Supply Sergeant 377th Infantry Regiment

During the war the officers received a liquor ration of one bottle of bourbon, one bottle of scotch and one bottle of gin each month. The companies in the regiment were to secure a requisition from the officers and turn it into regiment supply and our section would pick up the liquor and deliver it to the companies. There were some officers who did not order their ration and the company supply individuals ordered for them. I got into trouble one time for ordering for a Protestant chaplain.

During our venture down the highways and byways of Germany, we somehow came upon a storage area for V2 bomb fuel. One 55-gallon drum of the alcohol found its way, "accidentally", on to the tailgate of our supply truck. We discovered that the fuel mixed with grape fruit juice, obtainable from the food supply depot, made a refreshing, intoxicating drink.

Joseph W. Napier
Infantryman 377th Infantry Regiment

We finally got into a small village. Over there they had these farmhouses where the barn was connected to the house. Well, the whole company got in this one house. We had a new lieutenant, Nichols, which took over the company. The next morning we were walking out of that town. We were going to Boulay, France. Boulay was right next to the Maginot Line. As we went out of there was Charlie Arnold and I, he was a staff sergeant, the platoon guide. He and I were about 200 yards ahead of the company main body and as I walked along I noticed a hospital with a big red cross on it just off to my right. I told Charlie that we were setting ducks out here and he said, "What in the hell do you think you're out here for?" Anyway, we got on through and into another town and the people came running out and threw their arms around us and gave us wine and apples and some kind of bread.

As we walked out of town I asked Charlie, "What happened to all the people?" He said, "I don't know but something is up," and as we walked further out of the town we found out. Our objective that day was a wooded area in the Maginot Line off to our left, and as we went into this open field of frozen, ploughed ground we found out. They had some dummy looking places, what you thought were machine gun nests but weren't, and "Boom" they opened up and caught us in a cross fire from the right across the road. I could see them carrying ammo over there. When we left Metz we were well over strength. We had drawn a lot of new replacements we needed terribly. A guy right next to me was Glenn Ferret. He was hit and I talked to him but I saw he was badly hurt. There wasn't no getting a medic, everywhere you looked somebody was wounded. About that time I realized Lieutenant Nichols was hit, Sergeant Clark was hit and there was a guy back behind me over to my right that was hit in the lunges. You could see the bubble of blood come out of his back and bust. There was another guy screaming for help. He couldn't see, he'd been hit in the head. I saw another guy lying to my left and I guess the radioman was killed. Willie Bishop, who was the company runner, got hold of the artillery and called in for smoke. I saw this German carrying ammunition over to the machine gunner and I kept trying to hit him, but I guess I wasn't that good of a shot, but anyway he returned fire to me and lucky he didn't hit me, but the machine gun did. Anyway, smoke came in and an observer airplane came in right on the ground. I rolled over on my back and gave him a wave and he threw down some ore smoke. Lieutenant Nichols and Sergeant Clark could still walk and they said for anybody that could move to fall back. So I did, and as I did I saw a guy coming with wounded, he was holding his shoulder, and before I could get to him to help him he was hit again. I threw him on my shoulder and took him back and we picked up a jeep back there, the medics were there. They took us back to Boulay where the aid station was set up in a train station.

When I got back Willie Bishop, he was a private first class then, had more or less taken over the company I guess. We went back up and got to the Maginot Line and there was five of us left from my squad and platoon that made their objective. Toplift was wounded there, I never saw him again. I don't know what happened to him but a guy told me he was wounded there. We left Boulay riding tank destroyers and we were headed for Germany. I don't remember the name of the little town we were headed for, but I was just glad to ride for a while. We rode until we got into this little town prior to our next objective, which was another little town. As we came out of this town there were tank traps. The tank traps were about 30' deep and 20' wide, if a tank came along and didn't see it he would fall in it. If that happened you'd get down in there and have to get back out. It had been raining and it was foggy and miserable so they were filled with water. We came on up out of one of them, Fred Love, myself and Sergeant Barber, and a machine gun opened up on us and all three of us were hit. I was loading my rifle, pushing the clip in and a bullet hit my trigger housing and knocked me down. My hand was bleeding, my face was full of blood, I didn't know where I was hit. I looked over and Love had been hit in the shoulder, Barber was bad, he had been hit in the stomach. I grabbed up one of their rifles, I don't know who's, and went on. I got to a house and we overrun this machine gun nest and then I realized they needed help so I went back. Andy Northcut and I went back across the tank trap and I got a German medic and I told him to help me or I'd blow his head off and he understood that. We got Love up so he could get down in and out of that tank trap and the German medic took Love to that town that we just came out of. Of course Love had a pistol on him and I think the German was glad to be taken prisoner anyway. Andy and I found a ladder and there was a Laird, a Lieutenant Laird, I didn't know he was a lieutenant at that time but he helped us scoot Barber across the tank trap on a blanket and this ladder. Don't ask me how we got it done, but we did. We got him medical attention and left and went on to our objective.

It was still foggy as we got into the town and along with the bad weather a sniper opened up. Sergeant Tiner told me and Andy and Earnest Copland, and I think Laird went with us too, to go over to a house a couple of doors away and try to see where the sniper was firing from. So we did, as we walked into the house I noticed the fire was still going in the cook stove. Andy and Copeland went upstairs and shoved up some shingles on the roof from the attic to try and locate this sniper. I went ahead and was making coffee. Laired was standing over there, it was his first day up, and I reached over and grabbed him and jerked him back away from the door and said, "Don't do that!" I no sooner did that and a machine gunner came right down the doorsill. I told him to get a mirror and sit there and look in the mirror and not exposure yourself if wanted to look out. That night I found out who he was. I had to make an apology I didn't know he was a lieutenant [chuckles]. In the meantime the plan was for C Company to move through us. That was the plan I guess for the day. C Company in Metz was blown up, so these young men were replacements. These young men coming out of the wooded area were wearing overcoats. We mistook them for Germans and about that same time the Germans counterattacked, so we were shooting at them. A lieutenant came running down the street, he was hit in the leg, so I grabbed him and pulled him into the house where we were. I never got a cup of that coffee. I offered it to him and he drank it all. I was glad to give it to him [smiles]. I don't know who he was but I'd like to meet the guy again if he's still alive.

We went out of that town and went to Ishbach, Germany. We went up through a forest more or less. I remember the artillery was firing and we were sitting up on a hill waiting for them to lift. Andy Northcut and I sat there and made some coffee and had our dinner there. We had some good old pimento cheese and some hash or something. That afternoon we moved out and went down into Ishbach. We came in the back way on them and I was honestly worn out going down that hill, it was that steep. We ran into three or four houses there and took them. Nightfall came pretty quick because it was already late in the afternoon. You could see the 88's down at one end, they were firing point blank at us. Charlie Arnold and I were in this one house. We were supposed to be observing. We were up in the upstairs looking out the window watching these 88's fire. It was very strange, they would fire and hit the houses on either side of us but not ours, and we couldn't figure out why? We found out that night when we heard somebody leave our house. He had hobnailed boots like a German would wear, we could hear him leaving the house and running. Evidently we were observing from the same house and didn't even know it. The house was a duplex so he was probably over on the other side calling for fire. The next morning we move down into the center of Ishbach. I met a Catholic priest and I asked him if there were any Germans and he said no, that they had all gone to the hills. We could hear them moving out that night, the tanks and the other equipment, so evidently they went up into the hills. This was about December the 1st. I think we went in there on about the 30th of November, on the 29th I was wounded, so it would have been the 30th that we came into town. This was December 1st and late in the afternoon, probably about three o'clock the 1st and 3rd platoons went to find a supply route over to Oberlund, another town. So we had to go up this road and into the woods, and as we went up this hill, Andy and I and Copeland, were up the farthest part and as we went into the woods they opened up on us. There was machine gun fire, it was terrible, they had us pinned down. It just so happened that Andy and I and Copeland were well up out of it so we flanked them and came down on them. We knocked out the first machine gun nest and then took the second and the third. This is where I was awarded the Silver Star for gallantry in action. This is what it says:

Joseph W. Napier, Private, Infantry, Company E, 377th Infantry Regiment for gallantry in action against the enemy on the first day of December 1944 in the vicinity of Ishbach, Germany. On the evening of the first of December 1944 the 2nd and 3rd platoons of E Company, 377th Infantry Regiment were sent out from Ishbach with the mission of securing a supply route from Ishbach to Oberlund, Germany. In the woods on the West and Southwest of the former town, inside the woods the 1st platoon walked into terrific fire from German machine guns and rifles dug in on the slope of the hill. The platoon deployed quickly and vigorously with their rifles but it was apparent that the superior entrenched firepower of the well-camouflaged German forces had pinned down the outnumbered platoon. Risking his life to forestall this immediate counter fall Private Napier with two companions advanced boldly in the face of enemy fire toward German emplacements, firing from the hip and marching within grenade range Private Napier threw his own grenade at the enemy while dogging their grenades. Approaching the hostile nest Private Napier brandished the cold steel of his bayonet and with his two comrades closed in ruthlessly for the kill. In the ensuing fight they destroyed three German machine gun positions, killed two soldiers and captured six. This bold deed on the part of Private Napier and his two companions permitted the men of the rest of the platoon to completely fulfill their mission. The gallantry of his actions reflects great credit upon Private Napier and is in the highest tradition of military service.

The next day we moved out of there and went to Santa Barbara and then we moved on down to the Saar valley and went into Saarlautern and the Eldedorb, fighting down into that area. As we entered the town of Saarlautern we had some sniper fire, but it was late in the evening when we were moving in so we held up in some houses there. We moved out the next morning on down into Saarlautern, across the bridge. The bridge was intact, another regiment had captured it, I don't remember which one. We went on down and had some terrific house-to-house fighting in the town and about two days after that I became a sergeant.

Staff Sergeant Taylor was my squad leader and I was his assistant squad leader. Andy was sent to another squad. Andrew was wounded later on. Not too bad, he stayed with the company, but he was wounded in the hand. Then we went over across the Saar River to Fraulautern in the Siegfried Line. The pillboxes were all lined up for miles, one covering the other. Some looked like a filling station, some looked like a house with curtains up in the front end. We fought and got over in Fraulautern and Alvin Tiner and some of the other platoon boys got in a pillbox and couldn't get out because the Germans had them covered. Every time they'd open the door the Germans would machine-gun them. We went too far really and ended up staying all night in a house. Taylor told me that we were going to move across the street to a blue house. I always went last because I was the assistant so he went first and then the squad. As I was running I heard a shell come, it was one of ours. It hit the house where we had just slept all night. It went in the basement window and killed Pop Dudley. A friend of mine from Park Hill, Missouri, Alfred Betty, was in there and I run down in the basement and pulled him out. He had been hit in the stomach. I screamed for the medics and they took him back. I didn't know what happened to him then, but I later found out that he was OK and lived in Park Hill. I've met him since then.

This Tiner and a lot of them were in this pillbox so we had orders to pull back. We were going to pull out at 0500 in the morning so we decided to get some engineers up to blow up the pillbox so we could get those boys out that night. There was a bazooka man, his name was Sulack, and I had the furthest outpost. We were way over past the pillbox, next to where the Germans were in their pillbox. Could hear a radio and them laughing and talking in their pillbox. We laid there and waited and waited, Sulack and I from the number one position. When they said one that meant to get back and as we got even with the pillbox it blew. The engineers put a short fuse on it, my leg had gone to sleep laying there on the ground so I told Sulack to go on but he wouldn't leave me so we were just hobbling back when it blew. We woke up after a bit later and started back, we were disoriented and didn't know which way to go until finally we got into a factory that we had been in the night before and I realized where we were. When we got back to the company Andy Northcut halted us. I had forgotten the password because of the explosion and everything. I said, "Andy it's me," and he said, "where have you been?" We told him that we'd been out there and he let us through.

In the meantime we moved back to the positions where we had been before and had some more house-to-house fighting again. An airplane came in and scraped us and so on. They relieved us and we went to Hargortern, France to rest. The first night there they had a USO show come, but I was too tired and sleepy and wanted to rest so I stayed there. Just after dark they came in and told us to grab some men and get up in the hills because some paratroopers had dropped in. You have to understand that the 16th day of December was when the Battle of the Bulge started. They

had Germans dressed as Americans dropping in behind enemy
lines so Taylor and I and some other boys went up into the hills.
There was snow on the ground and we were looking for them up
in some caves up there. We didn't find anybody. We found some
tracks but we didn't find anybody. About two days later we went
back to the front lines. We went in to Walifang and we were in
more or less a holding position because of the Bulge. We were on
the outskirts of this town on patrols. One time Taylor would take
some then I would take some out on patrol. One night I took out a
patrol and ran into another patrol. Thank God it was an American
patrol. I was on guard one night about midnight and the Germans
tried to get in the house where Taylor was. We had two houses on
the outskirts of town. I had a radio; the CO called me and wanted
to know what was going on down here. I told him, "I don't know,
but I saw an explosion in Taylor's house." They were unable to
get in contact with him so I was told to go over there. I knew
Jerry was going to be over there and I didn't much want to go, but
I did. A German patrol had tried to move in on the house. We
were there several days and about that same time they called me
on the radio and I was told we were all expendable. The artillery
was going to fire, don't be alarmed, one round over us, one round
behind us. They didn't fire the third round. We were now zeroed
in. In case the Germans tried to overrun us. That was a very
unpleasant feeling, but that was the way it was.

Taylor came over later and said we were going to go on a
patrol. Anybody want to go along? No one wanted to go so I
volunteered to go. Taylor and I took off that night. We put on
our white suits we had made out of sheets taken from the houses.
As we walked along I noticed something moving, a stray dog, I told
Taylor to look. The dog would go back and then he would come
up again and get a little closer to us. I said you know I think that
dog is trying to spot us. Taylor said I do too. Let's lay some fire
down out there because you could see some bumps in the snow
and it probably was them. So we fired and took off. Well, you

know what happened then, flares went up and we got back to our house. Taylor got a phone call from his superiors asking, "what's going on down there?"

The next morning the Company Commander said, "I want to see you." Laird came in and said, "I found your dog." The dog is lying on the civilian hospital steps dead. We went down and tracked the dog in the snow across the street to the house where he had come from. We went into the house and there was a nice shiny helmet sitting on a table, the table was covered with plaster, the helmet was shiny. We went over to the hospital and a young fellow came walking by with his hand all bandaged up. We started to question him, a young man like that, you know he had been in the Army or should have been. The American people in charge of the hospital told us to get out. We told them that if any civilians came out of there we would kill them; we wanted them to understand that. The next day we received orders to go to Bastogne.

William W. Taylor, Jr.
Infantryman 377th Infantry Regiment

The next morning we jumped off. It was pretty foggy and we went down and kind of swung around towards this town of Rammelfangen, Germany, where Joe was hit. I went up a little hill and two men went with me, one of them being the man that knew he was going to die. When we got to the top of this hill the rest of the company was still swinging around. As I got to the top of this hill one man was on my left and the other behind me when the Germans opened with a machine gun. It cut the fellow to my left, the one that had the premonition, all the way across and he died almost immediately. The man behind me took some slugs through his field jacket, and with all those bullets flying, I didn't get a one. I jumped down in this trench that was there and when I jumped in this trench a German jumped out, but he didn't make it very far. So now I'm trapped in this trench looking at these jokers with the machine gun. I knew exactly where it was because I could see the barrel of the gun. I thought to myself, "Well, how do I do this?" So I put a fresh clip in my M1 and I shoved it up over the trench and fired three or four rounds. I immediately raised up after those rounds and luckily for me the German had ducked when I fired and then raised up behind the machine gun barrel. I could see him rising up and that was his fatal mistake because I put one right down the top of that barrel and got him. Just then another one came up and I nailed him too. About that time Charlie Arnold came up the hill behind me with two or three other men and that finished that little action.

We came back down the hill and went back into town. That's where Joe and Fred both got hit. I guess I was pretty lucky. Of course Joe wasn't hit too hard so he wasn't evacuated. We moved further up that afternoon in heavy fog. We walked right in to an 88 artillery piece. They didn't know we were coming until we were right on them because of the fog. We took them out and spent the night in a little town. The next morning we took off and went into Insbach. We got in there and occupied a couple houses, but I don't think the Germans really knew we were in town for a while. That night there were tanks sitting out behind this house and we could hear them crank up the engines and you could hear the treads squeaking when they moved. We spent the night in there kind of sweating, but we all made it. You could see out one side of the house where there was a Dutch door and up on the hill there was a German artillery piece and outfit. We thought, "Boy, if they see us and turn one of those guns down here they can get us with direct fire." Well, luckily they didn't do it.

The next morning the lieutenant came to me and said he wanted me to find a road back to this other town where we had just come from in order to get re-supplied. I thought, "All right," and took one man and went. While I was gone, they took the rest of the platoon over and had a fight on another road. They had a heck of a brawl over there; Joe was really up to his neck in that one. When I came back I told the lieutenant that I had found a trail where we could get a jeep up, but that was no longer needed because they had cleaned out this road while I was gone. There again I was lucky!

We moved on from there and went into a place called Wallerfangen, Germany. I was sick in there that day, but a couple people caught a chicken and were going to cook it. We were going to have chicken and mashed potatoes, but they didn't have any milk to put in the potatoes. So the guys found a goat and milked it. They put the goat milk in the potatoes and made mashed potatoes. I was never one for goat milk, but I ate a little bit of it anyway. From there we moved on over towards Saarlautern. Another unit had taken the bridge from Saarlautern to Fraulautern. We were supposed to go over there but they kept shelling the bridge. They had demonstrated a pattern to their firing however, so we went across during a lull.

We had a wild time in Fraulautern, at one point we were on opposite sides of the streets and our artillery was firing into the German buildings and their artillery as firing into ours. We were in a house there that had two stories and an attic with a tile roof. It pretty well took the entire tile off the roof from the shells hitting it. During the course of that stay I went down and was looking out of a long basement window. The ground was about knee to waist level outside of that window, and I was looking to see what I could see when an 88 hit the ground right outside the window. I didn't hear anything but I saw a bright flash and fire. When I came to I was lying in the middle of the basement floor with water dripping on my face from a pipe in the ceiling. I shook my head and looked around but didn't see anybody, so I got up and went into a different room where most of the squad was. I said, "What in the hell did you people leave me for?" and one of them, a big old Texan named Sulak, old Tex said, "Well, Sarge we thought you were dead." I said, "Thanks," and to this day I don't hear too well in my left ear because it blew it out.

We went on and hit the Siegfried Line right outside of town. There was a lot of activity in that area. The lieutenant and the platoon sergeant and one squad got in a pill box there and were getting shot up from another pill box. The pillbox was set up so that the entrance was on the other side so that other pillboxes could fire into the door. The lieutenant said, "For God's sake get us out of here!" They told me to take my squad and a few engineers to go out and get them out of the pillbox and then set explosives and blow the gun ports. So we went out in this mess and got them out. The engineers always say that they put enough fuse on a charge that you can always walk away from it, emphasizing always. Well, the engineers went in to set the charges and my God they came out of that pillbox on a dead run. We got out of there, but Joe almost got killed that night because it blew him off his feet. I don't know why, but they put a very short fuse on those charges. Anyway, we survived that without getting anyone killed.

There was a lot of activity there, shooting back and forth. I remember there was a man by the name of Charlie Arnold with us, he was simply a fantastic soldier. While we were defending on one side of the street we would try to go over to the German side and we would get all shot up and then they would try to come over to our side and the Germans would get all shot up and so on. One day they came across and Charlie was in the bathroom on the side of a building, it overlooked a little alley with a good view of the main street out in front of the house. There was a little iron fence out in front of that particular house, and Charlie was there in a perfect position. He just knelt there and waited and as the Germans were coming across. As the Germans would put one leg over the fence Charlie would pop them one by one. This went on for a while until they finally saw that somebody was doing this to them and opened up with a machine gun. The bullets went in the window, and Charlie rolled into the bathtub and kept shooting. I don't know whether he was left-handed or not, but he was sure shooting left handed, and he was getting them. The machine gun blew all the bottles out of the medicine cabinet, glass everywhere, and when it was over Charlie walked down into the basement, sat up against the wall, and just sat there. I guess he realized his own mortality. It didn't last long, Charlie bounced right back, but I thought that was quite a reaction from him. We finally left there and we went back to a place called Hargart just before Christmas.

Richard E. Hunton
Infantryman 378th Infantry Regiment

This is Richard Hunton, Company I, 378th Infantry Regiment, 95th Infantry Division. I was drafted on October 9th, 1943, while I was working at the United States Naval Observatory as an instrument maker. Because of my sensitive position I was deferred for three months, and then for two months and then for one month, for which I am grateful because had I not been deferred I would have gone in on D-Day. Finally, the deferments ran out about April 1944. I was inducted into active service at Fort Meade, Maryland. From there I went to Camp Blanding, Florida, where I took my basic training for the next seventeen weeks. Basic training was extremely vigorous. I started out in a heavy weapons company, but fortunately after two or three weeks of that I was transferred to an intelligence and reconnaissance company. That was a lot easier than lugging around machine guns and mortars all the time.

After a month or two in the new company the captain came along and told us that there were more riflemen being killed than I and R so they made us riflemen. It was real encouraging to hear that. They were recruiting more cannon fodder. After several more months of vigorous training, which included what was supposed to be a 25-mile march but ended up being a 30-mile march. It's amazing, at the end of a 30-mile march your feet are killing you, your back is breaking and you're about to collapse, but they had a military band at the end of the march and when you hear

that music you forget all about your aches and pains and it makes
you feel good again. Our company was the only company to go
through the vigorous training and never lose a man. Normally,
on a forced speed march with full pack and uniform you'd see
men lying all along the roadside, having convulsions, foaming at
the mouth, screaming with pain or something, but we never had
any of that. However, our commanding officer, a Swedish fellow,
said in a broken accent, "At the end of the column there will be
an ambulance following to pick up the dead bodies," now that was
real encouraging [Laughs].

Anyway, we finally made it through basic training and went
home for a couple of weeks of rest and relaxation before we were
taken to Camp [Pause, thinking out loud]…Who wrote the poem
Trees? Oh, yes, Camp Kilmer, New Jersey [Laughs]. Of course we
were heavily censored at that time and all the men were trying to
tell their folks where they were, so they would write the poem *Trees*
somewhere in their letters, but of course that would be censored
out. We stayed there a week or ten days before we finally were
taken down to New York City about the 2nd of November of 1944.
We loaded onto the *Queen Mary* and were put down into the bowels
of the ship. All of the engines were running and I thought we
were gone so I got sea sick, but we hadn't even left port [Laughs].
We left New York on the Queen Mary and it took us about four
or five days to get to Europe since we were zigzagging about every
five miles to keep from being blown up by submarines.

We landed at Greenock, Scotland, a small town about twenty
miles west of Glasgow. It was interesting over there. The people
were so poor and destitute from the war effort that they would
come out and look through our big pile of trash out on the fan tail
of the boat. They would go up and look through all this trash and
pick out half used toothpaste, used combs and anything they could
find to make life a little more comfortable. We got off the boat
at Greenock, Scotland and took a train down to Southampton,
England. We would have liked to do a little sightseeing on the way

down, but they had all the blinds pulled on the train so we didn't know where we were or what we were looking at. We missed a sightseeing trip on the way there, but we got on, I think it was an old Indian freighter, to go across the channel. About half way across we ran into another ship and I thought that would be the end of the war for us, but fortunately we didn't sink.

We made it to Le Harve, France where we got off the boat using rope ladders. We used these ladders to board a landing craft of some sort. By this time it was pitch dark and we got into the landing craft and headed for the beach. I didn't know anything about landing crafts, but the closer we got to the beach the faster this thing went. Well, you beach a landing craft at full speed to get on the beach as far as it can. We got off the boat onto the beach and immediately got out of there. We walked through Le Harve, France, which was still smoking and burning from a previous shelling. From there we loaded some trucks and then 40 and 8 railroad cars. Those are the dinky little box cars that could hold forty men or eight horses, but we had forty-two men, which I guess is equivalent to about eight and a half horses [Laughs]. If you wanted to lie down you had to lie down on somebody and if you wanted to sit down you had to sit down on somebody's lap. It was worse than being a sardine, but we traveled all the way from Le Harve, France all the way up to a little peninsula called Givet, France, just about two miles from the Belgium border. It was interesting. We would stop about every ten miles or so and the little kids would come up to the train asking for money or candy from the fellows. Of course we didn't speak any French and they didn't speak much English, but we did communicate a little bit. This one kid asked a fellow where he was from and the guy told him Chicago. The kid immediately went Bang! Bang! Bang! simulating holding an imaginary Tommy Gun like a gangster. All he knew about Chicago was that it had gangsters with machine guns.

There were a lot of funny things that happened along the way, even though it was extremely uncomfortable. Meals were C-rations. We had three kinds then: beans, hash and stew, but they were all cold and tasted just about alike. Very unpalatable. We took trucks from Givet and went down into Nancy and Verdun and some of those other World War I places that were famous during that time. We got down to a little place called Boinville-sur-Nied, or something like that, and joined the 95th Division. That was on November the 24th or 25th, 1944, and I finally joined I Company, 378th at a little town called Niedervisse, France a day or two later. We started walking up through several little towns that I can't think of the names of. I remember lying along the sides of a battered little road were a number of horses and cows, ripped and bleeding as a result of the previous day's fierce fighting. Many had been completely disemboweled by nearly direct mortar and artillery hits. One day about this time we started getting enemy fire. Our company commander said we had gone over to Kreutzwald, which is right on the German border, but there wasn't supposed to be any German soldiers there. We were there just to reconnoiter the place, but all of a sudden we started to get shot at from every angle, so we got out of there. We kept moving up over the next several days to a place called Falck and Dalem, where an interesting thing took place. As we were going through this little old town, liberating Dalem, there was an old man. He was standing on the side of the road with a bottle of wine in one hand and a glass in the other trying to get the soldiers to celebrate the liberation of his town. Of course we didn't have time to fool with that, but years later I somehow got in contact with a fellow named Alain Maas. Alain lives in Dalem, and I came to find out that this old man was his Grandfather.

We went up and liberated some other towns north of Falck and Dalem until finally about November 30th we came to a large hill called the Sauberg. This hill was supposed to be very important to the defense of the Saar River, which was only about four miles away. We had a terrific fight going up that hill. When we got to the top there was a dense fog, you couldn't see ten feet in front of you. We almost starved to death because we couldn't find the chow truck, well maybe not starved, but we were pretty hungry. Late at night, about eleven o'clock or so, the company commander said dig a fox hole and get in it, we're going to spend the night. So we got out our tools and started chopping on that stuff, but it was nothing but frozen rocks. We just had to sleep out on the open ground under half of a tent shelter while the Germans bombarded this hill with artillery all during the night. You can imagine how uncomfortable it was to just lie there and hear these shells coming and landing twenty-five or thirty feet from you. Every time one would land rocks would shower down and land on top of you. It was really a hairy night. As interesting as that is, I have a friend who lives in Neuforweiler, Germany, which is about three miles across the German border. My friend has a friend that lives up near Berlin, by the name of Rolf Grunewald. One day they were talking and the 95th Infantry Division came up. Because of me my friend began to compare notes with Rolf and it turned out that he was a nineteen year old, the same age I was, German soldier that was shooting a machinegun at us while we were shooting at him.

The Deployment at Saarlautern

Somewhere around November 25th, 1944 our regimental tank attack near Hirschland in Alsace with dug-in tankers, suffered high casualties in a counterattack. After that we came with five companies of infantry from the 901st Tank-Infantry Division and went into action near Saarlautern. On November 28th, 1944 we went towards Ensdorf with our armored personnel carriers. From there we marched through Lisdorf and Picard toward Saarberg. There we found a system of trenches that we used for our machinegun emplacements. Fortunately the sky was overcast and the clouds hung low so that the American bomber, the Thunderbirds and the Lightnings could not fly and attack us.

As soon as we got to the summit of the Sauberg there appeared about 150 meters in front of us an American Sherman tank accompanied by a number of soldiers. The tank commander tried to find our position by looking through his binoculars. After a firefight our machineguns directed their fire at the tank. A shot from the tank's cannon missed a couple of times, but the tank got out of the zone of fire. It didn't take long before the Americans started to move forward. To the right and left of us we heard heavy infantry fire. Quickly the attack advanced in front of us where only Americans were to be seen. In a mass exodus we got our company back in the direction of Picard. Our machinegun platoon received an order to cover the return with another machinegun, a howitzer and a tank gun. Soon reinforcements came for the American attack and we got ourselves back to the vicinity of Picard. Then the Americans began a bombardment with eight-inch howitzers. These shells made tremendous craters in the ground. Again and again we had to take cover. It was terrible that one had to have all of that thrown at him, but only by luck could he escape injury. Later in the night It was pitch dark when we arrived at Picard. It was a wonder that we lost so few men.

Suddenly fighting broke out around us. We threw ourselves back and I landed right in a manure pile. We sure smelled bad after that. Herbert Muller, our number two gunner, was a casualty. We tried to find him for a long time, but because of the darkness we didn't find him. Was he dead, or wounded, or was he captured? We hoped the latter, but didn't say so out loud. We were concerned because his Father was dying in a tuberculosis sanitarium.

At dawn on November 29th, 1944 our company went back across the Saar. At Saarbrucken from Ensdorf and

Lisdorf, an SS officer and his men wanted us to let them cross the border. The officer threatened to shoot our company commander. We got our weapons ready, but the situation soon relaxed and we allowed them to cross the bridge. In Ensdorf we were quartered in an abandoned apartment in a three-story house. We lay down and were sleeping right on the edge of the town square. I found a place on the top floor on a bedside rug. With a loud crash I woke up again. A shell had made a direct hit on the roof right over me. Ensdorf was under a severe attack. I was all alone in the apartment. After a few seconds I found the others in the cellar. They had sought shelter there and I was happy to see them. They said that the city had been under attack for the past half hour and I, totally exhausted, had known nothing about it.

After several days we got out armored personnel carrier back. We traveled to Lof on the Mosselle and then during the Ardennes Offensive in December 1944 we got ready to move there.

Rolf Grunewald
Machine-gunner 901st German Division

There was a huge tank trap just over the top of this hill. We had to figure out a way across this trap. Somehow we managed to cross this tank trap the next day, December 1st, 1944. We moved from there into, and liberated, this little town called Altforweilier. As we were liberating this town we started to get bombarded with mortars as we reached the far side. They had sirens on them so if the thing didn't hit you it would still scare the daylights out of you. We called them "screemin' meemies". It wasn't long until one landed about fifteen feet from me and knocked my squad leader Sergeant LaChance and me out. I came to and I was lying there in the middle of the road dying and bleeding to death and hollering for a medic, but all I heard was, "Hold your horses, you aren't the only one!"

They finally dragged me into an old barn across the street where they were all standing around congratulating me because I was going to get to go home [Laughs]. I was about half killed, but I was so happy about it because I would be going home.. I had a severe compound fracture of the right arm so they put sulfa powder and a splint on it and wrapped me up and gave me a half-grain of morphine. I was still able to walk so they told me to go back up the street to the company headquarters and they'll tell me what to do. I was walking up the side walk, which were pretty close to the houses, when all of a sudden a huge crash landed about three or four feet in front of me. It just so happened that a mortar shell had hit the tile roof of the house, all the houses had tile roofs over there, and the entire roof fell off about three feet in front of me. Two more steps and I would have had it!

I finally got up to the company headquarters. My squad leader was lying there screaming and begging for somebody to kill him and put him out of his misery. He had gotten a fragment through his back and intestines and was in real bad shape. I thought he was going to die, but a few years ago I found him alive and well and living in Florida. After it got dark an aid man started walking me back from the front lines to where I could get on a jeep. I told him, "I have got to lie down!" The morphine was really working on me and I kept telling him that I needed to lie down and go to sleep, that's all there was to it. He said, "No, you can't do that," and kept walking me on. If I had been by myself I would have lain down and died. They finally got me onto a little old jeep and drove me back to a field hospital where they put a better splint on my arm.

Anthony N. Petraglia
Infantryman 378th Infantry Regiment

We made our way inland into France. We went into the hedge-row fighting which was really, really tough because every hundred yards or so there would be another hedgerow. Hedgerows were built up high, they were actually trees but they were formed in rows of hedges. What the Germans would do, is they would bring their tanks on the opposite side of the hedge and like I said there was a hundred yards or so in between each hedgerow. This is more or less in the orchard part in the farmland through France. They would bring their tanks on the opposite side of the hedgerows and as you were coming through they would bring their 88's and put their gun emplacements behind there and fire point blank at you. They were really, really tough. They were mounted on Tiger tanks, which was an excellent tank. We had a lot of problems with their 88's, there were a lot of casualties due to these 88's and the hedgerows.

After we got through the hedgerows in France we made our way into village fighting, which was also tough, because we were going building-to-building, home-to-home, not knowing what was in the next room. I remember one incident where I made my way into this one room in a building and I went up to the second floor to check – there was like courtyard in between the two buildings – and the Germans were in the building next to me. I figured they were going to try to get over into this building next to me so I went up to the second floor to stand alongside this one window to see if I could catch any of them coming across the courtyard. As I was up there I heard a shell coming and I heard screaming, it came through the ceiling, there was an empty book case in the corner and it came through the ceiling right through the book case and landed about four feet away from me, right in that corner. It was a dud. I saw that and thanked the Polish saboteurs because they worked in the ammunition factories and it was their custom as the shells were coming through to pull the pin out of one out of every six shell. So every sixth shell would be a dud. That one dropped there was the one out of six that was a dud. They saved my life right there. I have thanked them ever since for that. As I think about that incident, it never bothered me at all at the time it happened or right after that because you just have to carry on and just keep moving, you don't have time to stand still and think about it. So like I said, at the time it didn't bother me, but right now it bothers me much, much more than it did then and I often think about that. I more or less get stewy just thinking about it. Like I said it bothers me now.

I remember one fellow that was in our division his name was Roy Paul. He came into the 95th as a replacement out of college. I believe he went to the University of Pittsburgh, he was in the ROTC program at Pittsburgh. I remember Roy as a young fellow, I was working in a grocery store after school before I entered the Army, this was an over the counter store before supermarkets. I would wait on his mother and Roy would come in with his mother at times to help her with groceries so I got to know Roy very well. So this one day we were in Indiantown Gap, Roy came in there as a replacement. He looked me up and I'll never forget it, I was standing on one side of the bunk and I looked over and there was Roy on the other side and I asked him what he was doing here. He told me he was coming in to our outfit as a replacement out of college. So I more or less guided Roy through his training and what not and as we got overseas, he'd always look me up. This one day we were being shelled pretty heavy and I'll never forget Roy crawled over to me and I told him, "Roy, you better be careful, we're being shelled pretty heavy, watch so you don't get hit." He said: "I will" and I said: "You better get back and try to dig in." So he left me and said, "I'll see you later."

He wasn't gone two minutes and another buddy of mine crawled over to me and said, "Roy Paul just got hit." He got hit as he was leaving me. After the service I happened to be walking down one of the streets of my local town in Pittsburgh with another buddy of mine who was just discharged. We were walking in front of this one tavern when all at once this gentleman was walking out of the tavern. He had quite a few drinks and he's staggering, he's having problems trying to stand up, so Ray, the buddy of mine that was with me, knew this fellow. He walked over to him, grabbed him and started talking to him. In the meantime this fellow was telling Ray about some problems of his and he said, "Ray, you know, I lost my son overseas" but Ray didn't know, so he started telling him this story about it. The guy took his wallet out and showed Ray a picture of his son, and you'll never believe it, but the picture was Roy Paul. Ray showed me the picture and I told Ray I said, "You know, I was very close to Roy, he was with me two minutes before he got killed, right alongside of me." Ray said, "tell him about it' and I did. As I was telling this guy the story, you'll never believe it but he sobered up. As I was telling him the story you would never have believed that he had had a drink in him. He started crying and said, "You're not kidding?" I said, "no way would I ever kid you about that" and he was Roy Paul's father, which was one out of a million that he was standing there. Yes, indeed that's a story that also stands out in my mind.

I remember in this village fighting, being in another home again and definitely at a window, alongside a window, you never stand in front of a window you stand alongside a window to look out. If you stand in front of a window they're going to pick you off, but I happened to look out and they were once again crossing these other buildings and I knew they were coming into the building, so I wanted to make my way out. I went to jump out the window when my trench shovel hit the edge of the windowsill and knocked me off balance as I jumped out. Before I hit the ground my hand and arm came up with my rifle, it was cold weather, and a sniper fired at me. He was in a stable across the road and he fired at me and it ripped the glove right off my left hand and the bullet penetrated my hand. I saw the blood coming out and I just wiped it off, but he ripped the glove right off my hand. Fortunately, he didn't get me dead center in the hand but he just scraped it on top and I could see the blood, but I made my way across the road into another building and we finally blew him out of that stable.

I remember quite a few stories getting back to Henson, a pureblooded Cherokee, he was like I said straight off the Cherokee reservation in South Carolina. We were very close also and in the states I have a few things to say about him. He was married at the time he had a little daughter. You often hear about Indians that can't hold their drink and all, and when we were still in the states he'd just have a few drinks and he'd come over to me and tell me that his wife was probably running around on him and that he was going to write her a letter and ask for a divorce. As he was getting a pencil and paper I said, "I'll write the letter for you Henson." I said, "dictate to me what you want to say", so he started dictating to me all his problems and what he thought and what not and I'd write just the opposite. I would write her a nice love letters and then he'd get a love letter in return and he could never figure out why he was getting love letters after what he was writing. I never told Henson what I was writing in the letters so he never knew what happened. You really had to know the guy to really appreciate the story cause he was an excellent soldier.

As we got into Germany, I do remember, we were being shelled very, very heavy this one morning and there was a shell, I heard it coming, but it dropped very, very close to me to my left flank, and I remember that and after that I can't remember too much. It dropped very close and I ended up in a field hospital and this was in Germany, so I was in a field hospital I can't say how long, but I do remember going back in an ambulance. I was in this field hospital in Germany until they brought me back to another field hospital in France. I can't tell you how many days I was in this field hospital when they transferred me to a field hospital in France and I was in the field hospital there for quite a while, I guess. But I do remember them flying me to England, they put me on a hospital plane, and I was in the hospital in England for quite a long time, in fact I was there and then they put me in another hospital in Bristol, England. So I was there for quite a while, in Bristol, England and I remember the excellent care they gave us. I remember the nurse coming over to me and asking me, "How long has it been since your mother heard from you?" and I said, "I really don't know".

She said, "I know you can't write to her but I'm going to drop her a her a letter." So she sent a letter to my mother and to this day I don't know what she put in it, my mother never told me when I got home. She did write the letter and that's how my mother found out that I was injured and that I was in the hospital.

This was Christmas time, I remember being in the hospital at Christmas time of 44'. Christmas morning of 44', I remember faintly that I woke up and I found, there was a priest that came to see me during the night or during the morning, I don't know which, but he left a card on my bedside. Then when the red cross was in they told me they'd left a pack of Old Gold cigarettes for Christmas and at that time [Laughs] that was my Christmas present [Laughs]. I faintly remember that. This was way after Metz, this was around Christmas as I remember. I was in this Army hospital in Bristol and one day my nurse came over to me and kneeled beside my bed and whispered in my ear, she said, "Don't repeat this, but I wish I was going where you are going." Actually she was from Boston, Massachusetts, just an excellent nurse. She said, "I wish I was going where you're going" and she looked at me and smiled and walked away. Afterwards I put two and two together to find out what she meant.

A little bit later they told me I was coming back to the states so they put me on a converted hospital ship, the *SS Brazil*. They brought me back to the states and they put me into Camp Edwards Hospital, in Massachusetts, to recuperate. I was in the hospital about six months and I recuperated at Camp Edwards and I was finally discharged out of Camp Edwards. They told me that my service records were lost. I was supposed to be discharged with a rank as staff sergeant, but they told me that my service records were somehow confiscated by the Germans and how they ever got my service records I don't know cause they never got me. I don't know how they got them, but that's what they told me. The hospital's medical colonel told me as I was being discharged, he said, "If you stay with us, stay behind three or four more months we'll try to straighten out your service records and get your rank and everything straight." I told him, I said, "Sir, I'd really like to be discharged." He said, "That's fine." So I was discharged in May of 45', in the end of May, I think it was 30th or 31st of 1945 that I was officially discharged as just a private.

Frank Bever
Infantryman 379th Infantry Regiment

After about a week of fighting the other units of our company F, 379th, along with units of the other regiments of our 95th had indeed penetrated the defenses of Metz and the city fell. I went back to join my company F after this and this is when we went on further after reorganizing and receiving a lot of replacements. We had very, very, very heavy casualties from this battle of going into Metz. I don't know the percentages, but I do know that I saw an awful lot of kids in my platoon that I had never seen before. After we reorganized we started out further. We didn't know for sure where we were going to go there, but I do recall being in the Maginot Line after we crossed the Moselle. That was a huge fortified area that dated back to World War I, I guess. I can remember walking, it seemed like lots of walking inside of that huge line of defense. We were going further north and eventually we ended up in Saarlautern, Germany. This was a cleaning process that we were going through to clean out the houses to make it safe for other troops to come through later on. This was on December 3rd, 1944. In the process of going through Saarlautern, a pretty good size city, we had a line of infantrymen across a regular size street with a tank in the middle. Obviously the Germans had us under observation and they fired a shell, I think it must have been an 88 shell because they had a high degree of accuracy with those things and they were quite respected, well they should have been anyhow by the US troops. Anyway, that shell landed in the center of the street, directed I think at the tank. It exploded and there was

one man killed from our company that was in these columns of
infantry on each side. Three more were injured with that particular
shell. I was one of the three that was injured. I was immediately
seen by a medic that was in our platoon. He doctored me up the
best he could. I had a facial wound and a wound to my knee and
thigh. My head was bleeding something radically as I remember,
but I could still see.

This led to my evacuation. It was a step-by-step thing. I went
back to the battalion aid station and then on back and I think my
actual surgery and removal of shrapnel took place in the Metz
area. Eventually I was put on C-47 plane along with a great
number other wounded men and we ended up back in England
for recovery purposes. They had excellent facilities and took good
care of me. I was proud of the United States from the standpoint
of taking care of the guys if they were wounded. I was back there
about three months recovering and of course we have to get back
into the idea of mobility and getting around. During this period
of time they started us out on a march deal in the winter months
of early 1945. While we were there I remember an outstanding
Christmas dinner, I remember getting word of the Battle of the
Bulge and reading it in some of the local publications. I was so
grateful indeed that here I was back there, but I felt bad that those
guys over there at the Bulge were subjected to that type of German
counter-attack. Eventually the US troops held firm after a period
of time to a degree at least in the Battle of the Bulge.

Paul H. Madden, Jr.
Infantryman 379th Infantry Regiment

After Plappeville the 379th went into division reserve while
the 377th and the 378th were attacking to the east along the Saar
River. About December the 2nd, part of the 379th, I think it was the
3rd Battalion, had gotten into the outskirts of Saarlautern. They
determined the bridge over the Saar River was still intact and was

the only bridge that hadn't been blown. They decided that a night attack might be able to capture the bridge, so the 1st Battalion of the 379th was selected to make the river crossing the next morning. We crossed the river and were successful in capturing the bridge before it was blown. The Germans kind of resented that I guess because we had multiple artillery barrages, probably the heaviest and most concentrated fire I had seen in several months of combat. Later our company moved from the bridgehead area into the town of Fraulautern, a little suburb, and then back and forth across the railroad tracks into Saarlautern-Roden. All these towns are now today called Saar Louis, which was the French name back prior to 1870 I believe.

I can recall on December the 2nd, when we were on division reserve, we were on high ground that kind of overlooked the Saar River and the Saar Valley as the Air Force bombed the town of Saarlautern, primarily the railroad yards. We found out it was the railroad yards later because there were a number of bomb craters there. I can remember one night when we were crossing the tracks I slipped and fell into a hole. We were in single file, and after I climbed back up out of the crater I fell in further back in the line, but for a few days after that I didn't get any mail. I used to get mail almost every day when it was available. So one night, after not getting mail for several days, I asked the platoon leader if I could go back with the ration detail to see if there was a problem with my mail. When we got there I asked the mail clerk and he said, "well somebody said you were missing and I was just holding your mail" [Laughs]. I assume that whoever was behind me didn't see me fall into the crater, or come out, either one, but that day I wound up with about twenty-three letters. That was the only time that I can actually recall the Air Force bombing. There were numerous times that it was requested, but it was almost always called off for weather and what not.

Our company made several trips back and forth across the railroad tracks, I think most companies that were involved in this area had the same experience. There were a number of pillboxes on the eastern side of the railroad tracks that caused difficulties from time to time for different units. I know that our company crossed the tracks at least four separate times before we finally stayed on the northern side of the tracks. When we first moved from the bridgehead we were in this suburb they called Fraulautern and I recall that part of our 3rd platoon had occupied a German house, these were stand alone houses as opposed to a number of them being row type houses. One of the machine gun squads set a machine gun up on the kitchen table inside of a window and unfortunately it was spotted because a German tank came up and put a round right through the window and killed one of the guys outright and I think two or three died later. I was in the adjoining room talking to our platoon sergeant and he had his back to the door of the room where the shell went off and of course as the shell went off everybody dropped to the floor, but the sergeant just kind of collapsed. It was almost like he was feinting. He just slowly sunk to the floor and he was dead. We found a very small wound in his back. A small piece of fragment must have got his spinal cord. He was acting platoon leader at that time, so that made the third platoon leader that I had the misfortune of losing a runner. That was not too good of an experience, but it happens. This was all street fighting at that time. Sometimes you would get into a row of houses and if you got into the first house on the block we'd stay in the houses and just blow a hole in the wall with a bazooka to get to the next house and the end of the block without ever going outside. When we would hit the bunkers, sometimes a squad might stay in a bunker to keep the Germans occupied and then the engineers would come up at night and set charges and blow it up or they may weld the steel doors so nobody could get in it later.

Our experience from the middle of December to the end of January was in the Saarlautern-Roden area. By this time the Bulge had started in the north. Around December the 16th the 5th

Division, which had been one of the main divisions in the capture of Metz, had gotten new replacements and equipment so they moved up and replaced the 95th on December the 16th. The 95th was to go into corps reserve for a period of maybe ten days but the Bulge hadn't started at that time. When the Bulge started the 5th was better manned than the 95th was so they elected to move the 5th Division up to the south flank of the Bulge into Luxembourg. So the 95th went back on the line and I can remember a company morning report that I acquired a few years ago showed that our company received 67 replacements one day in December, maybe the 26th or 27th. The next day we received 12 more. This gives you an idea about how reduced in strength we were after Metz. Periodically you may go into a battalion reserve for a few days and then replace another company after a few days and so on.

John G. Little, Jr.
Artilleryman 547th Anti Aircraft Artillery

December 1, 1944, our battery had crossed the German border. We stopped at a little village of Feldsberg on December 5, 1944. We then went on to Saarlautern (now called Saarlouie). On December 21, 1944, we moved back five miles to a rear area for a rest. This was during the Battle of the Bulge. We only stayed two days. We had to go back where we came from. The 5th and 90th Divisions were also in this area. We shot our first plane down near the village of Feldsberg. Fifty years later one of my friends went back and saw the plane. I was on a tour over there in 1990 and the bus would not stop in Feldsberg. We just drove through it. I wanted to look for that airplane. We stayed in Feldsberg until January 29, 1945. Then we made a twenty-hour road march to Houffalize, Belgium.

Leon E. Langford
Ordnance 795ᵗʰ Ordnance
(Light Maintenance) Company

From that point things get a little hazy. It did get interesting as we got thrown into the line. As we all well know the division fought well and took Metz and I guess we had a couple of scares about the Germans coming after us. I had always been concerned from the time that I was in the ordnance in Aberdeen some place in the training they told us that if you're in a support unit in the rear echelons that that is who the enemy like to take out because if they can take out the support units it leaves the poor GI rifleman up there without any support. He would soon run out of food and ammunition and everything else. I also remember that someplace it took fourteen other soldiers to support one combat infantryman. So I had always had a little concern about being in a support unit from that standpoint. I was always grateful that we didn't go into combat until the Germans were pretty well out of planes and a lot of that other stuff that could come back and get the support units like us, and even farther back.

We moved a lot. Of course the infantry guys were moving all the time. When we were with Patton's Third Army we were anywhere from thirty to forty miles behind up to within about a half a mile. I think we were in Boule, of course not everybody in the Army had a sufficient amount of the right kind of gear, so somebody decided that we needed combat boots. I'll never forget the day that I got combat boots. I was on guard duty (I was always on guard duty), I had just come off guard duty and up on the third floor of this concrete building, sitting on my fart sack. I had just gotten my combat boots, didn't have to wear leggings anymore, while I was waterproofing my boots one of Germany's fine bombers came screeching down and decided to drop a bomb. Fortunately, he didn't drop the bomb on the building. He dropped the bomb on the railroad track, which was right next to the building. I don't remember whether he hit it or missed it, but anyhow I thought that if this is what you get when they issue you combat boots, they can have them back, I don't want them. In that same incident there was a guy running from the slit trench, and as he ran a piece of that bomb cut his hand off. I think that was probably the only casualty from that bombing.

Martin H. Lincoln
Ordnance 795th Ordnance
(Light Maintenance) Company

We were always moving around from place to place. It was an interesting time, but those were the days. The division finally got up to the front. We were moved into a town just south of the Siegfried Line. I forget the name of the town, It wasn't Saarlautern, the first town began with a B, I think it might have been Bulay. We moved into this house that had been occupied by the Germans. There was this wicked stench there. I discovered later that the Gestapo had been there so they must have murdered some people and buried them around there because there was this wicked smell in the house and you couldn't get rid of it. Then we got into Saarlautern. The buildings were side by side in long blocks with about thirty feet between the rows of buildings on the north and south sides of the street. One day I started out the door and along comes a German plane. It came right down the ally firing its machineguns, but the bullets missed my head and slammed into the door. I jumped back inside the house as this guy went back to strafe a couple of times. After a few times he was getting pretty confident so he went to strafe some of the infantry and got shot down. The next thing you know I saw this guy walking around with a pair of boots that he said belonged to the flyer.

Then there was a rumor that the Germans had broken through in a couple of places and attacked units so we were all on high alert.

One night we were in this room getting ready to go to bed, and we all had our guns right beside us with orders to shoot anything that moved, when someone bust in. It was this captain that we thought was off for the night. He came back in through the door and almost got his head blown off. Fortunately we sat back and made sure before we shot. In that particular place there was a farmhouse owned by a German that had a beautiful daughter and made schnapps. Every night he'd come by and give us a big jug of schnapps. We got to be very friendly, and his daughter was very nice too, so we stayed with them for two-weeks or so until finally we had to leave there.

The colonel that was in charge of Ordnance from our area indicated that he was coming for a visit. Lieutenant Colonel Shawhan had everybody spick and span, particularly the division ammunition section. The Ordnance office said the colonel was coming to visit but they didn't know his name. The next day we were all in the office there and the door opens and in came a full colonel that walked up to me and shook my hand and gave me a hug. I had been a good friend of his when he was a lieutenant under Lieutenant Colonel Shawhan. He had now become a full colonel with Army. Colonel Shawhan almost had a heart attack when he saw who it was because now the full colonel was his superior in the area (Laughs). That was just a little turn around, a little justice I thought because Shawhan always gave Rawlings such a hard time the whole time he was under him. He escaped from Shawhan while we were still back in the states. He had gone down to Fort Sam Houston to become part of the Corps set up and went over to Europe ahead of us. He moved up fast after that!

Harry T. Hessler
Clerk 95th Quartermaster Company

I remember one run down into Saarlautern when they were down there to bring them out. We had some action there, we were shelled on the way out. Nothing critical, we did get out of there in good shape. We then moved up towards the Battle of the Bulge, but it was over by the time we got there. I stayed in that same capacity until the spring of the next year. They came around one day and told me I was being transferred and I wound up in a military government unit. There were 11 enlisted men and 4 officers. The first place we went was Stendle on the Elbe River. Stendle was an American area and we more or less established the government facilities to take care of things in that area. We weren't there too long and the English took over. From there we were sent to Weisenfelds, which was south of Leipzeig, and pretty much did the same thing there. We then handed that area over to the Russians. It was funny, up in Stendle the Americans were there and the British cam in and that was it, but in Weisenfelds all the Americans moved out before the Russians got there. That should tell you something about the Russians. We then moved to Heideland, Germany as a military government unit on the Mecau river just north of Heidelburg.

The Saar comes to an end

By December 5th the division had also defeated the enemy resistance west of the river and was prepared to transition to the task of the pending expansion. It was now one month since the 95th entered heavy combat. The long period without rest had taken its toll on the combat effectiveness of the Iron Men. In the division operations report of December 2nd, 1944, the "Combat Efficiency" of the division was listed as "Materially reduced due to heavy casualties and continual operations over an extended period. Replacements unavailable. Combat effective strength of four infantry battalions reduced to 55 percent or less."[5] With the capture of the bridge, the face of the division battle would soon be changed to reflect the expansion of the existing bridgehead and the establishment of a second bridgehead at Ensdorf.

With the towns of Saarlautern on the west side and Fraulautern on the east side of the river the 379th and 377th were given the mission to secure and expand the existing bridgehead. Until their relief on December 17th, 1944, the two regiments secured both sides of the bridge and expanded the bridgehead to encompass about 70 percent of the town. Close quarters combat was once again the nature of the operation as soldiers slowly cleared from one house to the next for another two weeks. To the south the 378th would take part in the establishment of the second bridgehead until the beginning of its ordered abandonment on the night of the 19th. The 378th began their mission on December 5th by crossing the Saar River under fire at Ensdorf. Unfortunately for the men of this second bridgehead, there was not a bridge at Ensdorf. Nevertheless, they fought valiantly to clear Ensdorf, hampered by the inability to effectively transport supplies and supporting heavy weapons across the river. Engineers were able to get supplies and heavy weapons across by December 16th, but this was only possible by ferry. A bridge was never constructed at the proposed second bridgehead, and as a result of the massive German counterattack in the Ardennes forest the corps directed the Iron Men to fall back to the original Saarlautern bridgehead. While parts of the XX Corps combat power headed for the Ardennes the 95th was ordered to relieve the 5th Division along the Saar and to maintain a defensive line in the vicinity of the original bridgehead. By the 21st of December the division was set in the specified defensive positions where it would remain through the month of January.

III. Continued Resistance

As the 95th headed for the Saar, Hitler was preparing his forces for the last great battle. He felt Germany could still win the war if they could mount just one more major offensive to demonstrate that the *Wehrmacht* was still capable of waging offensive operations. In order to launch this massive attack, the German staff had to begrudgingly maneuver valuable assets from the Eastern front to participate in the Ardennes offensive. The enormous battle that ensued from December 16, 1944 – January 25, 1945, would come to be commonly known as the Battle of the Bulge, referring to the bulge that was created in the Allied line. Fortunately for the Allies, the Germans weren't able to meet the logistical demands of an intense operation of this magnitude. Although the *Wehrmacht* achieved early gains, the Allies were able to halt and eventually stop the attack before the Germans could make any sustainable advances. The Ardennes offensive is most clearly represented in the staggering statistics of participation and damage. The Germans massed the equivalent of 29 divisions for this attack, while the Allies answered with 31 divisions. This put the total manpower participation at approximately 600,000 Germans, 500,00 Americans and 55,000 British. As a result of this one extended battle, the United States lost 81,000 men, with 19,000 killed, the British lost 1400, with 200 killed and 100,000 Germans were either killed, wounded or captured. Germany could not afford to sacrifice the massive amount of men and material that she exhausted in the Ardennes. Although losses were also staggering in the Allied ranks, additional manpower and material supplies were available to replenish those lost during the battle. Initial military training was abbreviated and production accelerated even further to meet the needs of the European forces. Germany manning and logistics on the other hand, had nothing left to give.

The end of the Saar and the Ardennes offensive provided a welcomed respite for the 95th Infantry Division. As a result of the last major German offensive the men of the 95th remained in their defensive positions from the latter part of December through the entire month of January. While not pushing through Europe the division was still engaged in combat operations, albeit of a defensive nature. Additionally, a cadre of officers and non-commissioned officers was ordered to report to Metz for the training of several thousand in-theater replacements from various other occupational specialties. This in-country on-the-job training program, along with stateside replacements, would be sufficient to bring the division back to nearly full strength prior to movement. As men and equipment were being rushed to the front, the remainder of the division repelled German probes and limited attacks.

Charles R. Fowler
Artillery Officer and Infantry Rifle Platoon Leader 377th Infantry Regiment

Then we went into Saarlautern and I remember artillery coming in while I was eating breakfast one morning. The kitchen was in the basement of this house we were in and the smoke came down in the basement so I ran out. As I came out a shell went just barely over the fence and exploded so I just went back in and drank another cup of coffee. The aid station was located across the street from us and during this same barrage a shell landed in the street and some of the shrapnel hit an aidman in the leg. They couldn't stop him from bleeding so he bled to death. Then we crossed over the Saar River, they had captured the bridge there so my platoon walked across. I had been transferred from the anti-tank platoon to an infantry platoon in C Company. They had lost the platoon leader earlier, in fact there was only one other officer in the company when I got there. We were in reserve once we got across to Fraulautern. In Fraulautern we had half of the town and the Germans had half of the town. We had all the houses numbered and the blocks lettered for artillery fire.

One night the Germans pushed in and captured some men in B Company. I was called out to get rid of the machinegun that the Germans had there raking up and down the street. So my platoon went into the alley and we set up rifles with grenade launchers to launch grenades over on to the house where the machinegun was. Then I took some plastic explosives and a couple of men down the street out of the range of the machinegun and crossed over to the machinegun side. We worked our way up while the rest of the platoon kept them occupied with the grenades. When we got to the house with the machinegun we took out the plastic explosives, put them on the house and pretty well blowed it down. Two or three Germans escaped out the back alley so me and the two men with me ran after them. One of them ran into a long shed and I went up to the window to shoot him and just at that time another German raised up over the fence and was going to shoot me. Luckily one of my men shot him. That pretty much took care of that machinegun problem.

William Lake
Anti-Tank Infantryman 377th Infantry Regiment

We got down to a town called Wallerfangen, one of the political officials of the Germans had a hunting lodge there and an estate there. We hop footed over to Saarlautern, where the 379th Infantry had made the river crossing and had a foothold. We got in to this little town of Fraulautern, gosh; I think we were in there for a week or ten-days, anyway, we got to where we couldn't go anyplace else. This was one of the strongest places of the Siegfried Line; it was what the Germans called the West Wall. About that time, this is

December 14 or 15, they took us back, now we had been on the line 109-days by then. They took us back 12-15 miles to some little towns where the quarter masters had showers set up running on creek water and they made it very clear that you had two minutes to soap up when they blew the whistle. You had one minute to soap up if you weren't ready, and in some cases you took your soap with you. We got brand new clothes at the far end, the other uniforms we had been wearing for a long time. Now I might mention that I was only 18 and I didn't sweat a lot so consequently my groin was fairly clean, but the older men, 35-40 years old, when I got to be those ages I saw the change in the body, you don't have to do much exercise and the groin in soiled. We got clean clothes and clean underwear and almost immediately they said get your gear and we went right back to where we had come from.

William W. Taylor, Jr.
Infantryman 377th Infantry Regiment

Hargart. This is getting towards Christmas and we thought we were going to have a Christmas party. Well, that's when all hell broke loose in Bastogne. So they shipped us back up and while we were in Hargart somebody saw someone jump out of an airplane one moonlit night back up in the hills and they got the usual suspect, they got me to go find this joker next to the parachute. We went up there, Joe and most of the rest of the squad, but we didn't find him. There was ice and snow everywhere and there were some strange boot marks coming down the hill. The tracks stopped at a little cave with a low entrance to it and we thought maybe he went in there. Being young and foolish at that time I just got down on my hands and knees and crawled in there looking for him. He wasn't in there and I guess I am lucky he wasn't there; maybe he was lucky I don't know. Back on the line the 5th Division had been off the line and we got replacements, we were shot all to pieces, so they put us back on the line, I think that our company took about a platoon position at that point, because we were so shot up. They sent everybody else off to Bastogne, so there went Christmas.

We weren't in Saarlautern, we went into a place called Linsdorf and had a few little experiences there. I had a 109 after me up there one day and we lived in these houses that had substantial masonry and so forth. I went up the door on the shed and this one ME-109 came up and he saw me there, so I just stood there and watched him and he turned and he came down, I guess he figured he was going to get me. In those days they had to aim the whole airplane at you, you could see him as he was giving it this and that to aim the plane. I figured at the last minute I would jump back in the door, just about then he opened fire. He went back and we had a gun there and they fired it at him but they didn't get him so I went back out and he came around again for the same drill. He was so close that you could see the man's face, he was right there, I'd dive and he'd fire. I brought him in there three times and they never hit him. He went away. That was probably the best experience I had right there.

One day I looked out the window and there was a Heffer coming down the street hungry, you know soldiers are always hungry. I popped that Heffer and looked at old Tex. He shivered and I said, "you haven't butchered any calves," and he said, "Oh, yes Sarge!" and I said, "Come on!" We went out on the street; unfortunately on the German side there was a little stonewall. Tex and I got down there and we cut our hind quarter and old Tex, who was right much of a man, got that thing up on his shoulders and stood up and when he stood up he ran to the house with it. We got in there, the house was boarded up because it was cold weather and snow. We grabbed it and cut off a big steak! For the next few days we would fry steak for breakfast, lunch and dinner. We lived pretty well there for a while.

Richard E. Hunton
Infantryman 378th Infantry Regiment

From the field hospital they put me in an old ambulance and took me to, I don't know what you would call it. I think they called it a hospital in Metz, but they were still shelling Metz at the time so it was rather a noisy place. They took me to the operating room and cleaned the wound and gave me an intravenous anesthetic in my good arm, my left arm. They told me to start counting and I got up to seven and passed out. When I woke up my left arm was paralyzed! They had stuck the needle in the nerve instead of in the vein. So there I was with my right arm in a big old cast and my left arm was paralyzed. They put me on a cot and if I wanted anything to drink they would put a rubber hose in my mouth and put the other end of the hose into coffee or whatever they had put on the floor and I had to suck it up. Later on when I had to go to the bathroom, the bathroom was a big room about twice the size of a hotel room with a GI 5-gallon gas can on a crate sitting in the middle of the room. I mean it was crude. Anyway, after two or three days there I was taken to the 7th Evacuation Hospital, somewhere near the French coast. I spent a day or so there in that tent hospital and finally they put me on a DC-3 and we flew across the Channel in a severe thunderstorm. We flew about one hundred feet above the water and I thought for sure that was going to be the end of everything, but we finally got over to England on this old DC-3, I think the army called them C-47's.

I was taken to the 187th General Hospital near Tidworth, England. This hospital was comprised of semi-cylindrical shaped Quonset huts. I was put in ward number seventy-three and they put me in a bed with white sheets and blankets and I said, "Don't put me in that bed, I haven't had a bath for six weeks." "I'm nasty and dirty and filthy and I don't deserve anything this good," but they seemed to think it was fine to get in this white bed, so I did. I started getting penicillin shots every four hours, day and night, had a new cast put on, x-rays taken and what not. I was getting to feel pretty good about this time and matter of fact I was made ward assistant cook. I would go in and make pancakes and scrambled eggs left handed until somebody complained about my cooking. I said, "Well, if you don't like it I'm going to quit then!" The very next day they came to me and said the fellow who took your place is worse, we want you back [Laughs]. So I went back as the ward cook. There was one fellow in our ward that was right pitiful. He had shot himself in the foot to get out of combat and nobody would speak to him at all. He was totally shunned and just pitiful. Anyhow, I guess he deserved it.

I don't know how long we stayed in that place, but I got to where I could write V-mails left handed pretty well. I remember the first one I wrote, I think it was about twelve days after I got hurt. I wrote on the bottom, "writ by hand," and you could sure tell it. We were eventually taken from there to a hospital in Bath, England. Of course we were walking wounded so they put us in tents in back of the hospital. It was the middle of December and of course it was really cold, I mean cold. The only heat we had was an old 30-gallon drum in the middle of the tent that you had to put coal in to make it burn. Since I was able to walk better than some of the rest of them I was the left-handed coal carrier for the tent.

Frank E. Shaffer
Infantryman 378th Infantry Regiment

I was just a farm boy and I got drafted into the Army and went up for an examination and they said: "What do you want? Army or Navy?" I said, "Navy," but he said, "Well, you're in the Army." I took my basic training at Camp Willard, Georgia. We did 13-weeks at the IRTC, Infantry Replacement Training Center, and they told us that when we were done we would go directly overseas. The war was going on, so after I was done with basic training, it was around Christmas time then, they put us on a plane out of Georgia to New York so we could get over there faster. We shipped right away out of New York harbor. We were supposed to go to Liverpool, England, but instead we had to pull up on an island off of Scotland because there were so many German subs in the channel. I got over to the theater in January, because I wasn't home for Christmas.

Louis O. Vogt
Infantryman 378th Infantry Regiment

I was with the second battalion of the 378th Infantry. A replacement in Company G, the third platoon, first squad of the 95th Infantry Division. Prior to the Army I was married on the 8th of July 1944, and I had received a deferment from the government, my father had a farm and a rendering business. We were farming and a gentleman came to one of our farms in Ort Valley, just outside of Lewistown, Pennsylvania, and said, "Louis was drafted." After that I went into the service on August 28th, 1944, wondering if I was going to make it back or not.

Right before I left, my uncle, my mother's only brother who was in the First World War, said, "Louis it's better to be a live coward than a dead hero!" I reported to Harrisburg, what the devil is the name of that place, I don't remember, but from there I took my basic training at Camp Blanding, just outside of Stark, Florida. We got our Army issue clothing, shots and everything else. I think at that time our training was supposed to be 15 weeks, or something like that. I only knew one fellow from town, he was our squad leader, a Wilson boy, Paul Wilson. Paul was from Reedsville, Pennsylvania. When we got down to Florida, where our training was setup, I was in an infantry rifle company. The same as you see on television or in the movies, they have calisthenics, hikes with all your gear, bivouac, rifle ranges and other military things like that. It wasn't too hard; I was a young fellow, nineteen

years old, from the country so I was used to being around guns
and physically working, so I didn't have any problems in basic. We
were really trained for the Pacific but then the Battle of the Bulge
came along and they cut our training short, telling us that we would
get advanced training overseas.

I had seven days leave before I shipped overseas, so my parents
drove down with my wife, to Noland, Florida. Noland is just
outside Camp Blanding, but just outside equals twenty-six miles.
So I told my lieutenant I was getting off the train a little closer
to Noland and he said, "Vogt, you have to be on the train when
it pulls out of Blanding!" Just as we left Blanding there was this
curve that we had to go around. As the train slowed down for
this curve, I threw my duffel bag and jumped off. I grabbed a bus
up to where I was going to meet my parents, and had a wonderful
seven days leave.

I reported to New York after my leave and got on a ship, it
was the *USS Wakefield* I think or maybe it was the *Manhattan*? In
1941 it had burned out but they had converted it to a troop ship,
so I'm not sure exactly what it was named when I rode on it. We
went over to Europe by ourselves, unprotected, no convoy. I don't
remember any problems on the ship. At night, they put us down
in the hold, I don't know how many holds were on the ship, but
we were locked down in the hold at night. Fortunately we weren't
torpedoed or anything. You well know the United States lost a lot
of ships right outside of New York Harbor in the Second World
War from German torpedoes. They would lay in wait right off the
coast and torpedo ships within view of the coastline. Anyway then
we landed I think at La Havre, France. I think they called it the
repo depot, replacement depot, or something like that, where they
assigned new and returning personnel to a unit.

Eugene M. Wroblewski
Infantryman 378th Infantry Regiment

Everybody else in the whole outfit, because they did replace everyone, was a "replacement". This is how I met Louie Vogt, who joined us later in our battle history. When a replacement is assigned to your outfit, you are not necessarily on the friendliest terms with him. You realize that this person can drag you back and he's got a lot to learn, so you try to pass on as much of your experience or lore as possible as an "old" infantry guy [Laughs]. But it's a problem with trying not to get too friendly with someone that might be killed the next day. You don't want to develop a real friendship with anybody, but at the same time you do depend on these new guys for your continued existence. You've got to have cooperation, you've got to work together and so forth. I remember Louie and the fact that he was a replacement. He was relatively short, wore glasses, was strong as an ox and was determined as hell. Since I carried the BAR, the Browning Automatic Rifle, which weighed about twice as much as any other rifle and I had to carry lots of ammunition because it was the one automatic weapon we had in the squad (Add note Forty p. 124 and 113, BAR 19.4 lbs. with a 20 round magazine as apposed to M1 Garand 9.5 lbs or the M1 Carbine 5.2lbs). We had to have a bunch of people carry the ammunition and I think that Louie was one of my ammunition carriers; I think I had about two of them. I was the big guy with the Browning Automatic Rifle, I hated it, but I had to do it. I remember that I was also trained at one time to work with flamethrowers to be used against the pill boxes in the Maginot and Siegfried line, but after seeing the devastating power of that weapon and how you get to be targeted by the enemy as the guy to wipe out, I tried to get out of it and fortunately did. I was not targeted [Laughs].

One of things I have to say about the military and the war is the fact that they always tried to give you one good hot meal a day, even on the front lines. There were many times when you'd be up on the lines in foxholes and early in the morning you would sneak back and they would have hot breakfast for you with the pancakes and everything else. The cooks usually were several miles back and trucked everything up to the lines in insulated containers so you got a hot meal in the morning. They distributed C rations in cans or K-rations in boxes and I believe you got the evening meal too if you weren't on the move. For Thanksgiving and Christmas we got the FULL turkey dinner, that's really something. However, one time we were marching a long distance in the rain and cold. We marched in galoshes, raincoats and hot overcoats until we finally arrived at our destination. We expected a hot meal, because we had gotten kind of spoiled by then. At the end of any long march the cooks would prepare the meals and then put it in the thermos containers, bring it out and serve it to us at our destination, especially if we weren't right up on the front lines. This night we waited and waited and then we finally got the word that the cooks had found a few extra bottles of red wine, drank them and were feeling no pain. So much so that when they were carrying all this stuff out to us they drove off the road overturning the truck. All that good food was dumped into the drainage ditch on the side. That night we had K-rations instead of a hot meal [Laughs]. At the place where we were waiting for this hot meal, which was some sort of a house where we were going to stay, across the front door was the body of a dead German soldier. I can remember we had to push him out of the way in order to be able to get into this place. Another time I can remember walking into a house in a battle area, and there were several dead bodies of American soldiers lying on the floor. Apparently the Graves Registration people, (those are the ones that pick up the dead bodies) had tags on them and I could see this fellow lying there with a small hole in one side of his head and a larger hole on the other side where the bullet had come out His tag gave his name, rank and serial number but written in pencil on the bottom was "entitled to the purple heart." I could never forget that particular scene.

Three Rivers

Well over 50 percent of the Iron Men were replacements by February 1945. The division had been on the defensive since December, but now that the Germans had been contained the Allies were ramping up to continue their drive across Europe. The 95th was transferred to the VIII Corps and was ordered to assemble in the vicinity of Bastogne, Belgium. General Walker, the XX Corps commander, commended the division for its professionalism and outstanding sense of mission accomplishment prior to departure. The 95th sterilized their uniforms and equipment and headed for Bastogne as ordered. Upon arrival the division was designated the corps reserve, receiving a be prepared to mission to exploit a breakthrough resulting from the corps attack from January 29-2 February 1945. The sights and conditions of the Battle of the Bulge were fresh in Bastogne. There were not enough hard shelters to house the division from the bitter cold, and the battlefield was still littered with destroyed or abandoned equipment, land mines and frozen corpses.

The division's stay with the VIII was short lived. On February 2nd the 95th received the order to move to Maastricht, Holland for assignment with the Ninth United States Army. This meant that the Iron Men of Metz would no longer be a part of Patton's famous Third United States Army. The Ninth United States Army was located along the Roer River and was planning an enormous attack, Operation Grenade, designed to penetrate all the way to the Rhine River. Even though the Allies had gained offensive momentum following the defeat of the Ardennes offensive, weather had once again delayed the beginning of another attack. Flood conditions allowed the division, acting again as a reserve element, to continue training and recuperation. In the meantime the 95th was again transferred to a different headquarters, albeit temporarily. This time the Iron Men were attached, for operations only, to the Second British Army, an arrangement that would last from February 16th to the 22nd. The division was given the mission of holding a 15-mile defensive line along the Maas River, thus allowing the commitment of a British mountain infantry division elsewhere. The Germans, licking their wounds from the Ardennes, were uncharacteristically docile during this period. By February 22nd the Iron Men were back with the Ninth United States Army at their assembly area in Maastricht.

Back in the assembly area, the division planners were notified that the 95th would remain in reserve for the initial portion of the long anticipated Operation Grenade. The operation kicked off with preparatory fires in the early morning hours of February 23rd. As the corps reserve the 95th (-) was given two be prepared to missions. Both missions depended on the condition of the Adolph Hitler Bridge that spanned Rhine at Uerdingen. If the bridge were captured in tacked the 95th (-) would exploit this success and immediately reinforce the 379th, which had been attached to the 2nd Armored Division for this purpose. If the bridge were found to be demolished the 95th (-) would link up with the 379th and continue to attack north. As with the majority of the bridges encountered along the Allied push, the Germans had completely demolished the Adolph Hitler Bridge by the time a scouting party from Company F, 379th Infantry had arrived.

On the morning of March 4th, the 95th was given the order to attack and seize the west bank of the Rhine near Rheinhausen. The division only encountered light opposition and as a result rapidly seizer and expansion of the bridgehead. The 95th continued its advance facing light opposition for the remainder of the operation. By March 30th the division found itself again in the defense and attached for operational control to yet another headquarters, this time the XXII Corps. From February to March the division had crossed the Maas, Roer and Rhine Rivers. Along the way they began to encounter a different face of war, the beginnings of military government. The personnel intensive tasks of weapons collection, segregation, interrogation, prisoners of war, displaced persons, etc., were now added to the combat duties of the regiments. Because of the repetitive movement in the face of light to moderate opposition, and the new duties of military government the late winter and spring operations of the 95th Infantry Division began to blur together for all but the higher-level planners. Unless designated by evacuation, return or another truly memorable event, the Iron Men were simply pushing further and further into Germany. With the light at the end of the tunnel, this entire period is commonly referred to by private soldiers "mopping up" or "sweeping" from Belgium to Germany.

Charles R. Fowler
Artillery Officer and Infantry Rifle Platoon Leader 377th Infantry Regiment

A few days later we pulled out of town. Our division was pulled out and as we were leaving a German tank shot and hit the jeep behind me and it went up in flames. I told the driver to stop and we jumped into a bomb hole. We waited and waited for at least an hour until I finally said lets get out of here. We jumped back in the jeep and just as we rounded the next corner the tank was still sitting there. He hit the corner of the building and the jeep driver said he was going to quit. He said that it was just too dangerous being a jeep driver, he'd rather be a rifleman [Laughs]. We got out of there all right and then we moved to Belgium.

We stayed in Belgium awhile until the trouble at Bastogne. Since the German push was on we were called out to help, but by the time we got to Bastogne they had already pushed the Germans out. We stayed at Bastogne, there was a lot of snow on the ground when we got there. Me and my sergeant had to go for a meeting when we got there. When we got back the platoon had found a cowshed and were asleep, but there wasn't any room left for us, they were all lying side by side. I remember racking the snow off the ground and laying down one blanket and covering up with the other blanket. The two of us slept together for warmth. The next morning we had to evacuate one guy for frostbit feet. We went on and crossed the Rhine River, going into the Ruhr pocket and fighting there. I had started out in the anti-tank platoon, then I was with an infantry platoon and then they transferred me to the heavy machineguns and mortars. We were moving and we came to an opening in front of this big wooded area. We could see two small villages across this big wide-open area. The new company commander had evidently gotten lost. He was supposed to attack one of the towns and another company was supposed to attack the other town. I remember it took me a long time to convince him which one was the right town. He was convinced that the he was supposed to attack the town on the right but finally we got it straightened out. He was a West Point graduate and he was a little bit arrogant about the thing. Luckily the first sergeant was on my side so we convinced him. As we were going across this big open field mortar shells started coming in. I had a phosphorous grenade with me and as I jumped over a fence the grenade went off. I don't know whether I hung the pin or it was hit, but it went off.

So I was wounded and evacuated. I had gotten some shrapnel earlier when we were in Uckange after we had crossed the Moselle, but not enough to be evacuated like this. I was evacuated to a hospital in Germany and then I was sent over to England. After a bit I was put on a boat and sent to O'Reilly Hospital in Springfield, Missouri. They did skin grafts on my hands and legs where I had been burnt by the phosphorus. I was medically retired after that because I wasn't physically able to do the duties of a rifleman.

William Lake
Anti-Tank Infantryman 377th Infantry Regiment

The Bulge had started, the Battle of the Bulge. So we held and held and held and I guess it was February the 8th, when we were relieved from the 20th Corps, which was 3rd Army. We moved north toward the Bulge; the Bulge was officially closed on the 12th of January. When we got up there we went to the outskirts of Bastogne and bivouacked at a little town called Foy, about two and a half miles north of Bastogne. We saw battlefields there that you could never imagine. If you looked without moving your head you could count 22-23 vehicles that were driven and had ran out of gas or whatever had happened, they were still there. The church there was just, well, everything was pretty torn up. We stayed there for a while and then moved up to Belgium and there they were waiting for the weather to change because the Ruhr River, which we were going to have to cross, was high because the Germans had opened the dams in the Hurtigen forest. So we were waiting in the controlled areas until the water level went down. While we were there I got a four-hour pass to go to Liege, Belgium. When I go there it was like a flea market, everything shoulder to shoulder. I'm a naïve Christian boy and although I saw he lines for the houses I did not participate. I found a movie theater that showed the movie "Wings" in French and I went in and saw at least part of that. Then we got some chow, went back on the trucks and eventually we went up to the British 2nd Army area for less than a week.

Joseph W. Napier
Infantryman 377th Infantry Regiment

We left for Bastogne that evening on trucks. We pulled the headlights on the trucks and away we went. We were on wet mountain roads and the truck that I was in slipped off the road and Taylor's truck coming behind us went off the road and rolled over. We ran down to them, only the medic was slightly hurt. We went on through Bastogne and on the other side of town there was a little farm village. We moved into a house where the roof had been blown off. We went upstairs and found an old iron kettle. We wired the kettle up and started a fire in it. Didn't have to worry about the smoke because the roof was blown off. Later on in the evening "Bed Check Charlie" came over and we were afraid he would see the fire. The next morning I went upstairs, after guard duty, to get Charlie Arnold to go on guard. When I saw him I couldn't believe my eyes. He was lying there with his head on a three- foot shell. I said, "Charlie look where your head is!" He said, "I'm too tired to care."

We were there for a couple of days and then they put us on a detail of picking up the dead. I didn't mind picking up the Germans and throwing them in a truck but when I picked up the GI's, there were several that got to me. There were Germans lying on top of GI's in their foxholes. We piled them up along the road being much more careful with the Americans. My brother-in-law was in the 9th Armored Division. The 9th Armored Division was in the Battle of the Bulge in Bastogne. There was a burnt out American tank along the road and I went up to it. The driver was still sitting in the seat dead, badly charred. The Tank Commander was lying dead on the ground, I thought it was my brother-in-law but it wasn't. My friend Andy checked his dog tags to make sure.

Frank E. Shaffer
Infantryman 378th Infantry Regiment

We went across to England and France and then went up to the front. I remember we got to the unit around 12 o'clock at night. I got to the division when they were on the Siegfried line after Metz. The majority of Metz was over and I was one of the replacements. The Germans were up at the top of the Siegfried line and we went in at the bottom. This one time we had a machine gun set up on the second floor of a house and we stayed there for a bit. We thought we'd have a nice place to sleep, me and my friend Cross, there was a so called bed and we thought we were going to get a good night's sleep. Instead a shell hit the building and blew part of it away. Needless to say we got out of there.

We were so close that we could see the Germans up in their pillboxes and on the lines, the tanks from their platoons all out in front of us. In the towns we moved back and forth from building to building. One day my squad leader had his canteen shot off while we were clearing houses. My squad leader went and knocked a door down and went in this one house. There was a mirror on the wall and they saw a German in there. We took him and turned him upside down and tied him with cord and put him in the corner. Every time we went by him we'd say, "now there's a good German."

I don't want to discuss this a whole lot but after awhile we had to go on the big push. I was the ammunition bearer and George T. Jones was the BAR gunner. We were on an outpost one night and we saw Germans come beyond the houses up through the field. My assistant squad leader and the other fellows went down to the right on the road down by the bridge and waited. We let the Germans get up further to us and then we opened up on them [Pause].

It was cold and we froze our feet. George Jones froze his feet pretty bad. He was a good fellow, he never complained about anything. He took that old BAR, it must have weighed 35-pounds with the tripod. One day there was a big counterattack. We turned the German's back that day during their counterattack, at least me and George did. We captured a German fellow too. We sent him back to the CP and he said they had us all zeroed in, all they had to do was just fire and they would have gotten us all down in the woods while we were on patrol. We were supposed to go down and find out what was up on the front. We were supposed to go until we got shot at and come back for the artillery to fire that day. He said we were all zeroed in and his commanding officer wouldn't let them fire. In other words we were surrounded, but the war was getting over then and they had all but given up. You still had to watch though. The next morning we pushed off I think there was a dozen dead German bodies lying around our position.

I was the ammunition bearer and I had two bandoliers, two hand grenades and my cartridge belt full. You could say I was loaded down with ammunition. We went marching fire, shooting from the hip as we spread out all across the field. One day we all jumped across an irrigation ditch, all but me that is, and I said to myself, "They did it I can do it!" I jumped over but I fell back in and I got all wet. It was cold and now I was wet and even colder. We went on up through Germany. We would move along and sometimes we would get tied down with fire, we couldn't go anywhere and we would have to call tanks and they would come up and shoot to clear the way for us. We went through Germany, France, England, Belgium, and Holland. We were one good bunch, the 95th division.

Another incident I remember is when we were marching and a fellow was intoxicated. He came down with a weapons car and crashed into some of our fellows and hurt them. So the captain came to me and said, "You stay here and guard him. You're responsible for him. If anything happens you're responsible!" He said he'd send the CP back to pick him up. Well, I had to stay there and I often wondered if I would have shot him or not. The captain said, "You're responsible for him, if you have to shoot him, shoot him!" I never thought too much of it then, but whether I would have shot him or not [Pause], well, it's quite a thing. They came back and picked me up in a Jeep and took me up to the front again. Lots of things like that you don't think about until afterwards.

William W. Taylor, Jr.
Infantryman 377th Infantry Regiment

Then we came out and they said we have to go to Bastogne. So they loaded us up on trucks and we drove and drove, we took an air raid I remember jumping out of the back of the truck to get in a ditch. I jumped out and I tripped on my rifle and it dug deep in the ground and got all plugged up. Fortunately they had a bunch of ring mount .50 calibers in the convoy and they opened up and the plane just made one pass at us. After that we loaded back up again and went. That night we were driving along and I was sitting at the end of the seat on the driver side by the tailgate and it was so black out you could see anything and the road was built up. All of a sudden I felt the truck start to go over, as it started to tip I jumped, I don't know how I did this but I jumped clear of the tailgate and landed down the hill. The truck came down and turned over. They had a couple of logs there and they fell on and hurt a few people. I thought I was lucky I missed that one. Joe was in the truck ahead of mine and from there we went on to a little town outside of Bastogne.

The fighting was over in Bastogne when we got there. We got in there and there were bodies everywhere. There were 101st Airborne people in holes with dead Germans all around them and everybody was frozen stiff. We moved in to a house, I don't know how we got a whole company in this house, but it had a barn beneath the house and it had cattle in there. A big hole had been blown in the roof. We were on the very top floor up there with the family that lived there. We put a whole rifle company in there with the family and their cows? Snow would come in through the hole in the roof and some of the guys got a big iron kettle that hung up in the attic to heat water. They built a fire so they could boil water and keep warm when they slept at night. We stayed and we policed up the battlefield and hauled dead bodies. We took litter jeeps, we put 101st Airborne people on the litters, I think four litters per Jeep, and we tied a rope around a whole bunch of German's legs and tied it to the back of the Jeep and we would drag the German's out. We would put the GI's as best we could in the field, but we stacked the German's like cordwood beside the road, a long big stack of them. It was very cold and they had given us these shoepacks that had felt liners in them and our feet would freeze. We would wear the shoepacks and our feet would perspire and get the felt wet and it would freeze. If you kept walking you were all right but if you stood still you could feel it as the things began to freeze. It was a little frightening.

Anyway at some point we left Bastogne and I guess that's when we went to Holland? We went to Belgium and had a break, which was the first real break we had had. There were some interesting things in Holland. We used to find whatever alcohol we could find and drink it, it was a wonder we didn't drink go blind or something. We were living it up in this little town. The company commander had a command post down the block from where we lived and one night a few of our guys got drunk and they used marching fire on the company CP. So Lord have mercy, I guess the regimental command post wasn't too far away and the regimental commander heard the firing and called the company commander wanting to know what was going on down there. I guess the regimental commander told him that he wanted to bust all these people. So they busted them. My friend was turning in a lot of stripes when they busted him. Anyway we went on and it seems to me that next time we were on the line I was walking along out there, we were firing away and the company commander came up to me and asked where my friend that had been drinking was. I said, "you busted him, remember?" He said, "oh, yes, yes." Well my buddy made all his stripes back in short order because he was a real good soldier.

We went from there where we occupied a position that we took over from the British, they were supposed to move and come by in front of us but they never did. They fired artillery forever up there and they finally moved us out of that area.

Louis O. Vogt
Infantryman 378th Infantry Regiment

I really don't remember how long it took to get to Europe, but it wasn't very long. Because from the time I left New York on the 1st day of January 1945, twenty days later I was in the middle of the Siegfried Line in Saarlautern. They told us in Blanding that we would get an additional twenty days advanced training overseas. Well, we got advanced training, the Germans were on one side of the street and we were on the other. That was advanced as it gets! My squad that I went to had lost seven men out of the twelve. I think there was twelve men to a squad and seven had been wounded, either way it was over half of the squad. I got to the platoon in the evening and the lieutenant said, "you carry the 50 caliber machine gun barrel." I can remember as plain as day, we were standing there and a soldier came in from the communication line, a man was stringing telephone lines, and a young soldier had stepped on a mine had his leg blown off! Then the sergeant said to me, "I don't care what you done and how they trained you in Camp Blanding", he said, "you listen to me and you will live a lot longer!" "So when the Germans they send up mortars, don't freeze", he said, "they'll bracket you." "They'll shoot a mortar over you and the next one will be in front of you and the next one will be in your hip pocket!" "You just keep moving!" After that we went up into a house that was on a big cross road. We set the 50-caliber machine gun up and pulled guard, you were on two hours and off one hour. You wouldn't any more than get off and lay down before the sergeant was waking you up to come up and be on guard duty again. They started to shoot 88's over us, Phoom! Phoom! and they got closer and closer until the next one hit about the middle of our building. I was scared to death, and down I fell over the 50-caliber, down the stair steps I went. That was my first day in combat, no problem, we had our advanced training [Laughs].

Well, right after that, I don't know how many days I was there in Saarlautern, but we had to cross the Saar River when we left. A Kochenderfer boy from my same valley in Pennsylvania, Ferguson Valley, was with the 26th Division, but I didn't know it at the time? The 26th relieved the 95th and we crossed the Saar River at night. Twenty days after the 26th relieved us the Germans threw a big counter attack their way and my friend from Ferguson Valley was blown from the second story of a house down to the first story.

He was wounded and headed home. We went from there, I can't really remember clearly, but we went by six by six trucks and ended up in Hoist, Holland. Why we went there I don't remember, but then we walked and walked for a long time after that.

One day we were advancing along and we went into a house where there were about half a dozen Germans. The squad leader said, "come on, come on" and another fellow that had got a hold of a P-38 and a 10x50 Zeiss binoculars earlier ran out and left them hanging on the doorknob. Since he left them I grabbed them before we started up a paved road. When I grabbed this P-38 and binoculars, they told us that if you were captured with this stuff they would shoot you on the spot. We were walking again and about three or four-hundred yards up this road there was a big stone house, and all at once the Germans started to shoot at us. The bullets were ricocheting off the macadam road so my squad immediately jumped down in a ditch beside the road. Our 2nd Lieutenant, a "90-day wonder," said, "I'll have you fellows all court-martialed!" Well, we weren't going to get shot right there, walking up the road. So we told him to call up a tank destroyer instead. He called up a tank destroyer, they were 90-millimeters I believe, and it shot three rounds into the stone house. Several Germans came out and we just kept on advancing.

One night we stayed overnight in an old barn. I never had any trouble in the service with my fellow soldiers, except one big polish boy. I hung my rifle up with the muzzle down where we were laying in the straw. Gene asked me to move it and I said, "you can move it." Well, he got a little huffy and then I said, "I guess we will have to go outside." Fortunately he backed down and I got to be very good buddies with him after that. Gene Wroblewski. *(Gene recalls that he had to testify in a Court Martial prior to Louis joining the unit. A soldier had not secured his weapon properly and it had fallen, accidentally firing a round into his foot. As the "old" veteran he didn't want to see that happen again).*

Eugene M. Wroblewski
Infantryman 378th Infantry Regiment

When we were in Saarlautern, which was separated from the Saar River by a big open field, our outposts were in the line of buildings right behind the Siegfried line. We were on one side of the street and the Germans were on the other side of the street, or maybe a block back. We maintained this particular relationship for what seemed like several weeks. All of our mail, and all of our food and all of our ammunition had to carried by the darkness of the night across this big open field between the river and that particular town. The Germans fired powerful magnesium flares in parachutes to light up the whole area. They were monochromatic, everything looked silver, there was no color and the only way the Germans could actually see you is if you moved. I can remember my mother baking me a big chocolate cake, getting this cake in the mail and carrying it across that huge open field into our outpost. Of course when I opened it up everybody in the squad wanted a piece of that delicious cake. There was a lot to go around, but I got very little of it [Laughs]. It was a great treat for everyone, though!

Our 2nd battalion received the honor of the Presidential Unit Citation for our accomplishments in the battle of Metz. That was a special honor that given only to our battalion and we wear a special badge as a result. Nobody else in the division could wear it. It's worn on the right hand side of the chest as opposed to all the medals worn on the left hand side. Those of us who were in the battle of Metz received this honor. I felt pretty good about it even though it's just a little piece of metal. At one point when we were in the Ruhr pocket we captured some SS Troops who were not very cooperative. I can remember our officers trying to interrogate them. They had the obvious SS lightning emblems on their uniforms. Our translators kept hollering at one SS Trooper to tell them his name, rank and serial number but the SS Troop just spit at them. The SS Troops were just unbelievably arrogant.

Paul H. Madden, Jr.
Infantryman 379th Infantry Regiment

On the 29th of January we were relieved by the 26th Division and then we moved north through Luxembourg up into Belgium. On that trip, I suppose I froze my feet earlier, but on that trip I froze my feet pretty bad so I was hospitalized. At that time they just tried to be sure that you didn't develop trench foot. General Patton didn't like trench foot. I'll say this, we usually got a fresh pair of socks everyday with our rations when we were with the Third Army. At the end of January we transferred to the Ninth Army and my experience from that period is just from talking with the fellows in the company and reading about it. The division was in Holland for about two weeks in relief of a British division from the Second Army, while the Brits were making some adjustments in the Maastricht area. After that two-week period they came back down and my company was around Fort Ibanamill, Belgium. From there the division moved into the Krefeld area and on into the Rhine and Meuse and later the Ruhr pocket. All during this time after I got out of the hospital with frozen feet I was in the Repo depot system going back to my unit. I knew something was wrong with me so one morning I went on sick call. They said I had Jaundice so I went back to the hospital.

John G. Little, Jr.
Artilleryman 547th Anti Aircraft Artillery

On February 2, 1945, we were in the vicinity of Tongres, Belgium. We were taken out of the Third Army and placed into the Ninth Army Reserve. We were staying in Heure Le Romain, Belgium. We lived in homes for eight days. We noticed the very first night that the old couple we were staying with left with their bedding. We didn't know where they were going. We found out later on they were going to a bomb shelter. Half of the village was blown away by the V-rockets that were being dropped all over Belgium and England. We went to Holland for awhile. The 95th Division was there assisting British troops.

Leon E. Langford
Ordnance 795th Ordnance
(Light Maintenance) Company

There were a couple of other fun times. The captain moved us up into an area, I'm not sure what river it was, but he decided that we needed to be billeted about a half mile from the infantry and those units that were up just across the river. It wasn't the Moselle or the Saar; it was just a little bigger than a stream. He moved us into a school, I don't remember the town, but all during the night when we were sacked out on the floor it kept rumbling. We came to find out that the Germans had been shelling a bridge not very far from us with one of those- what do they call them, one of those "Long Tom's"- some kind of an artillery piece that is mounted on a railway car. They didn't get the bridge that night, but the captain decided in his infinite wisdom that we needed to get out of there so we moved. The next night they got the school where we had been. That was a fortuitous decision on his part. As history tells us, when the Germans started the Battle of the Bulge we had gone into the line and replaced the 5th Infantry Division. They pulled them out for a rest, but when the Bulge happened, Boom! We got pulled back out of the line and were sent up towards the Bulge. Of course as we went we were in convoy, driving at night. During the daytime this one-day there was this one lone ME-109. He picked our unit out to strafe and that's when Faruchie was killed. Fortunately, he missed the rest of us, but the trees were just clipped like when you go through the combat course in training where they're shooting live shells over you. That's exactly like it was when we got out of that little steam. Every little tree was cut off about 2 ½' over our heads- [pause] but we only lost that one guy.

Our unit never really got that close to the Bulge. Some of the infantry and artillery and some combat units did, but it was really over by the time the division got up there. We went up to the north side and eventually went into Germany through Aucken and up through Dusseldorf until eventually we occupied at Recklinghausen where we stayed for the balance of the war. I know that a lot of our units went up with the British under Montgomery for a while, but then we were back with Simson's Ninth Army for the balance of the war. Some of the units, I think, got up to the Elbe River and met up with the Russians.

Martin H. Lincoln
Ordnance 795th Ordnance
(Light Maintenance) Company

Ultimately came the Battle of the Bulge. That's when we got orders to move north. The division moved up along the highway. That's when we lost the only man from the ordnance company, Feruchi. A plane came over and strafed and it killed Feruchi as he was running for cover. Just a couple of weeks before that his brother left the signal company and went up with the infantry for a two week period of time, when they needed replacements. He had gone into an open window in a building to look through and he got blasted by the Germans. So two Feruchi's were killed within two weeks of each other.

We continued on and ended up in the Ninth Abby for a while and then the division's section got moved up into Holland for about a month with the British first Army...I guess it was the first Army. I stayed up there for a while and then the division stayed with Simpson the majority of the war. Both went into Germany and we went on line with them and those were the days! We were in Salispot in Germany and had taken over a doctor's house. We had the division's ammunition in the house with the six of us and no fraternization went on with the Germans because you could go out and walk around town if you wanted too. So two of three of us were walking around Main Street or Saliscottn and we came by this hotel with big glass windows and there were a couple of girls in there. The girls came and opened the door for us and we went in. They had snaps in there, so we had a lot of fun. So the next night we went back again and they invited us to a big party but there was no fraternization allowed so we had to be careful. The chief of police's daughter was one of the girls so we had to go on the back of the hotel and avoid the MP's. Then we went from one farmhouse to another around lake Teggety. We had to go through many stables and go around cows and finally we ended up at the chief of police's house. On the second floor there was a large banquet. There were about 12 guys. There were three or four of us, along with a bunch of infantry guys. They put on a beautiful meal for us. After the meal a bunch of fellows and girls went into a large bedroom under a bunch of comforters and started wrestling around for about an hour. The mother and father were in the next room. We had a great time at the party but as soon as we got back to the house that night we got the word that we were moving out again. While we were visiting those girls in the hotel Hitler came on the radio for a one-hour speech and the girls said "still, still the Fuher, the Fuher" [Laughs]. I said still, we listen to the Fuher and see what he has to say tonight. I heard him two or three times in different parts of Germany.

I remember going up to a big cement building on one side of the river and the Germans were on the other and we were receiving artillery and were hitting them with artillery and the infantry was all around. We were in the middle. I can't remember the name of the city, a big city but it was on the way down to the Bulge and we spent a couple of days there till they finally wiped out the Germans on the other side of the river. We kept moving along in the Bulge.

Recklinghousen was the last town I ended up in. There were nice looking girls all over the place there. The war was kind of petering out and then the Russians started coming and they were all scared stiff of the Russians. They loved the Americans at that point in time. We kicked our landlady out of her house and took her house over for our six-man unit. The next day she brings us strawberry short cakes loaded with whipped cream [Laughs]. We were right next to an old German beer garden and we had captured a brewery and they were serving all over the place. We had a great time while we were in Recklinghousen. I had a girlfriend there and one day she said her husband was in Italy and she hadn't spoke with him in a long time. She could speak enough English that I could understand her. She told me he was in the SS and then showed me a bunch of his uniforms. He was Colonel in the SS, but he was over in Italy and I don't think he ever came back.

The Ruhr Pocket

By April the Axis cause was all but lost. Allied forces were hopping from island to island in the Pacific, and in Europe Allied planes and tanks moved in the face of only harassing opposition. Germany's industrial might had been destroyed by coordinated Allied efforts. The final push of men and material had long since passed for the once mighty German *Wehrmacht*. Every available male, with little regard for age, had been thrust into the defense of the fatherland. While organized resistance had almost been eliminated, small pockets and bands of die-hard troops still carried the battle to the Allies. Without contact or support from a higher headquarters in many instances, the remaining German soldiers fired wooden bullets, conducted battlefield re-supply and continued to fight in isolated cells. While Allied planes enjoyed air superiority and Allied tanks raced by destroyed and stranded German Panzers, gasoline production in Germany had been cut by an estimated 90% by this time, Allied infantrymen still had to deal with the possibility of death around every corner. Wooden or not, the direct fire battle of the infantry was no less perilous in Hamm than it was on D-Day or in Metz. Regardless if the war was about to end or not, houses still needed to be cleared, rivers still needed to be bridged and battlefields still needed to be crossed. It was up to the Iron Men and their infantry counterparts to accomplish many of these difficult and dangerous tasks.

In late March 1945 the 95th took part in the clearing of the Ruhr pocket. The Ruhr pocket was significant to the last hopes of German resistance because it was the leading industrial area of Germany. Further adding to the importance of the region was the earlier loss of the second largest industrial area, Silesia, to the Russians. The Ruhr was an industrial powerhouse, equal to or greater than the eastern American industrial centers. As a result, a final push of replacements and material had been consolidated in the region. This final effort included loyal SS troops and idealistic youngsters prepared to go to an early grave for the *Fuhrer*. With this in mind, the 377th, referred to as Combat Team Seven with its attachments, preceded the division with the 2nd Armored Division for the initial envelopment of the Ruhr pocket. The Germans managed to provide stiff resistance, reinforcing key terrain in an attempt to impede the rapid success of the "Hell on Wheels" Division and its attachments, but by the beginning of April the task of 377th was complete. With elements in place, the Allies were preparing for the second phase of the Ruhr Campaign, reduction of the Ruhr pocket.

For this task the 95th would keep the recently returned 377th in reserve. The 377th was given the be prepared to mission of passing through and either clearing the western portion of the division zone to the Ruhr River, or seizing Soest and clearing the eastern portion to Moehne River. The 378th was to cross the Lippe-Seiten Canal and seize the Hamm railway center. The 379th was to cross the Lippe River and clear a designated regimental zone, with additional be prepared to missions of either seizing Soest or continuing the attack in the western portion of the division zone. From April 3rd to the 7th the regiments worked hard to accomplish their assigned missions. The 378th met stiff opposition in their zone. To give an indication of the fierceness of the battle for Hamm, the 378th encountered specialized units such as the 200-man SS battalion that fought until only four remained alive. The 379th also met determined resistance but continued on to accomplish their be prepared to mission of attacking in the western portion of the division zone, while the 377th eventually executed the Soest mission. The mettle of the SS troops was not possessed by all, as there were many willing German prisoners taken in each of the regimental zones. Likewise, resistance could be characterized as uncoordinated with sporadic periods of increased intensity dependent on unit moral.

By April 7th the regiments had once again reorganized. This time the division and its attachments would assume responsibility for the seizure of the Ruhr pocket to the south and southwest. Initially the XIX Corps had been responsible for the Ruhr pocket and the drive to Berlin, but because of the rapid advance on both fronts this dual task was no longer feasible at this time. Task Force Twaddle, a force of over 35,000 troops led by General Twaddle, was now responsible for clearing south to the Ruhr River. The primary components of the task force were the 8th Armored Division, the 378th Infantry Regiment, the 379th Infantry Regiment and Task Force Faith, consisting of the 377th Infantry Regiment and several other separate regiments, battalions and companies led by the assistant division commander Brigadier General Don C. Faith. By the time Task Force Twaddle reached the Ruhr River they had collected over 325,000 prisoners. Fortunately for the Iron Men, German command and control was no longer in place, preventing this enormous amount of combat power from conducting coordinated attacks of any considerable size. April 14th was recorded as the last day of combat operations in the Ruhr pocket, and subsequently as the last day of 151 straight days of combat for the division in the European Theater of Operations.

William Lake
Anti-Tank Infantryman 377th Infantry Regiment

We did a lot of driving; then we came back down and started the attack toward the Rhine River and the big cathedral town Cologne. We went side by side with the 84th Division and that is the only place we got strafed; we had a 50-caliber machine gun set up on a big tripod and it jammed. The kid that was on the gun he tried immediate action and ripped the gun off its stand, he couldn't get it to work. So then we rested for a while until we went up and crossed the Rhine River, up close by Wesel. The 17th Airborne had jumped over there and they shot at everything that moved, they had better supply of ammunition that we did, at least we think they did. They seemed to be doing an awful lot of shooting. We traveled at night; we went through towns that were burned from the front end to the back end. Tanks would go past us and we would go past tanks. We got stopped and Lieutenant Lanes, he was my platoon leader from Macon, Georgia, came back and had a hand full of papers and he said in his southern accent, "We are going to get on our trucks and we are Task Force B and we are going to be in Berlin." We got going and for two-days we went day and night and then they took us off and put some other infantry division with them.

We started to circle this industrial area, even though there were a lot of industries there, there were also a lot of wooded areas. The war was just about over and we were going down a nice gentle curving road, the sun was shining and suddenly the Germans opened fire on us and we ended up with three men wounded out of about 30 men in our group. Corporal Zorb got shout through the shoulder, it went out his shoulder blade. My squad leader got shot somewhere up around the eye. The third guy I can't recall what his injuries were, but we got fire going up to where the Germans were and finally there was no more fire coming from them. We wanted to just leave, but they said no, we had to go look and see if there was anyone up there. After that we went into garrison and lived in houses, estates, inside buildings and the like. This was springtime, near Easter. All this didn't happen just like I brought it out here; this one area we were in the Germans had an awful lot of 20mm antiaircraft automatic weapons, and oh boy, they would shoot at the houses we were in. We would get on the floor and get up towards the front wall because we thought in our haste to survive that it would be safer there, that the things coming in through the windows would go back and fall down a little bit. It scares you, not to mention is was dangerous.

Then we went into military government and here came all these displaced persons; we had some military camps that we had Polish DP's, displaced persons in, along with Russian DP's. They fought each other all the time. Fighting and stealing each other's women and they would go back to the farms where they had been slave labor and tear the family up and take the best beef cattle and have a barbeque. We couldn't control them. All the time they were finding stuff to drink, there always seemed to be a lot of stuff to drink around. You couldn't understand them half the time; they were talking dialects, an unknown number of dialects in Eastern Europe of the slaves. I guess some of those communities had their own lingo and they couldn't talk to someone 25-miles away. They had these little wooden carriages with wooden wheels on, sort of like oversized baby buggies. Everybody had a pack on his back, I can't remember seeing anyone bare footed. We stopped every once in a while to check their identity cards; everybody in Europe had an identity card from I guess when they were about 10-years old. Some of these people had cards and some didn't, depending on where they came from and where they had worked. I remember seeing a group of guys, nice blue uniforms and garrison military looking hats and at first we thought they were some kind of an auxiliary that Hitler used. It turned out they worked for the train. We thought we had captured some high-grade military fugitives.

We settled down in a town called Recklinghausen and painted our trucks and lined them up on the street of what we would call a suburb. All the houses looked similar to each other. We were still eating military food, but the higher echelons always had steak and so forth and at night the different beer halls would be open. Inside the beer halls, the waitresses would actually fight for the cigarette butts in the ashtrays. If one waitress was in someone else's area and dropped a cigarette butt in her apron, there was some major yelling going on and shoving around. I'm still a non-drinker and coke hadn't caught up with us yet, so drinking was sort of far between for a while. But they finally go their shipments of coke coming. Coke syrup came in gallon jugs and of course you had to carbonate it to make it halfway decent. We hung around there and did nothing but calisthenics in the morning and then we couldn't leave the area, but we didn't have anything to do. You could read or whatever.

In June I guess, they motored us back across France to Le Havre and we got on the USS *General Gordon*. I don't know if it had been a luxury liner or not, but it was a pretty big ship. We hit the most fantastic storm I had ever imagined. I don't know if we were supposed to have landed in Boston or not. Of course everybody wanted to go to New York and be in the big street parade, but we ended up because of these storms down in Newport, Virginia. We got off the ship and here we go, there were all these German prisoners working with the American women and they were giving us the Victory sign and the girls were hugging them, I mean it was just ridiculous. We got over to the big mess halls and they told us, "Now, everything in here is cooked by German cooks. When you people eat fresh eggs they eat powdered eggs." You know people that work with food aren't going to do that, but we stayed there a day or so, got haircuts and got our clothing drawn for issue. By then we had orders for 30-day furloughs and they put you on troop trains so you didn't have to fight with the civilians. They got you all the way to your service center, mine was the 6th at Fort Sheridan and then from there you traveled by bus or horse cart, or whatever was available.

Joseph W. Napier
Infantryman 377th Infantry Regiment

From Bastogne we moved into a rest area in Mastric, Holland. We got orders to relieve a British Brigade. So we relieved them with the understanding that their artillery would support us. We spotted a German boat going up the Moss River. I radioed back to the Brit artillery with coordinates to fire on the German boat. He came back on the radio and said, "I'm sorry mate but I have fired my quota for the day." Being a GI we went back to where the artillery was and found a discarded German gun. We fired on the boat with the German gun. Afterwards we asked the British how the Germans were and he said, "we leave them alone and they leave us alone." I thought to myself, "how the hell do you win a war that way." We were relieved three or four days later by a Scottish Outfit, bagpipes and all!

We moved back to Belgium and Sergeant Tyner received a battlefield commission to 2nd lieutenant. We had a formation and along with Sergeant Tyner five or six others were commissioned to 2nd lieutenant and I received a bronze star from 16 December 1944. It reads:

The bronze star medal is presented to Joseph W. Napier Sergeant Infantry US Army for marathon achievement while serving in the European Theater of operation on December 16, 1944 in the military occupation against the armed enemy of the United States during World War II, Sergeant Napier performed his duties in active ground combat was in the keeping of the finest tradition of

America's service and reflects great credit upon himself and the 377th Infantry Regiment of the United States Army. Signed by Adjutant General Fast and Secretary of Army White.

We were assigned to the 2nd Armor Division nicknamed "Hell on Wheels" for four days as part of a task force mission. We crossed the Rhine River into Dortmund. We were to protect the tanks from any ground resistance. When that happened we would take prisoners to be sent back to the rear echelon. We moved very fast on the Autobahn. I was amazed at how they could keep fuel in the tanks moving so quickly. We went into the Ruhr Pocket in April and then on 8 May 1945, the war in Europe was over.

William W. Taylor, Jr.
Infantryman 377th Infantry Regiment

At some point we went down and we met up with the 2nd Armor Division, *Hell on Wheels* and crossed the Rhine River. We had tanks, with some infantry riding on tanks and other infantry riding in trucks. We rode for a week and of course there was no sleep. You were either riding or nodding, or the thing would stop and you had to attack some town. Sometimes we would find warm food on the tables, and take it back to the trucks with us. We did that for about a week. We went in to a place called Obersdorf, in Germany, on April fool's Day. We went in there and got bogged down. The whole company was lined up around this village and we were sitting there and it was a *Hell on Wheels* tank there with guns pointing towards the village. I went in to the village, I started out with two men, I lost one and two of us made it in. As we were going towards the village the gun around the tank put a .50 caliber on the village right in front of us and I was thinking, "I hope this man is good with that gun because we were right there," but he was good. I've always thought the world of the *Hell on Wheels* since then because he moved that gun around and kept it just right in front of me. We went in and took a few houses and spent the night while a lot of houses were burning. In the morning we took off and drove a couple of blocks up through there. When we reached our objective, we stopped.

The next thing they did was load us up and take us back. I remember going in to a house and lying down and I slept for 14-hours. After about 3-days of no sleep and constant operations if you think you're running but you're really not, you're walking. You're putting everything you've got into it and you're walking. Then you get on a radio and you hardly know your name. It does that to you, three-days is about what you can do and be any way at all efficient. Anyway we came back and after my 14-hour sleep my kindly lieutenant came to me and said, "it's time to get your squad, I will give you some more men in the squad because I know you are short." " You have to guard a warehouse that it's full of food and people going to try to loot it." So we went up to the warehouse and he gave me a half a case of c-rations and said, "I'll be back in a couple of days." We stayed there and stayed there and stayed there and I had hunting parties out hunting these big old rabbits, they had some humongous rabbits over there. We would also hunt chickens and steal potatoes and cook up stuff to eat. This went on for several days and I didn't know where the rest of the company was. One day a vehicle drove up and there was the lieutenant. He said, "where have you been?" I said, "right where you left me?" He said, "we're going to move out." I don't know if they put anyone else in the warehouse or not, but we moved out.

Frank E. Shaffer
Infantryman 378th Infantry Regiment

One day there were Germans coming across the field. We were in a big building, a big brick barn type building, and my assistant squad leader Andy, one of the fellows and I left the building. I guess the Germans didn't know we were waiting for them in a ditch. We left them get half way across to the barn and we opened up on them. My squad leader was wounded and the fellow that was trying to get him out of there got hit in the leg. That was just one of the experiences we had. That was our Easter, I'll never forget it.

When we were in the Ruhr pocket we would call for fire a lot. We would get $10 if we called fire in on the tanks. But we found out that tanks fire too! We were trying to save ammunition while we were in the Ruhr pocket. Some of our artillery shells would fall short and hurt a few of our fellows. I often thought about it.

In the Ruhr pocket there was an attack we had. I remember we would land in a ditch and the Germans would show us an airburst. They shot artillery about 15 feet from us, there was a big shell that landed right there in the mud and it didn't go off, good thing it didn't! Some of us saw our shells falling short hurting some of our fellows, but I guess you have that. We slept wherever we could, nights in a barn, piles or holes, anyplace. We always put our guards out. Some people didn't mind getting shot at but when they get pretty close what do you think about? I often thought about that drunk guy I was guarding, whether I would have shot him or not. Quite a decision to make, I didn't think much of it then, but I often thought about it afterwards. We had three days in Holland somewhere about that time. We stayed at a big hotel and I could hardly believe it! We were well taken care of.

One day we captured a German from North Carolina as we were guarding a road from a ditch. We waited until he got about a few feet from us and jumped up and poked our guns at him. "I have no rings, no watches, no souvenirs on me. I can speak American very well," he said. We questioned him a little bit and he said he was from North Carolina but he got caught in the draft and they put him in the German Army.

We had a bunch of guns laid out on a big pool table in the City Hall in Hamm and we could take what guns we wanted. I took a pair of .32 pistols with shoulder holsters in case something happened to our rifles. We could just pick up what we wanted. It would be just like somebody had moved out of their house and left everything there. We would come up to any door and we would kick the latch right off and you could pick watches or anything. I brought a little money back. The problem was what were we going to do with it? The pistols we could bring home and we rode the train when we got home with them on us and they let us do it, but you could only carry so much.

Louis O. Vogt
Infantryman 378th Infantry Regiment

As we were walking, I can remember it one guy wanted me to carry his galoshes, I mean four buckle arctic's. We had gas masks, rifles and full packs. You would get so tired with just your rifle, but can remember one guy wanted me to carry his BAR, which was 20 or 25 pounds, much heavier than your rifle. As a result of being so tired we would throw away nonessential equipment like our gas masks. We were doing nothing more than mopping up, so the Germans weren't going to hit us with gas? The Battle of the Bulge had broken Germany's back, if you want to see a good movie Van Johnson stared in "The Battle of the Bulge." For the Germans that was it. It was their last big offensive, the big push, when all of their big Panzer tanks were caught out in the open. They had run out of benzene, which is nothing more than gasoline. Fortunately for us, the United States, the fog lifted and they caught all of the tanks out in the open, because they were headed for Liege, Belgium.

We kept going after the Battle of the Bulge, always moving, mopping up and crossing the Rhine. One time my outfit took over this house where we were going to sleep for the night. The lieutenant told the lady that owned it that she had five minutes to get out of the house. She didn't understand him very well since she didn't speak English, so he was pointing his gun at her stomach and yelling at her, "You have five minutes to grab what you need and get out!" I couldn't help but stand there and think, "what if this was my mother or grandmother?" That was just no way to act, but I guess it was war, because we did a lot of things over there [Reflective Pause].

On the 6th of April we were pushing forward. Going, going and going outside of Hamm, Germany. In a little town called Berg, we took two towns and then about 500 yards difference between the two towns where the railroad tracks ran. Then we pulled back and they put a nine-man outpost out. Well, it wasn't over an hour or two hours when the lieutenant came along and said, "I need nine more volunteers." "You, you, you and you…" he pointed out. I was one of the lucky ones that got to go to the outpost.

The outpost was in a big brick house, now that was on the 6th of April. There was a paved road right in front of us and we had a man at each side door and upstairs in the back window. Wroblewski was in the back door and I was in the front door. I knew our outfit, the second battalion, Company G, first squad, was going to attack, that we were going to move out shortly. We were there all night and the next morning at 6am three young boys came running up through the orchard and I hollered, "halt!" They hit the ground and started to shoot. They had American uniforms on, kaki, not kaki but maybe our wool kaki because it was April. Anyway, the first bullets were wood. They hit the wooden frame and you could tell they were made out of wood. The Germans had been fighting on several fronts, they were fighting on and on and they were running low on ammunition by this point in the war. They had wooden bullets instead of metal, which I have one at home right now, plus the steel 8mm. So I stepped back inside, and I have my right arm on my left side, I'm a lefty, and I stuck half of my helmet around the corner of the door frame. A young German boy, who was a real good shot, put one right through the middle of my forehead, but high enough that the good Lord sent it around exactly where I part my hair and creased me through the skull. I had a little bit of blood come running down my cheek and a Jewish boy said, "your hit, your hit" but I was scared they would come over and throw hand grenades. The Germans had concussion grenades, our grenades were fragment grenades which breakup, I believe, into forty-eight different pieces, but the Germans had what we called "potato mashers." So I ran upstairs and pulled open the windows, their windows opened up from the inside. When I pulled the windows open, the boy put one through the windowsill, up through the ceiling and a ricochet went about two inches low. I thought, "man, that is no place for my head!" We kept firing for a little bit, but I was a little shook up. By the time I went back downstairs the medic had already come. He shaved my head and put a bandage around it. The one German boy was brought over, he was only thirteen years old. they sent him back to the aid station with me. It is unreal how they can be shot up and still live, but he actually bled to death back there when I was in the aid station. From there I think I went back to England or France, they flew us back in a C-47.

Actually I had another friend that didn't make it back, a boy by the nickname of Wyoming. He was killed. I wasn't there, I already left for the aid station, he was killed on April the 7th 1945, Wyoming was his name. After I left, the remainder of the outpost had to keep moving. They moved to another house that they ran into, I was not there understand, it's only through Gene Wroblewski that I found out what really happened fifty-two years later. Twelve German boys, or soldiers, were upstairs and they threw hand grenades down and my squad ran out. Wyoming, I can't tell you his name but I always called him Wyoming. He stuck his head around a corner, I'm telling you I wasn't there, but anyway Gene told me, he said, "I've never seen any redder blood in my life" he said, "when Wyoming stuck his head around he was hit through one temple and out through the other and that was it, he was dead."

I have to back up a little bit. When I got back to the first aid station after the medic shaved my head and wrapped it up a lieutenant colonel said, "soldier you don't want your helmet." "No" I said, my head was ringing and [Pause] I think an 8mm is like a .31 caliber, but if you ever shot mark think of when you shoot through a tin can and where it went in the front of my steel helmet it made a little hole but it blew the whole back out. I brought my helmet liner home, I have it today yet and I gave it to my one grandson, Zachary Ryan Vogt. Zach was commissioned a 2nd lieutenant of Infantry on the fifth month, the ninth day of 2002 at Fort Benning, Georgia. I was there and his brother, Tobias Vogt is a captain in the Infantry. Toby fought in Desert Storm, Africa, and both Toby and Zach were in Iraq. All three of us have combat infantryman badges and bronze stars! When I was wounded I had this P-38 and Zeiss binoculars, beautiful binoculars. The supply sergeant told me that when I went back to the hospital that they would take them from me, so I gave the binoculars to my supply sergeant, I forget his name. I kept the pistol though, and I brought it home. I was married before I went into the service, and when I got home I needed some extra money so I sold it to my brother for fifteen dollars. Incidentally, he still has it today, but I never saw the binoculars that I entrusted to the supply sergeant again!

Eugene M. Wroblewski
Infantryman 378th Infantry Regiment

Now, let's fast-forward to the time of April 6th, 1945, when we were in a mopping up operation in the Ruhr. We realized that the war was coming to an end and we were sweeping up all the enemy soldiers in this encirclement type of operation. In the typical way that an infantry group operates, after a day's advancement, and the attainment of a particular position, at night you maintain an outpost at that position while the rest of the group moves back to a safer area. This is what happened on the night of April 6th. As a matter of fact we were back there and somebody found several bottles of wine and some of the guys had a lot to drink. I was not a drinker in those days so I didn't get involved. My vice was chocolate. I traded any wine I found for a bar of chocolate. A fellow we called Wyoming in our squad got very drunk and particularly obnoxious. In fact, he started to cry and said, "we're going to get killed tomorrow, and we're going to die". I told him to pipe down, that this is not good for the morale, keep it to himself, and wouldn't you know it, he was one of the people who was killed during the battle that next day.

We were in this back position when we heard that the telephone line extending out to the outpost was cut and that the enemy captured the guys in the outpost. We had to send out another group, and it turned out that Louie and I were in it.

Ten of us went to this ill-fated house outpost. Half of us were on guard duty at a time. The rest of us tried to sleep on the floor. We switched every two hours. On the 5 to 7 guard shift, Louie was guarding the front of the house and I was in the back of the house. At dawn, about 6 o'clock in the morning, I could hear conversation on the inside. They said something about nine enemies in the house next to us, so I was very alert. I was sitting out there by myself at the back of the house and all of a sudden I heard shooting around the front of the house. Well, in order for me to participate in that battle I would have had to shoot left handed around the corner of the building. Since I couldn't shoot that way I decided to stay out of that battle and that's the one where Louie was fighting these three young German soldiers who were trying to cut our phone lines and give battle with our people inside the house. In the meantime I turned around and looked out ahead of me and I saw three soldiers standing there about 50 feet ahead of me. We saw each other at the same moment. I whirled around and fired a few shots at them with the BAR and then I dove for the ground. When I looked up they had also gotten on the ground. I fired a few more shots from the hip and they took off. I had a clip of, I believe, twenty rounds and I fired everything I had at them. I didn't hit anything as they took off. I sat there and waited.

I had actually captured a German Lugar pistol from a soldier the day before. I carried it in my belt. I decided that I didn't want to be captured with this enemy weapon in my possession. As a matter of fact I looked into my pocket to see if I could pull out a white handkerchief in case I needed to surrender, because I had the impression that we were surrounded. Instead I pulled out a khaki colored, government-issue handkerchief. I decided not to surrender. I threw the German Lugar under a pile of firewood. In my crouched position I started to tremble to a point where I had to open my mouth so I wouldn't bite my tongue. I was totally inoperative at that point but after a few minutes I was O K. Soon that battle was over and I was able to come around to the front. There was Louie, hit by a bullet right in the middle of the helmet. I thought he was hit in the forehead because there was blood all over his face. I couldn't tell whether he was fully cognizant. He was kind of stunned by the whole thing, as you can well imagine, but in a few minutes you could see that he was the same old Louie. Fortunately, the wooden bullet had lodged between his metal helmet and his reinforced plastic helmet liner. These were kids, German soldiers that were firing wooden bullets and they were all wounded. Louie did good job of mowing them down. Three guys that were still alive but they were riddled with bullets, I don't know how they ever stayed alive and, as Louie mentioned, at least one of them had died on the way to the hospital.

After we licked the wounds of that first morning battle we regrouped to investigate another house, down a diagonal road from the main intersection in the town of Berge. This house was sitting out in the open field by itself and had many windows and doors facing us. We approached the front of the house and then moved left around to the backside where there was a big open door. A squad of soldiers always searches out a house by the first three people moving into the ground floor, the second three going upstairs and a third three downstairs. I was the fourth one in so I started to go up a set of stairs that was to the left just inside the door. As I started up the stairs I looked upward to see three German soldiers standing at the railing above me. They had rifles pointing down at us. In the meantime one of them had taken a potato masher hand grenade, it looks like a tin can on the end of a stick, and dropped it at our feet and I yelled out "GRENADE!!" as loud as I could and we all rushed for the door. The concussion of the grenade hit the last guy through the door. The concussion threw him out of the house and his jacket was all shredded by the shards of metal that came from the tin can but his body was never touched. His jacket was ripped, that was all. As we came out we realized that we were in a very vulnerable position because they could throw hand grenades down on us from the second story. We had noticed that the right side of the house was a blank wall, no windows or doors, so we all congregated behind it. In the meantime, one of the guys, his name was Wyoming, put his head around the corner to take a look around the front. A German soldier was in a window at the front corner with his rifle pointing right out. When Wyoming put his head out there he was greeted with a bullet in the brain. He fell like a sack of coal and spurted vivid red arterial blood. It was quite a shock.

At that point we all got together to figure out what we were going to do. We had a walkie-talkie, or whatever they called it in those days, and we called for a tank destroyer, or a TD, to come and help us out of the situation. Fortunately one was available and was dispatched to our aid. As it came down the diagonal road headed for us we knew we had to get away from the house. Since I had the most combat experience, our lieutenant suggested that I take a run for a ditch about ten meters away that ran parallel to the right side of the house that was providing us with cover. Before I got to it I saw bullets hitting the ground near me. I dove into the ditch. The ditch allowed me to move around to the front where I got behind the walls of a blown out house. I also had a good view of the front of the house. There were a lot of windows, so while the rest of the guys did the same thing I did, I covered their escape with bursts from my BAR. With the BAR you usually fire the first bullet in the lower left hand corner of a target and since the gun has a tendency to rise and pull to the right as it fires, it's a natural for firing into enemy windows. The tank destroyer came along and put five great big holes in the side of the house, and just about when the fifth shot was fired I apparently turned my body. Next, I felt as if somebody had hit me in the back with a baseball bat or a building block or something like that.

I had a hard time breathing and collapsed. It turned out that a bullet entered my back near my spine and traveled through my left lung. It was a ricochet because the bullet didn't go completely through my body. If it had been from direct fire it would have gone right through. Afterwards I was able to feel the bullet in the chest muscle under my left arm. Just as I was wounded, a white flag appeared from this building and seventeen enemy soldiers crept out of the house. A medic came over to bandage my wound and give me sulfa pills. He said: "Soldier, you got a million dollar wound." A million dollar wound is the best wound a reluctant combat infantryman could get because the war is over for him and the wound is not life neither threatening nor disabling as in losing a leg. I was concerned, at that time, that he was just trying to keep my spirits up and that I actually had a ten thousand dollar wound which was the amount they paid your family when you die on the battlefield.

As I was lying there thinking about this everything started to grow dark. I was going into shock. I felt I was dying. I can remember my thoughts at the time, that "Damn, here I am just a kid, 20 years old, I haven't really seen life, I went to school, that's all I've ever done, I never had a job!" But the thing that ticked me off more than anything was that I had never slept with a girl. That was the worst thing that I could imagine. I wasn't thinking about my parents or God or anything else like that, it was the thought that I was still a virgin and that I hadn't tasted life. Then a few seconds later everything started to clear up and I could feel the breeze on my face, I could see the leaves on the trees and the birds flying in the blue sky and the clouds and hear the birds chirping. I was totally back to life! It was a fantastic experience [Laughs]!

They put me on a stretcher and took me by a Red Cross jeep, to a temporary field hospital, which was located in some sort of a German château. This became a problem because I insisted that I wanted keep my German Luger with me in the ambulance, clearly against Geneva Convention rules. (I had retrieved the Luger from the fire woodpile in this morning's battle.) I insisted: "I fought for this thing, I want it!" They conceded to my logic and put it in a bag under the pillow they had placed under my head. I still have that particular pillow at home. I took my pillow and Lugar back to the large, tented field hospital where I was surgically made able to breathe again. They removed the bullet a few days later. The doctor gave the partial bullet to me on a piece of tape but I lost this valuable souvenir a few days later.

This tent hospital was in the middle of a field somewhere. I have no idea where it was. During the ten days I was a patient, one of the medics came along and offered to buy my Luger. I told him it was not for sale. He said: "Well, I'll give you a hundred dollars for it." At that time that was a lot of money. (My combat military salary was about 50 dollars a month) I said, "sold!" So I sold my precious Lugar for a hundred dollars [Laughs]. In the field hospital everything was clean and fresh, something we hadn't experienced for months. It was so difficult for me to be comfortable on those fresh white sheets with your body all caked with blood and dirt picked up in battle.

A little vignette: When I was in the hospital I asked one of the medics how he had ever gotten to be a medic. He said, "well, when I was drafted they asked me where I worked and I told them I worked in the Dr. Pepper Bottling Plant." "Oh, you have medical experience" the interviewer exclaimed, "and here I am, a medic" he said [Laughs].

As soon as I could I wrote a letter back to my parents to allay their fears. I actually wrote two letters, one was by V-mail and the other one was by regular mail. I sent them out telling them that I was wounded but not to worry about me. Fortunately both those letters got to my parents in the morning of the same afternoon they received a telegram from the War Department saying that your son Eugene has been seriously wounded in action in Europe. Having just received those letters from me made the shock of receiving such an ominous telegram more bearable.

After ten days in the field hospital they put us on a hospital plane for my first airplane ride. The plane brought us to a large military hospital in England. We flew very low because many patients had chest wounds. This made breathing much easier and the views were spectacular. They piled four stretchers on each side, one above the other and I could see down at the ground. It was a beautiful sight, a beautiful sight! In England I stayed in the hospital for about a month or so while recuperating. Finally, they put us on a hospital ship bound for the good old United States. Our arrival in New York was an emotional experience. As we passed the Statue of Liberty, everyone lined the port side ships rails. I almost had the feeling that the ship listed in that direction.

Not long after we arrived in New York and I had a chance to visit home, they shipped me by train to a Memphis, Tennessee military hospital. After a furlough, I was discharged at Camp Upton, New York. The advantage of being a wounded combat veteran is that I was discharged with a CDD, or a Certificate for Disability Discharge. With these credentials I was able to get out of the service faster than many veterans who had more service time than I did. I did have a year of combat experience, so that should have counted for something [Laughs]. With the CDD I was also eligible for the new college educational benefits: Public Law-16, PL-16. As a result, I was able to go to MIT for four years at no cost to me. They paid for all my tuition and they gave me living expenses besides, and that was fantastic. Even at this point I still receive a pension that I use for good causes.

With all the trials and tribulations of a war, certain benefits come out of the experience. Many of us have developed a bond of brotherhood with those who faced the same wartime hardships. Division-wide and individual reunions are exciting. These few paragraphs could never fully explain the shared experiences of a difficult life. Being in the war, being in the "actual" war where bullets are really firing at you, is an unusual experience for most people. Fortunately I survived this special, brutal experience. Many did not. Looking back, I'm glad I went through it; I would never want to do it again.

Frank Bever
Infantryman 379th Infantry Regiment

Eventually after my recuperation back in England I was sent back to my unit and by that time they were in Dusseldorf on the Rhine River. I don't remember how I got back there as a lone soldier, but I did. I went up through Belgium, I remember being in Liege, Belgium, and eventually getting back and being greeted by the few survivors from company F in the beautiful city of Dusseldorf. We were there looking across the river where the Germans were on the east side of the river. We were trying to cross and eventually did, but I don't really recall any specific details other than that from the Dusseldorf area, but we got across apparently and established beachheads.

Our closing days were pretty much dedicated to clearing out areas in Hamm, Germany, and Dortmund, Germany. We took an active interest in getting those cities clean of any Germans. I remember snipers here and there that made it difficult for our unit to go any further. I think Dortmund was one of the largest cities that the 95th was credited with capturing and making them safe for the rest of the people in the area. After that we went on with the cleaning process until May of 1945. I can remember one early spring day we were advancing forward with not too much opposition and you could hear planes in the distance in back of us. I think that was on of the most joyous sights I ever saw as a service person, looking overhead and seeing those huge bombers with the star of the United States military on the sides. Obviously there was still resistance on further east of us. That early, bright, warm spring morning after all the blood and the guts and the cold and the mud from previous days and weeks and months. That was the culmination of a lot of activity from the United States military and I was grateful I was on the side of those planes that had the star on them. I remember the talk of the capitulation of the German reign and eventually it was indeed over. I can recall great hordes of German prisoners walking down the autobahn. I have a mental image towards the tail end of the war of a great number of German prisoners coming with their hands up.

Another noteworthy "happening" during the dying days in WWII that I still recall was in March or April 1945, I believe. Our Company .F, 379th Infantry unit was involved in "cleaning out" an area in the Krefeld, Germany region. Our platoon and my squad happened upon a forced labor camp that was devoted to helping the German war effort. Apparently the forced labor personnel in that large building knew that their liberation was at hand and they streamed out of that structure leading the German person who had issued them orders for who knows how long. Anyhow, they ended up bringing that individual to me and demanded that I shoot him on the spot to make up for past atrocities that he had undoubtedly done to them. I couldn't do that, it was just not the American way. Instead I sent him back to my company commander under guard of a couple of squad members. I never did know what eventually happened to him. I do know however that there was a bunch (25-50) of Lithuanian forced labor people that were more than gratified to see us. Another little sidelight at this time was that I had carried in my backpack one of those K-ration hard chocolate bars. I had carried it for some time, waiting for a good time and place to eat it I guess. Those forced labor human beings coming out of that camp appeared to need something to eat a lot worse than I and I recall giving that bar of candy to a young lady in that group. I have long considered that to be one of my greatest gifts [reflective pause] simple as it was!

IV. Change of Mission

The Allies raced to divide the lands of their conquered European enemy. The question of the post World War II division of the world was one that would plague the coalition throughout the latter days of the war. Conference after conference resulted in many fruitless discussions as a unified war effort gave way to the realities of occupation duties with less than desirable post-war alliances. One of the most significant undesirable divisions of post-war Europe was that of Germany. The final agreement concerning Germany was to quarter the country, with the United States, Soviet Union, United Kingdom and France each taking a share. To further complicate matters, Berlin, which was located in the Soviet sector, was also divided equally. This additional division of Berlin was designed to weaken the traditional German seat of power. With Allied relations quickly cooling as the war came to an end, experts were unable to devise a stable plan of dispersion, relying instead on the goodwill of the Big Four to govern in unison for an indefinite period.

The once industrial powerhouse of Germany had been reduced to a shell, and in many instances rubble, of its former existence. The early days of Soviet occupation were without electricity, water, sewage removal, food and security, to name but a few luxuries of modern existence. What had been spared by the war was then ravished by Soviet soldiers as they unsystematically and then systematically looted the country. A common theme among references and one that Thomas Parrish devotes an entire chapter to in his book *Berlin in the Balance 1945-1949* is, "Frau...Komm!"

stemming from the massive amount of rapes inflicted on German women and girls during the early unrestrained Soviet occupation. An example of the conditions in Germany immediately following the war is the deplorable state of the once pristine city of Berlin. Following the war, and the two-month Battle of Berlin, the city lay in shambles. The stench of death filled the air as bodies lined the streets and floated in the city's waterways. Thousands of victims of Hitler's final orders to flood the subway, washed out from under the earth. These bodies further competed for space in the canals with the raw sewage that leaked from the destroyed sewage systems within the city.

Although V-E Day didn't come until May 8, 1945, the war in Europe had wound down to little more than a police action for the 95th by mid-April. The division posted military government orders in English and German as the preceded through the Ruhr pocket. From April 16-May 20, 1945, the majority of the division participated in the supporting operations of the military government in the vicinity of Dortmund, while the 378th moved to the Bremen Shipyards from April 19- May 8, 1945,to provide security for the naval task force, USN TF 126. The naval task force had been ordered to prepare the Bremen, and later Bremerhaven, harbors and docks for use. For the majority of the division, the largest problem of this period, in addition to policing and rebuilding a large war-torn population, was the administration of over 100 repatriation camps. These camps were responsible for handling between 60,000 to 112,000 displaced persons, along with several tens of thousands more Allied prisoners of war from various nations, that had been repressed by the NAZI government.

On May 29, 1945, the division received orders to redeploy to the United States. Because the 95th was a "young" division, committed to the war following D-Day, they were directed to return to the United States to prepare for redeployment to the Pacific Theater. The V-E Day celebration and upcoming stateside leave upon redeployment were now overshadowed by the knowledge that the

95th would soon have to assault the Japanese Islands. The 377th was the first to embark for the United States on June 21, 1945, departing on one of five ships that carried the Iron Men back to the United States. Upon their arrival they were given a heroes return at several different ports along the East Coast. In 24-hours the men had eaten a wonderful home coming meal, phoned loved ones and been sent to personnel centers in their home states. At the respective personnel centers they received back pay, new clothes and leave orders for 30-days, with directions to assemble at Camp Shelby, Mississippi, in early August for additional training.

Transition to the Pacific

In the Pacific General MacArthur eventually fulfilled his promise and returned to the Philippines. The journey from Pearl Harbor had not been an easy one for the soldiers, sailors and marines fighting in the Pacific Theater. Many of these young men laid down their lives during bitter island fighting and in deplorable detainment camps before the General returned. Guadalcanal, Tarawa, Kwajalein, the Marianas, Saipan, Guam, Peleliu, Iwo Jima and finally Okinawa are a few of the bloody battles that bring chills to the surviving veterans of the Pacific. Tarawa is an excellent statistical representation of American determination. In the seizure of the island empire, Allied servicemen killed approximately 4,700 Japanese at a cost of 1,000 dead and 2,300 wounded. Sadly enough, statistics can only convey a quantitative summary of any story. In the Pacific, the men charged with assaulting beach after beach were concerned with little more than survival. While the sights and sounds of combat were horrible in the chilling European Theater, the Pacific took on the distinct realities of amphibious and jungle warfare fought against a fanatical enemy. In his book, based on his experiences as a Marine infantryman with Kilo Company, 3rd Battalion, 5th Marine Regiment, part of the 1st Marine, E.B. Sledge shares the realities of combat in this demanding theater:

Peleliu

It was gruesome to see the stages of decay proceed from just killed, to bloated, to maggot-infested rotting, to partially exposed bones-like some biological clock marking the inexorable passage of time...Added to the awful stench of the dead of both sides was the repulsive odor of human excrement everywhere. It was impossible to practice simple, elemental field sanitation on most areas of Peleliu because of the rocky surface...Added to this was the odor of thousands of rotting, discarded Japanese and American rations...the stench varied only from foul to unbearable.[6]

The island of Peleliu was a mere six-miles long by two-miles wide, located within the Caroline Island Chain. It was nothing more than a hot, heavily defended piece of coral in the middle of the Pacific. In temperatures of up to 115 degrees the Marines pushed forward, suffering casualties in excess of 50 percent in a month and a half of fierce fighting. Although the type of landings varied between islands, the statistics and conditions from Tarawa and Peleliu are an excellent indicator of the personal battles that raged between infantrymen in the Pacific.

While not part of the Japanese home island chain, Okinawa, because of its geographical and historic importance, was seen as the first Allied test of attacking Japanese soil. During the same period that the 95th was pushing through Hamm, the Pacific forces were contemplating what was speculated to be their hardest battle yet. Carriers had conducted raids on Okinawa since October of 1944, but regardless of massive aerial and naval preparation it would be necessary to put men on the ground to neutralize the islands formidable defenses. Many of the "Three Island" veterans of the Pacific had been rotated out, leaving a mixture of experienced men and replacements to take Okinawa. The island of Okinawa was remarkably different than some of the earlier battlegrounds in the theater. The island is sixty-miles long by eighteen-miles wide with a large ridgeline running through the center. Much more like the main Japanese islands, Okinawa was the home of a considerable civilian population, trees and wildlife. The climate was cooler, but the island was still prone to tropical rains. It took the Allies almost three months to complete the seizure of Okinawa. In that time, a great deal of foreshadowing for the pending invasion of Japan could be derived from the conditions set by the enemy, terrain and weather. This one passage from E. B. Sledge is sufficient to dispel any of the misconceptions concerning the glamour of combat, and represents the horrors of war that run through the minds of many veterans:

Okinawa

The situation was bad enough, but when enemy artillery shells exploded in the area, the eruptions of soil and mud uncovered previously buried Japanese dead and scattered chunks of corpses... If a Marine slipped and slid down the back slope of the muddy ridge, he was apt to reach the bottom vomiting. I saw more than one man lose his footing and slip and slide all the way to the bottom only to stand up horrorstricken as he watched in disbelief while fat maggots tumbled out of his muddy dungaree pockets... We didn't talk about such things... Nor do authors normally write about such vileness; unless they have seen it with their own eyes... But I saw much of it there on Okinawa and to me the war was insanity.[7]

Lieutenant Colonel James H. Doolittle had taken the war to Japan in April of 1942, with his famous air raid on Tokyo. His initial raid set the stage for the American land based preparatory bombing of the Japanese home islands that had begun once the Marianas were seized. The Army Air Corp bombed and burned Japan with extreme prejudice, but the Allied leaders fully understood that the Japanese would not surrender based on air power alone. With Iwo Jima and Okinawa under Allied occupation the land-based forces had a staging area for the final push into Japan. While invasion planning continued, it was commonly understood that a massive amount of men and material had to be assembled prior to the possibility of assaulting Japan. With Victory-Europe Day complete the Allies could now afford to transfer the much needed combat power to the Pacific. When the Big Three met at the Yalta Conference in early 1945, President Roosevelt had lobbied intensely for the Soviets to declare war on Japan. After receiving several major concessions, Premier Stalin agreed to enter the war against Japan once fighting in Europe was complete. Russian troops and equipment were eventually maneuvered to attack from Manchuria, but in the summer of 1945 the new American President Harry S. Truman, was faced with a larger problem. He was now forced to decide whether or not to introduce a revolutionary weapon of enormous proportions, the Atomic Bomb. Nevertheless, the Allies continued to prepare for the dreaded amphibious invasion of Japan until the historic flight of the *Enola Gay*.

Thirty days of leave flew by for the young men of the 95th Infantry. Thoughts of long awaited time with loved ones and friends were marred by the impending attack on Japan. By August the Iron Men had closed on Camp Shelby, Mississippi. Still today the debate over the use of Atomic weapons rages between academics, policy makers and other individuals who were not facing the impending slaughter of an amphibious assault on Japanese shores. The argument is much easier for those that were faced with conducting the assault; there is nothing but gratefulness in their voices as they recall the fear of knowing what had to be done, one way or the other. On August 6, 1945, the United States made an atomic strike on Hiroshima, Japan, followed by another atomic strike three days later on Nagasaki, Japan. These two cities felt first-hand the devastating power of this horrible new instrument of warfare. In the meantime, August 8, 1945, the Soviet Union

Declared War on Japan, and immediately penetrated into Japanese held territory in Manchuria. Faced with the devastation of the atomic strikes, the Soviet entrance into the war and the impending Allied invasion of the home islands, the Japanese government sued for peace on August 10, 1945. Victory-Japan Day, September 2nd, 1945, would officially end the Second World War and allow the millions of Americans supporting the war effort to return to a more normal life. The few remaining old soldiers of the 95th, along with those receiving medical discharges, were able to obtain the 85-points needed to process out of the military prior to beginning Pacific invasion training. The replacement members of the division were not so lucky. V-J Day removed thoughts of a bloody invasion, but even with the points lowered to 80, many of the men had to be transferred to other duty stations after the division was deactivated on October 15, 1945.

William Lake
Anti-Tank Infantryman 377th Infantry Regiment

In June I guess, they motored us back across France to Le Havre and we got on the *USS General Gordon*. I don't know if it had been a luxury liner or not, but it was a pretty big ship. We hit the most fantastic storm I had ever imagined. I don't know if we were supposed to have landed in Boston or not. Of course everybody wanted to go to New York and be in the big street parade, but we ended up because of these storms down in Newport, Virginia. We got off the ship and here we go, there were all these German prisoners working with the American women and they were giving us the Victory sign and the girls were hugging them, I mean it was just ridiculous. We got over to the big mess halls and they told us, "Now, everything in here is cooked by German cooks. When you people eat fresh eggs they eat powdered eggs." You know people that work with food aren't going to do that, but we stayed there a day or so, got haircuts and got our clothing drawn for issue. By then we had orders for 30-day furloughs and they put you on troop trains so you didn't have to fight with the civilians. They got you all the way to your service center, mine was the 6th at Fort Sheridan and then from there you traveled by bus or horse cart, or whatever was available.

In those days I don't think that the trains charged you anything, you just showed your ID card and your travel orders and you got on there with your baggage. Then in a lot of the cities, like Chicago, in the streetcars and trains there was no fare, you had your uniform on that was your ticket. Of course in those days we didn't use postal stamps either we just wrote free in the upper right corner, but then eventually, all those benefits disappeared. Rightly so, you can't have benefits like that forever. I didn't get any citations for extraordinary heroism, but I was awarded the Infantry Combat Badge. If you understand what that badge is about, it is more than anything else you can get. The only qualification for it is to be in an infantryman in combat. The artillery, the engineers they all got in good fighting. Especially the engineers, they were in front of you getting the boats ready if you were going across the water, and they didn't give them anything. Incidentally, we got $10 hazardous duty pay in these infantry units. The Air Force was in more dangerous situations, so they got more money. Add the parachute jumpers; I won't say they're any different than any other man in the infantry. Instead of walking to the job, or driving a truck, they come by parachute, so they got their jump pay too.

After leave I went to Fort Sheridan and they organized troop trains to Camp Shelby in Hattiesburg, Mississippi, not too far from the Gulf of Mexico. They had buildings there that had wooden awnings that went out that you propped up with a little board. When it rained, which was a lot of the time, you let those down, and they had screens up for ventilation. Malaria was not unknown in those parts. We got our little exercises, we were moving around pretending we were doing something. We didn't have any rifles. We were ready to go to the Pacific and they dropped the bomb and they still said, "No, you're going to the Pacific. You're marked for it and it is chiseled in stone. We can't change the orders."

We had some problems after that. Nobody wanted to go to the Pacific. So one day General Twaddle gave us a 7-minute speech. Control of the men was always automatic. We didn't have a lot of shirkers or people dragging their feet; we had go-bricks, but when time came to hit formation, they hit formation. When they were given the commands most of them, at least on the outside of the formations were right with it; they weren't playing around. Playing around really accomplished nothing. After a while it was so remote that the only thing you could do was wait for them to trap you. You were going along real good and all of a sudden they would give you a rear march. Well you can't beat that to mom's apple pie. You'd run in to the guy who'd just turned around in front of you. We marched there and of course he is on a raised speaker stand and he had a PA system. I don't honestly remember anything else than that they started catcalls.

You can do a catcall without doing any silliness. General Twaddle was an exceptionally fine person; he was a politician. I've never found an autobiography on him, but he came out of Washington DC, picked his own headquarters' staff and trained that division from start to finish. These Army Specialized Training people that we had they were treated shamefully. I didn't realize how much until after the war and especially after I got to read some information on it. Many of them gave up rank to get this education, some dropped out.

So some of the guys started this big campaign of writing their congressman and calling home having their families bellyache to Congress and finally out of the blue, they decided that the division would be disbanded. A lot of the divisions at that same time, that came home after us were being disbanded at the port. Say they came in to Camp Shanks, New York, poof, that was the end of the division. They were infantry just like us. We couldn't figure out how come there were five divisions that were high priority, that were going to go to their state for a 30-day leave and right out to California and off to the Pacific. I can't say for sure but I think one did actually get to California before they finally disrupted this program. But you had thousands of people in the states who had never been anywhere.

When the division was disbanded I didn't have near enough points to get out, so they sent me to Fort Sheridan. At Fort Sheridan they put me in a service company and I was with the labor battalion. We were down there in the warehouse, bundling up shirts and pants in bundles of 25 and throwing them on freight cars where they were being sold as surplus. Well, working with us were German prisoners. That lasted about an hour and then somebody said, "That's enough of this" and we all walked off and said, "You get those guys out of here and we'll do the work, but we're not going to work with them." Well, the Captain said, "This is insubordination, and you're going to do he work!" There was a little rumble about that and they took us out and then they had me working in a gas station. We were pumping gas and checking oil and we had one German working there. His main job was to make the coffee.

I got word that they were forming up a prisoner of was escort unit and since anything would be better than what I was doing, I went down there. We were going to take them to New York, get on the boat and take them all the way to France. Spend seven or eight days over there get on the boat and come back. Well, heck you can't beat that. So I got in to that and went up to Biliewenchal Field, Milwaukee, to get all the prisoners. We had a guard at each end of the coach with a carbine, I can't remember if we had ammunition or not, I doubt it. When we went to Chicago, those guys couldn't believe it, they bombed that place according to the propaganda that they had. We got off at Fort Custer, Michigan and hung around there for about a week, still guarding prisoners and I was on bed check in the barracks. The barracks orderly is supposed to meet you at the door and tell you how many men he has and how many are in the hospital. The barracks were neat as a pin and everybody was sleeping. Anyway, we got another load of prisoners and they had two barracks bags full of shoes and they had these big thick comforters that they rolled up and carried. They were supposed to have shakedown inspection of fountain pens. They could have one fountain pen, one pocketknife, or whatever else they were supposed to have. We got them loaded up and got them to Camp Shanks, and that's where our program ended. They said, "No, we've got other people that are going to do the escorting on the water." So, we went back to Fort Custer and I stayed there until late March when I had enough points to get out.

I went to Camp Grant at Rockford, Illinois and there they decided that I had tuberculosis. I had been in service for two-years and boy, I'm tough, I may have some bad teeth, but I certainly didn't have tuberculosis. They told me I could go to the VA or you can go to the hospital here so we can decide what this is. I got in the hospital here and they had big rubber hoses that they ran up my nose to take gastric stuff out and supposedly analyze it before they disposed of it. After about a week they declared that mine was inactive. That was it, I got $300 mustering out pay, my separation paperwork and all of a sudden I was on my own. You had until four o'clock that day to clear the post, after that you were trespassing. It kind of shakes you up to hear that, I hadn't thought about it you know, after four o'clock you're subjecting yourself to disciplinary civil police.

I was not a bright student. I was always barely pushed up to the next grade. I couldn't read, they never tested for reading in those days. I can't remember my mother ever reading to me. After two years of high school I didn't get any more school. When I got out of the Army everything was full and I knew one thing, I didn't want to work on an assembly line. What else was there for me to do? I didn't have much experience, so I thought I'd take the easy way out with the peacetime Army. They said, "You can go to Infantry, Armor or Artillery." I chose Armor and was going to learn how to be a mechanic. I enlisted for three years and went to Europe and got up to Buck Sergeant in six or seven months and was transferred to a recoilless rifle outfit in Augsburg. One time we got overnight passes on Labor Day, but we had to go to a military facility to stay overnight, so I was going to go to the old unit. By the time they were handing out the passes they were cancelled. This young corporal and I decided to go anyway and got turned in for missing bed check and got busted all the way down to private.

I got my GED done, I took a couple of correspondence courses and finally got back up to corporal and got discharged and by then the Air Force was taking people so I went in the Air Force and I got the good treatment. I wanted to go to Aircraft mechanic school. I had good numbers and such, but they said no, they were going to put me in military police, since I had all this training on weapons. I kept bugging them and they decided to get rid of me and sent me to atomic energy in Albuquerque, New Mexico, where you were boxed in for18-months. I had gotten married just as I entered the Air Force and by then we had our first baby and coming out of there I went to aircraft mechanic school at Shepherd Field in Wichita Falls, Texas.

Fred B. Love Jr.
Infantryman 377ᵗʰ Infantry Regiment

They put us on a plane and we flew back to England with a group of planes. Somehow the plane we went on, a C-47, veered away and landed at the airport in Paris. He had a tire blow out I guess because it ran off the runway and there was about 30 of us guys that had been wounded in combat on the plane and the pilot came back and said, "You boys just had the closest call you've ever had in your life!" We laughed and I said, "You don't know what a close call is!" They unloaded us there and fed us a hot meal, hot dogs with some kind of sauce on it and some vegetables and that was the best meal I ever tasted!

We stayed in Paris over night and they put us on the plane the next day and sent us on to England. We landed in England and they put us on a train and we rode and rode, we didn't know where we were going, they never told us anything. If you weren't top boss, you didn't know what you were doing. They unloaded us in London, England and they unloaded us there and put us in hospital wards. They were nice buildings with wounded guys lying all over. I thought I was pretty lucky because I had all my parts, a lot of them didn't. Even though I couldn't use my arm, it was paralyzed and it stayed paralyzed for several days. The nurses went in and started pulling the bandages out from each side of my arm. It took a week or two to get the bandages to come out of my arm. It healed up properly without getting an infection inside. As soon as they let me I started taking a shower. They would put a thin rubber wrapping around the bandage of my arm and then I could go take a shower. I had gone eleven weeks without a bath or a change of clothes and laid in mud, water, rain, ice, and snow, as we were live in holes in the ground like animals. I had a long beard on my face too, this was the first chance I had to scrape it off. I started taking those showers and you talk about it feeling good, I was taking two to three showers a day. The nurse said, "Why are you taking so many showers?" I said, "If you had gone as long as I did without a bath you'd feel dirty too!" There was a lot of dead skin and it would peel off as I showered. When my arm healed they started talking about taking it off, because I had no feeling. But then, before that happened, I started getting a tingling in my fingers and it started coming back and I regained full feeling as the nerves healed. The feeling came back mostly, but I've never been able to use it as well as I could before. As it happened I was left-handed, partly left-handed anyway. It caused me problems like that, I'd bat a ball right-handed, chop wood right-handed and dig with a shovel or a how right-handed. If I do any of that ever since

World War II it hurts to bad I can't sleep. I have to be real careful about any work I do with that right arm, I still have to use the left arm. But I did heal up and they put us in tents to heal up before we went back to the front.

Well, in the mean time they examined me. They give you this complete physical. They said, "How long have you had this sinus condition?" I said, "I didn't know I had sinus problems?" They said, "You sure do." I guess it had developed in that three months I had been living outdoors. My sinuses were in pretty bad condition so they irrigated them, they punched a hole in them and flushed them with saltwater. They did that several times and gave me antibiotics. That was the first time I had gotten antibiotics and they really worked. But they said they wouldn't put me back in the field because of my sinus condition. They said they were going to find something else for me to do. I was now a class V; if I had been a class VI they would have sent me home. Eisenhower said: "Keep every man who can do three hours a work a day."

After two months in the hospital they discharged me and I went to the replacement depot, which is where the requisition guys would fill the different units. The units requisitioned the bottom ranked guys, privates, because they all wanted to make their own Non-Com's. As it went on they got higher and higher ranks and there was nothing left but Sergeants. There were 42 guys left in the group I was in and I was the lowest ranking guy, a Buck-Sergeant. They never gave me Staff Sergeant when I was a Squad Leader, they never got it through for me. But I was Squad Leader with Buck Sergeant rank. They put us in the MP Company, it was kind of amusing there, they took us out and put us on guard and I told them I couldn't stand guard because of the night air and they agreed with me so I didn't have to do anything, I just sat there. One night this Corporal of the Guard, he was an MP corporal, told this one infantry staff sergeant to stand guard. The staff sergeant said, "You stand guard and I will take your place." That corporal got mad and told the Commander, "That staff sergeant wouldn't stand guard when I told him to." The Commander instigated a court-martial against that staff sergeant for not obeying the corporal. When they read the charges in the courtroom the board said, "are you crazy, a Corporal doesn't order a staff sergeant around." A staff sergeant orders a corporal around. Because of that they ordered the Commander to reorganized the company and put the top ranking sergeants where they were supposed to be. They completely reorganized that company, but we didn't stay there that long, they sent a bunch of us up to the front. A Lieutenant up there said, "We are going to separate the men from the boys. We are going to send you up to Germany." We had already separated the men from the boys before and we were the men.

I ended up in an MP Company; an infantryman wears a blue braid on his cap and that is a badge of honor as far as we were concerned, so to end up in an MP Company, well, it couldn't get much worse. That was awful, well, they took some of us that had combat infantry badges and put us on the administration of a prison stockade. We had 1800 German prisoners. So I served my time there, I had an interpreter and I worked for German Affairs as an administrator. Then came time to go home and the Lieutenant came up to me and said, "Love, if you agree to stay around for ten months, I'll get you another stripe." "I said, "I don't want any more stripes, I want to go home." "Well", he said, "alright, you've got enough points." We were on a point system, I had a medal, and had done time in combat and had enough points to rotate home. They sent me to England to catch a boat to go home. Don't you know I sat there for two months waiting for a boat! I had a new daughter at home, she was born on December 16 1944 and now it was 1945. I got home on December 20th, 1945. My daughter was a year and four days before I saw her. In fact, she was 20 months old before I even knew she was born, because the communications were so bad back then.

They sent me right home and discharged me, and when I was going to leave they said, "You have got some disability; you could file for disability income." I was afraid it would keep me from getting a job, I had a job to go to, but I was afraid it would keep me from working, so I said, "No, I don't want it." The Doctor said, "I'll write it in your records, so if you ever want it you can just apply." Well, I was out for five years and a milkman came around the house, he was a disabled veteran, and he found out that I had been in the service and my wife told him that I had been wounded. He said, "Why don't you apply for disability?" I had been out for five years but she wrote in, I wouldn't do it, and they sent some papers and we filled them out. A short time after I got a letter saying I got 50 percent disability, which was big money, about 75 bucks, with dependants it came to about 100 bucks a month! Oh, boy if I had had that I would have gone back to school. I had about 72 hours of college, but I already had another child and I wasn't quite settled down after the war. You have to be awfully solid not to be shaken up by war. I was pretty shaken up. I didn't talk much about my combat experience, but I started talking one day to someone who hadn't been in the service and he said: "I don't want to hear that, you guys come back and tell a bunch of tall tales, I don't want to hear it". So I went for years and didn't talk to anybody about it. I couldn't, I'd get the shakes talking about it; it made me a little shaky today talking about it. It took me several years to get completely adjusted again. I went back to my old job I had had before going to war, at the oil fields for Ohio Oil Company, and it paid pretty good. But when I got that disability pay I was thrilled. As a footnote to that I recently applied and they raised me to 100 percent, I've got 140 percent disability now. I've got different things wrong with me and they are all combat-related. I've got hearing aids in both ears from that tree that blew my ears out. I've got 30% disability in my right arm and it all adds up to 140 percent, but they pay me a 100 percent. They were good to me, they did all they could and took care of me when I needed it.

Daniel F. McCarthy IV
Supply Sergeant 377th Infantry Regiment

After returning to the United States and starting to draw equipment for a transfer to the South Pacific, our orders were cancelled. I was at home when I received orders to report to Fort Leonardwood, Missouri, for discharge. The Army had an Army bus to receive applicants for the Army Reserves. I was in line to sign up when a bus bound for Kansas City came. Being the only transportation between Kansas City and Fort Leonardwood for 24 hours, I decided to go to Kansas City rather than spend another day in an Army camp and didn't sign up for the reserves. I am glad I didn't because some of my college classmates who were in the reserves were called for the Korean War.

Joseph W. Napier
Infantryman 377th Infantry Regiment

We were sent to a displaced person camp with Russians and Poles. The Russians would get out of camp and rape the German woman and kill their livestock. We Americans would get blamed for it because they were wearing American clothes. We had to capture them and put them back in the DP Camp. They didn't like that at all. This all took place in Lipstock. When we went to Rayelti we were told we were getting a 30-day leave back in the states and then we were going to be shipped to Japan.

On June 1st, 1945, I had an appendicitis. I was sent to a field hospital thirty miles away and operated on for a ruptured appendix. I was there two weeks and then sent to a general hospital in Liege, Belgium. I was at this hospital for another two weeks. Now it was July 1945, and I was sent to La Harve, France to be shipped back to the states. I was waiting for a ship to go back to the states when we dropped the atomic bomb on Japan. I didn't have enough

points to get out so I was sent back to Belgium. I was assigned
to an Engineering outfit. My service records were sent back to
the states and then my records had to be reconstructed. I was
an infantry buck sergeant with a construction foreman rating. I
built roads, Army barracks, water lines and took up oil lines from
Antwerpen, Belgium to Russell, Germany. I had a large crew, a lot
of equipment and German POW's for the labor force. The POW's
were classified into different work groups, plumbers, electricians,
and carpenters. They were paid 80 cents a day. Then I was down
in Belgium working on the roads. During the war ammunition was
placed all along the roads for quick access. While we were there
they had started to collect all of the ammunition and take it back to
a central depot. During the time in Belgium we also moved water
lines. We were based out of a trucking company building. We ate
our meals there since there were only seven of us that went down
to Belgium. There were a total of fifteen of us. The other eight
men stayed up in Remand, Holland. They were working towards
Russell, Germany.

On February 22, 1946, we had a truck driver come down from
Remand, Holland and he asked me to ride back with him, I wasn't
supposed to go back into Germany because I guess they thought
I had bad feelings against the Germans, but I didn't. Anyway, this
truck driver pleaded with me to go along back with him. I could
see the handwriting on the wall. He wanted me to sign the troop
tickets so his buddies could go to Holland to visit their girlfriends.
I finally agreed to ride back with him so I could listen to the band.
Well when we got there the band wasn't playing that night. The
truck driver said to me, "I'll get you a girlfriend and you can go
to the movies." I said, "No, I'll go to the movies myself," but he
finally persuaded me to meet this girl called Rosalie. We went to
a Marx Brothers movie that was very funny and then I took her
home. She didn't ask me in because she didn't want her parents
to know she dated an American. I asked her if I could see her
again and she said, "yes." We went out the next night to listen to

the band and we had a great time, but her sister had to tag along, I guess she had to have a chaperon. We dated two or three more times and then she wanted me to meet her parents. I did, and it went well. I fell for her and I told her I loved her and wanted to marry her and she accepted.

So then I had to go back to the company, get the Company Commander to view her and have her sign papers that she wasn't a collaborator with the Germans. All of the other necessary paperwork had to be taken care of at this time too. I went to the American Counsel in Rotterdam to see if I could bring her back to America with me as my fiancée. They told me to get married over here so the American Government would pay for her transportation instead of me. So that's what we did. I signed up for an additional sixty days overseas. Right after I extended for sixty days I was called into the office and the CO told me I was going to be shipped back to the states. I told him I had extended for sixty days to get married. He told me I had five days to get married. I telegraphed her right away and asked her if we could get married right away. We had to get papers from her government in Mastrik, where she was born. We got the papers and then on Saturday, June 1st, 1946, we were married. Four days later I was on a ship to the United States. I arrived the 28th of June and was immediately discharged. My wife arrived the 19th of July 1946.

Richard H. Schoen
Medic 377th Infantry Regiment

After my recovery in the hospital I was sent back to France. I was below induction standards so they put me into an SS camp in Lemon, France. The camp was full of SS prisoners and I was in the dispensary there. I found out something else there, all these guys, SS or not, still had a wallet with a picture of their mother and father or brother or sister or wife. They weren't a hell of a lot different than I was actually. I hate to say this, but it's true.

They weren't arrogant or anything, they were just like our special operations guys, just a good bunch of soldiers. We were all put there, both sides, what else could we do? It came time then when the war was over that they were sending divisions back. I found that my division was at La Harve or Camp Old Gold or Camp Lucky Strikes or something, so I hitchhiked up there to see if I could go home with these guys, but being below induction standards they wouldn't take me. The division was coming back to go to war with Japan, I didn't know that at the time, I just wanted to be with my buddies. So these guys came back and they were going to go to war with Japan, but fortunately the atomic bomb was dropped and they didn't, they were instead disbanded. I eventually got discharged on points, 105 points I think. It was quite an experience, but I wouldn't do that again for a million bucks!

William W. Taylor, Jr.
Infantryman 377th Infantry Regiment

Eventually we hit it out of there, came back on the trains and went to camp Old Gold, got on a ship and came back to the states. The battalion ahead of us had a train wreck and totaled the tracks and delayed us for a while. We came back and were down on the ship at Old Gold and took off right on the tail end of a hurricane. We went above deck and they put us in life jackets but I wouldn't put one on, I said, "if this thing goes down out here I might as well just go." The ship would hit the waves and the water would come up over the bow and it was just terrible! The company commander was up there and I have to say that the company commander and I didn't get along very well. We had never been the best of buddies, we didn't see eye to eye. He said, "where is your lifejacket?" I said, "I'm not wearing one." I was eating a banana and he was seasick, it was actually pretty funny.

Anyway we made it all back and went down to Camp Shelby, Mississippi, to the 28th division, *The Bloody Bucket*. All you had to do to get into a fight was have somebody see your patch. We were training because we were supposed to go to Japan and land there. They had a big war plan where we were supposed to go in. One day, hallelujah! somebody dropped a couple of bombs. Talk about celebration. A lot of people in this country complain to this day about us bombing the Japanese. I thought that was one of the greatest war heroes we ever had. I still believe that and I will continue to believe that until the day I die. We wrestled around there and finally they deactivated the division and sent a lot of people home. There was a lot of celebrating going on. I remember the VJ-Day celebration down in Hattiesburg, Mississippi and the people were crazy down there. I asked, "what is the matter with these people?" After hearing it was VJ-Day I went back to the barracks I had a bit of booze. The taxi drivers would sell booze and I had a bit of booze in my duffel bag so I went back to the barracks and tried to drink that. I didn't do too well though, but it was a big celebration because the war was all over with.

After it was all over I got out of the Army and went back to college, I stayed in the reserves though, I didn't want to loose all my stripes. I said to my Platoon Sergeant, "we are going to fight Russia and when we do I don't want to have to start all over again as a Private!" Low and behold, the Koreans got into it over there. I had put in an application for a commission, as the first two grades out of World War II could apply for a commission, though some got in and some didn't. I had planned for that thing before the Korean War broke out because I was having thoughts about the Army, I should never have gotten out. I thought I had found home and didn't know it at the time. I got orders to report to Fort Campbell, Kentucky on the 3rd of October 1950, so I retrained with all these reserve people, we were better people than they were, the Army had gone down hill pretty badly at that point. The company commander tried to get me to reenlist for the Airborne, but I couldn't see getting out of a perfectly good airplane.

Willis E. Young
Infantryman 377th Infantry Regiment

When the Battle of the Bulge happened they captured a whole battalion of the 106th. I looked down the road and here come a whole bunch of GIs and then I realized ain't none of them got any guns. The Germans were marching about 1400 of them down the road. When they came in the front gate the Germans took what few Americans that were already there out the back gate. Then I ended up in Stalag 7-A. In a week or two I started going to Munich on work details everyday. We did everything from filling bomb craters, to repairing railroads, to putting those old tile roofs on the buildings over there. About the 1st or 2nd day of April there was a big thousand-plane raid on Munich that bombed all day long and that night they decided that we weren't going back to camp anymore. They just locked us in our boxcars along the railroad tracks. That's where we were until the 42nd division and an armored division came through Munich. We really got turned loose that morning about an hour before the Americans came because the Germans took off a runin' and they grabbed all the guards they could, but two of our guards got away. They came and unlocked the boxcar doors so we could get out. One of them was a German boy that was built like Charles Atlas. He wore a leather motorcycle trooper's uniform and his outfit was just in shreds. He must have put up a heck of a fight. The other one was an old fella about seventy-five ears old, but they both got away and came and unlocked all the boxcars and said, "take off because the SS are coming to shoot you." They didn't have to tell us anymore because we made ourselves scarce in a hurry.

I think it was about the 30th of April when they came through town and about eight or nine days later the war was officially over. I think it was the 12th of May when they finally came with trucks and loaded us up and hauled us out to Dakau, the famous concentration camp where they had DC3's lined up on the runway. They loaded us up and flew us back to Camp Lucky Strike out on the Cherburg peninsula. We were there about ten days and they deloused us and gave us a bath and burned our close. There wasn't nobody going to get any souvenirs of their own clothes because they burned them to get rid of the bugs and lice. They wouldn't let us have any candy or anything because the day before I got there two nineteen year old boys dropped dead from eating a candy bar. I guess the sugar content was just too much for their bodies to stand. Anyway, that's what they laid it onto, they said they ate too much candy.

After that we got on the boat and went to the southern point of England and picked up a bunch of boys that had been wounded. We left for the United States in a big convoy with probably seventy-five ships because there was still some submarines that hadn't surrendered yet. We got to the States on the 3rd of June. It was dark when we got to Fort Dix and they had supper already for us. They put two big steaks on everybody's plate and there wasn't anyway we could eat all that. Nobody could eat one, let alone two! I told the guy that he might as well take one of those steaks back, but he said, "orders are everybody gets two," and that's the way it was, everybody got two. I got to Fort Sheridan in about three days and they turned me loose for a sixty-six day recuperation furlough. It was better for Momma to fatten me up then the Army I guess [Laughs]. While I was at Fort Sheridan for those few days I met one of the guys who was put on KP with me when I first went in. He thought it was real funny, he never even had been to basic training and he was a staff sergeant still in the same mess hall.

From there I went to Miami Beach to be reassigned and we sat down there for about a week with our feet in the ocean and picked up cigarette butts in the morning on the beach and things like that. Next thing I knew I was in Camp Crowder, Missouri. They had 800 of us ex-prisoners there and they announced that they were going to make us the cadre to discharge the rest until they started interviewing us and we started telling them what we thought the situation was, the kind of bunch we thought they were and so forth. They didn't like it that we weren't very complimentary to them so they put us on railroad cars with wooden seats and sent us to New Orleans to train rookies. I was down at Camp Plouchet, Louisiana just outside of New Orleans until I was discharged on the 29th of November 1945.

Richard E. Hunton
Infantryman 378th Infantry Regiment

I finally got out of the General Hospital and went back to Southampton. I don't know when this was, but I'm guessing about the middle of February 1945, when we got on an old Victory Ship. By this time I had on a body splint. It went all the way down my stomach and back and all the way up my right arm. I looked like a statue, but it was so I wouldn't get hurt on this old rickety boat that we were going to take home. We were up and down so bad on that boat that it's a wonder we didn't get submarine pay, because we were under water half the time [Laughs]. It took about twelve or fourteen days to get back and we landed at Newport News in Norfolk, Virginia.

From Newport News we were taken to Camp Pickett, VA to the general hospital there. They removed my big old cast and put a hanging cast on. I was there about five months with eight or nine months all together in hospitals, but finally the time came for discharge. I ran up to get my discharge papers on August the 6th, 1945 and they had typed on there, "Date of Discharge, August the 6th, 1946." I said, "Hey that doesn't look right?" So I had to go through the whole thing over again, but they finally fixed everything and I left and went back to my home in Washington D.C. I got on a street car there to go out to my house and I heard all these people talking about this bomb that had been dropped over in Japan that had destroyed an entire city. I said, "No that couldn't be, because

I have been in the Army and I know they don't have such a thing." Of course they did, but they just forgot to tell me. Anyway this has allowed me to claim responsibility for winning the war. The story I always tell is that when my commanding officer found out I was being discharged he said, "Oh my, how are we going to win the war without Hunton?" He said he didn't know, but he called President Truman and told him and the president said, "I guess the only thing we can do now is drop the bomb to make up for losing Hunton." So they dropped it and we won the war [Laughs].

Frank E. Shaffer
Infantryman 378th Infantry Regiment

When the war was over we left France. We had a train wreck about three o'clock in the morning when we were leaving. Unfortunately a few guys were hurt. Coming back I remember there was a bakery right there by the train tracks, and the French bread tasted pretty good. Then we got on the boat and ended up in Boston. We went to Camp Shelby Mississippi, we were supposed to go to the Pacific our unit, and so we went to Mississippi for training. I read in the paper they had it all planned, we were going to make one big push. It showed where each division, I think there were three or four divisions, were supposed to go and that was supposed to be it. I knew some of us were going to be killed, it would have been really dangerous if we would have invaded Japan. Anyway, they dropped the bomb and I was discharged from Fort Dix.

Louis O. Vogt
Infantryman 378th Infantry Regiment

All right, going back to this repo depot again and then back to my 95th Infantry Division. The division kept losing people, a couple of fellows didn't mean anything, they just kept moving on and mopping up. Now, I was wounded on the 7th of April

1945, and the war ended on May the 8th of 1945. My 95th Infantry Division was up at Bremerhaven, the big submarine base, when I got back. One of the men out of my squad, I think his name was Wells, told me how he was standing guard over a big submarine. When they came back from Bremerhaven, I caught up with my company. Before this though I met a boy from Lewistown whose name was Dick Marker. I met him in Worms, Germany. He remembered me from home. After I made it back to the 95th we went to Liege, Belgium where the Germans were pushing forward. The big American supply lines were in Liege, Belgium. I can remember this very well, we were staying in a house upstairs and one of my squad mates had the GI's, dysentery, and every night he would run down the steps and he would leave a trail all the way down the steps. During the day there, I love to fish and hunt, so I took hand grenades, the people there needed some fish, and went fishing. I would pull the pin out of the hand grenade and drop it into the canal and Poof! fifteen or twenty fish would come up and the people would gather them up.

When we left Liege, Belgium our artillery train was going full steam ahead but they couldn't make the steep grade and were backing up when our troop train, 40 men to a car, 40 and 8 something like that they called them, hit them. It was about 3 o'clock in the morning our packs and rifles were hanging around the car and I had just woken up. I had to go to the bathroom, so I relieved myself and I was ready to lie back down when the next thing I heard was clunk, clunk, clunk? I knew we were off the track and all of a sudden the car upset. The cars in Germany were hooked together with chains and big bumping blocks one on each side with springs in them. One of those came right through the head, fortunately, we didn't have anybody killed right on the spot, but there were about ten guys that died later on. Broken arms, legs, ribs, and stuff went through their lungs. I can see a fellow yet, the reinforcing rods that help keep the cars together were over this poor devils neck so I grabbed it and tried to create a little space so he could get out, and not choke to death.

After V-E Day we weren't allowed to fraternize with anybody. We were only there like a month or so after the war because they shipped us back to the states for additional training. I think it was Camp Lucky Strike that we left from; I don't remember anymore, that was a couple of years ago you know. My outfit was to embark for the Pacific, but we come back to the United States and ended up in Camp Shelby, Mississippi first. We didn't get much training. The 95th had something like 145 days actual combat, and we had a lot of divisions and stateside replacements that didn't have any combat. So, in the mean time I telephoned to my wife and she came down to Mississippi with me. We rented a couple of rooms down there. When we turned the lights on at night there were cockroaches everywhere! Wow, I can still see them scurrying around. We went to a hardware store to get something for cockroaches and bedbugs. We were from Pennsylvania, we weren't used to anything like that. I had never seen anything like that in my entire life. The cockroaches, some about 2 inches long, would sound like elephants running. You'd turn the lights back on and away they would scatter. Anyway the war ended. I didn't have enough points at that time to get out. You had to have so many points, I don't remember how many, but since I was just a replacement I didn't have enough points to get out. After August the 14th of 1945, the war ended and the points dropped, but I still didn't have enough.

I do believe the atomic bomb was the best thing that could have happened, it saved a lot of lives. It took a lot of lives, but we saved a lot of American lives too with those bombs [Pause]. Right, Ok, now I didn't have enough points to get out so the major read on my form, one of the forms you fill out when you go in to the Army, that I was a "cooker man." They didn't even know what the rendering business was. So anyway, the major saw that I could cut meat, and the paperwork said I could cook, so he said, "your going to be a cook." I said, "I don't want to be a cook." So, he said, "you're going to be a cook anyway." I never went to cooking school and from Camp Shelby, Mississippi I ended up in Fort Monmouth, Red Bank, New Jersey. There I went into a kitchen. We had a bunch of German prisoners and a bunch of Italian prisoners. The Italians, it's surprising how many people don't realize that the Italians fought against us, they were with the Germans in the Second World War. But anyway, the Italians got to go into Long Branch, New Jersey once a week because Long Branch was mostly all Italians. The Germans had to stay in the compound. We had three American cooks, a sergeant, and a company of men, I think at that time there were about 220 men in a company. I was a sergeant then so I had three American cooks and eight Germans, the Germans actually did the cooking and everything else. I ate right with those fellows; I didn't have any ill feelings against those boys. They were drafted the same as I was and I was from German dissent anyway. I was born in the United States of America, my parents were born here too, but my grandfather was born in Essen, Germany and my grandmother outside of Heidelberg, Germany.

I think it was a T-4, sergeant then. I just missed being a staff sergeant before I got out. But in the meantime I had leave and went home hunting. I stayed a little longer than I was supposed to [Laughs]. AWOL. I got a good discharge but there are three days on my discharge paperwork listed as AWOL. When I went back to Red Bank they had my bed and everything moved out of my room. I remember being scared, standing there at attention. The lieutenant snapped his fingers and said, "I'll have you court-martialed young man!", I snapped my heels together like the Germans did, and said, "Yes sir!" He gave me seven extra days in the kitchen, which was excellent. I wrote letters everyday and it turned out all right but my wife was madder than a wet hen, even today, after fifty-eight years with the same misses, she still brings it up. She goes on about my parents letting me go hunting and being AWOL [Laughs]. So then from there I went to, well I'll have to think about where I was mustered out, [Pause] Fort Meade, Maryland. Fort Meade, that's correct, my parents came down with my wife and I was separated from the service on June the 30th 1946.

Frank Bever
Infantryman 379th Infantry Regiment

Eventually we were all reassembled after the armistice in Germany and then we went back to the Le Harve area, and then back to the United States on the *USS General Blatchford*, I believe it was. We were then given a month furlough. I remember coming into Boston and what a sight the city was. To come through there seeing orderliness after seeing so much destruction, I was grateful to be able to get on a train and head towards the state of Indiana. What a relief it was to be back to an area where you did not have to worry about security at night. It made a big impression on my young mind at that time. We went back with our month furlough and then reassembled at Camp Shelby, Mississippi, in the early part of August, something like the 6th or the 8th. I remember being on the streets at Camp Shelby, Mississippi, extremely hot weather again, and getting word of the dropping of the atomic bomb on Hiroshima, Japan. I could not comprehend the size of this bomb when they told us about the casualties and the tearing up of a whole city by dropping one bomb [emotional pause]. [Continues with a heartfelt account] At the time I was really joyous that President Truman decided to drop it. Since then I have talked to ministers and so forth. They pretty well side with me, saying that if it weren't for killing all those Japanese people there would have been that many dead Americans, I feel. I've thought and thought and thought about it. I've also thought how I got to come back home while that guy across the street got his throat cut and died instantly [emotional pause]. I get kind of emotional, but I guess all the years give you a long time to think about these things. One minister said, "in the long scheme of things you have five boys with a good Christian upbringing, and a grandson in that category that seems to pursue a Christian outlook"; but I've struggled with that for a long time, and I still do. I'm truly gratified that indeed I got to come back and that I'm here today. In spite of all the medals that they could heap on a person, I see no glory in war.

Then after this happened it was just a matter of time, my particular F Company as I recall, those that had a certain number of points were reassigned to the 44th Infantry Division. We eventually got our discharge in Arkansas through the 44th I believe. I had sixty-eight points at that time, they were releasing personnel by points but I don't remember the exact number. When we were discharged, a friend that I had gone through a great deal of combat with was from California, so we decided to hitchhike there and visit his folks for a week or so. After that I hitchhiked home to Indiana. I don't know how I could go virtually across the United States hitchhiking, but people were not reluctant to pick you, I had great luck coming home. Just coming across all those states is another high point in my military experience.

Roger A. Bushee
Infantryman 379th Infantry Regiment

When I got back to my unit the mail came in and that's when I found out that my brother had been killed. It really had to be terrible for my parents. They got a telegram from the War Department saying your son went down with his ship, so they thought it was me that had been killed coming home on a hospital ship. Later on they explained more that it was my brother and not me. He drowned, I guess, in an airplane crash. He was a bombardier in a B-24 Liberator. They crashed off of Montauk Point, Long Island during a low-level bombing mission. Apparently the pilot was a new member of the crew and their radio contact was fine amongst the squadron but when they tried to talk to the base back on shore they couldn't get through. Because of that the squadron leader told them to pull out and return to the base. Well, the pilot immediately dipped his wing to pull out and turn and that's when the wing hit the water. The plane cartwheeled and went down as a result of this. There was a fishing boat nearby so it stayed and circled the area until the coast guard arrived. Unfortunately, there were no survivors. They never have found the plane, it's still on the bottom of Montauk Point, off of Long Island. The squadron did go on and rehearse their practice bombing mission but [emotional pause]. So anyway, he was nineteen years old when he died. The Red Cross didn't ever get a hold of me. Apparently they tried, but I didn't find out until I got back to my outfit that my brother was gone.

There was not much activity by the time I returned. There was an occasional resistor that would harass you and they would send somebody out to make him surrender, and that sort of thing. Not much going on at all. We had air and ground superiority and by that time they were just giving up. During the military government time we went to a German factory that made wooden gas tanks. The Germans would put these tanks on airplanes and fly them until the tank was empty, and then they dropped them and used their internal tanks to return. They had Russian workers and these Russians were really tough. They wanted to go out and rob and rape all the farmers and steal their gold and silver. We had a tough time controlling them, saying, "Hey, the war is over, you can't do that!" The women would wash our clothes for us and helped to feed us, but the men really hated the Germans. They probably were displaced from Russia against their wishes. There were so many Germans that were in the service just as I was, because I was called. They told us either you kill or be killed. They kept brainwashing us in that respect, but anyway, that's as much as I remember from the occupation portion.

I can't remember the name of the boat, but we came back to the United States as a unit. After a thirty-day delay en route we assembled at Camp Shelby, Mississippi. Then of course the atomic bomb was dropped and the war was over. I admire Truman for dropping the bomb. I think he saved a lot of lives. We would have had a lot of men killed, from what I heard, if we would have had to invade Japan. I know there were a lot of civilians killed there, but we didn't start the war, we just tried to end the war. A tough decision for Truman, I'm glad I didn't have to make it. I didn't have enough points to get out, I only needed two more points, but I guess it was about two months longer they made me stay in and I went to Camp Swift, Texas for that. I was discharged from there.

In Oklahoma City there is a memorial museum for the 95th. I was one of the original members that started that. I was the treasurer. We would make monthly trips from Bella Vista, Arkansas to Oklahoma City when we first started the museum... We all would get together and send memorabilia to me and the other guys. We worked on the museum and the people of the 95th at the General Twaddle Reserve Training Center were very cooperative. Originally the room was on the second floor but as we got more and more memorabilia we were able to be instrumental, I think, in the center winning the Army Excellence Award. Because of this award the center received one hundred thousand dollars and a portion of that money went to moving our museum to the first floor by enlarging and cleaning what used to be an old gun range. After the EPA finally approved us, we were delayed because of the de-leading, we completed restoration and it really is very nice now. We are really very proud of it and it really is a very nice tribute to the 95th Division.

Eldon L. Knuth
Infantryman 379th Infantry Regiment

During the winter of 1944-45, thousands of us got trench foot. I had never heard of trench foot until I had it, and don't remember being cautioned about preventative measures. Trench foot results from a combination of circumstances that lead to no circulation in the feet. We had been pinned down for five days, my feet were wet, we never took our shoes or socks off, it was cold and the end result was impaired circulation. I didn't lose any toes but a lot of my buddies lost toes and some of them lost parts of their feet.

I was in various hospitals in England and Scotland until March. In March I was sent back to the States. We left through Glasgow on the hospital ship *Aquatania*. It was the sister ship to the *Lucitania*. As we left Glasgow we felt a jolt and heard a large thud. We heard that something foreign had been detected in the water and that a charge had been released. After ten days on the rough north Atlantic, we arrived at Halifax, Nova Scotia. From my stretcher, I caressed the American soil.

After nine months in the hospital I was discharged August 8th of 1945. That was just about the time that we dropped the bombs on Japan. By acting promptly I was able to start school for a third time -- at Purdue University.

During and after the fighting, the military took quite a few photos of the actions in and around what then was Saarlautern and now is Saarlouis. As one of the many ironies of war, my family stems from Saarlouis – I still have relatives there. Since the war, I have visited that area often, and have been able to locate and photograph the sites of a lot of the military photos. In the Ninety Fifth Infantry Division History, one finds a photo taken in Roden, a suburb of Saarlouis. The fighting was particularly severe there. This photo includes a village square where one sees a pile of personal possessions: suitcases, boxes and such things. Some of those possessions belonged to my relatives. When they were told to evacuate they were told to take what possessions they could carry; what they couldn't carry and wanted to take they were told to take to this square. These possessions would supposedly be taken to them later. They never saw them again, but they are in the photo taken by the 95th Division.

During the fighting in Saarlouis, many of the houses were either destroyed or damaged. Among the damaged houses was the house where my family had lived in the 18th and 19th Centuries. It was a more substantial house than most; it's a historical monument now. After the war, the present owner of that house (a medical doctor) restored it to its original design as best he could. I happen to have a picture of that house taken in 1912. I gave the owner a copy of it and we were both pleased to see that his restoration was quite faithful to the original architecture.

Looking back at my life, I feel lucky that I returned from military service with only a relatively minor medical problem – and that I was part of "The Greatest Generation." Since I had a medical discharge, my first four years of college were paid for by Public Law 16. My M.S. studies were supported by a Research Assistantship, my Ph.D. studies by a Guggenheim Fellowship. When I finished my Ph.D., the aerospace industry was knocking at the door. Three years later, when I decided to go for an academic career, the transition was easy. Research grants and supplemental consulting positions were easier to obtain then than they would be today. I am glad that I am not a freshly baked high school graduate starting on a career today.

Paul H. Madden, Jr.
Infantryman 379th Infantry Regiment

After all that I really didn't get back to the company until May the 3rd and by then they rumors the war would be over. Our division was in military government by that time. They established eighty-five points as the discharge system, so we lost some High Point men then that were transferred out of the division. I recall that my squad leader, Sergeant Kloyd, when we joined the company had been drafted at the age of forty-one. I didn't know this at the time, I knew he was older than a lot of us were [Laughs], but several years ago a friend of mine in Milwaukee helped me get a copy of his discharge and sent it to me and I noticed that he had been born in 1901. He was a High Point man along with my original assistant squad leader. Sergeant Carter became the squad leader later, but I remember he was older too, married with two children.

I rejoined the company in a little town named Hudlehof, which was north of Paderborn, Germany. I believe we had moved back to the area of Hamm Germany by the time that the Germans surrendered. My company was in the small town of Bulkamhovel, a suburb of Hamm, participating in military government and of course there was a non-fraternization policy at that time. I believe it was our battalion executive officer that always tried to catch you talking to the German citizens so he could give us a fine when we were there. I forget what the fine was, but it was all right if we were getting the German women to wash our clothes for us. I can remember this lady, that two or three of us were carrying our uniforms to so she could wash them, she had a daughter that I think was maybe sixteen or seventeen years old. One day there were these two individuals in British uniforms out at the fence gate talking to her. I was getting my laundry and I heard this conversation going on. I finally figured out that there was a British soldier there that couldn't speak anything but English. He had his buddy there that could speak French, they had an Italian displaced person there that could speak Italian, French and German. So the Englishman was trying to get a date with this German girl by talking to his buddy in English, then his buddy would translate it to the Italian in French and then the Italian would speak to the German girl in German. Then she would answer and it would go back in reverse order. I thought that was very amusing, but I guess where there's a will, there's a way. [Laughs]

We stayed in that area until early June and during that period the 95th was one of the four divisions that was picked to go from Europe to the Pacific. Fortunately we came back to the states for thirty days leave. I remember we left Germany on my birthday June the 12th, so that was a pretty good birthday present. I was 20 years old that day. We came back to La Harve by train and where the division had gone over on two ships, I'm not sure how many ships came back, but I know that only our regiment was on the troop carrier called the *General Blatchford.* We got through a north Atlantic storm and as I recall from the time we left La Harve I stayed in my bunk, I didn't get sick [Laughs]. I just stayed flat on my back until we saw Boston again. Somebody brought me a box of Baby Ruth's from the ship's PX and that's what my rations were for the trip back home.

From the port at Boston we went back to Camp Miles Standish and we were broken up into groups by area of the country. Being form Louisiana I was in a group that went down to Camp Shelby, Mississippi. We drew our thirty days leave from Camp Shelby and I know other members of our company went to Fort Sheridan for their leave and others went to Camp McCoy, Wisconsin and different posts around the country. After leave the division re-assembled at Camp Shelby, Mississippi, right below Hattiesburg. During our thirty day leave the bomb was dropped on Hiroshima, and I really appreciate President Truman authorizing the dropping of that bomb because I feel that it saved a lot more lives than what were lost in those two bombings. The division was still slated to go to the Pacific and our Commander General Twaddle said we would go if we were ordered. I remember there was a little bit of unrest. Stories were written to news people that the division was assembled one day in an open field at Camp Shelby and the general announced that we would be going as ordered, but I think within about three or four more days they elected to just deactivate the division there at Shelby.

I think the last company morning report that I have is from around the 8th or the 12th of October, with only two fellows left in the company. The company clerk Eugene Beeler, who had been in the company from the beginning, and Fred Gidry, who joined the company in Indiantown Gap out of the ASTP program. The division was scattered to different directions at that time. The High Point men were gone. The original members of the division from Camp Swift, Texas, that hadn't already been discharged went as a group to Camp Chaffee, Arkansas, to the 44th Division and most of them were discharged from there. Some of the lower point men went to Camp Atteberry, Indiana, a group to Fort Meade, Maryland, and other places. I happened to be in a group that went up to Fort Hancock, New Jersey, an old coast artillery post on the end of Sandy Hook, where I was discharged November the 3rd, 1945, which coincided with my parents wedding anniversary. They said they had a happy anniversary that year.

Adolph Massa
Infantry Rifle Company First Sergeant
379th Infantry Regiment

I stayed in the hospital for the next few months and it wasn't until the war was over that I rejoined my unit. When I got back to the unit Burton Spalding was first sergeant. Lieutenant Brown picked me up and brought me back to the unit and the first thing Spalding said when I got back was, "Here Massa, you're first sergeant." Captain Howard at the time said, "Well, I guess you're it Massa." So I became first sergeant and Spalding went back to his fourth platoon. After the war ended I believe I was the only one in the company that had enough points, I had over 105 points, meaning I was suppose to be one of the first ones to rotate back to the states. I took my war souvenirs and a P-38 that I was suppose to try and locate a Private Hill, a medic from our outfit that was wounded on the night the short round came in, and return the pistol to him. I was taken by jeep to a collecting point and from there I traveled by truck to Bremerhaven.

When I got to Bremerhaven they had large tanks of buzz bomb fluid, almost identical to setline welding tanks. Bremerhaven was the area where they would fire these buzz bombs at England during the war. A few of us sergeants decided to have a little fun with those so we turned them over upside down on a ramp and we'd knock of the ends. They'd shoot up in the air, the same as when you blow a balloon up and let it loose. We thought it was quite a bit of fun. Well, we were having fun until a vehicle came by with a major in it and one of the tanks almost demolished his vehicle. He jumped out and said, "You SOBs! I fought the war from Africa to here without being wounded and now you're going to kill me with one of these damn buzz bomb tanks!" So we felt pretty bad and we immediately discontinued our pleasures [Laughs].

I was called in and interviewed to fly back and go on a bond tour with General Eisenhower because my original home was in Kansas and Eisenhower was from Kansas. I declined and said that I would rather not participate in the bond tour. That was a big mistake because then they shipped me to the 69th Division. They took all the low-pointers out of the 69th and filled it with high-pointers and sent us to Hattingen, Germany. There, most of us being sergeants, our job was to help set up the demarcation zone when they divided Germany up between Russia, England, France and our country. Our sector was with the Russians. We had to work with the Russian soldiers so I got acquainted with a Russian first sergeant. At the time I was a little upset. I had high points and wished that maybe I would have went with Ike, but I did gain a lot of experience with this other assignment. I stayed there until the early part of June. Later I went on rest and relaxation to Le Harve, France and while I was there the war ended and the next day the *Stars and Stripes* released, "The High-Pointers Will Be Going Home Immediately!" The 65th was to be one of the first ones to rotate. Well, here three of us first sergeants were down in France while our unit was up in Germany. So we went to the airport and asked to terminate our leave and fly back to Frankfurt and then go onto where our units were. We were informed that they couldn't do that because they had a return R and R schedule to maintain, so we had to wait out our full seven days.

When we got back to Frankfurt we commandeered a vehicle from the Military Police, not to their knowledge [Laughs]. We drove back to Hattingen and when we got there our unit was already to leave. They were on trains, so we hurried and located the battalion commander. When we found him he said, "Boy, we didn't expect you guys back. We transferred you three fellows to the 555th Engineers in Frankfurt." He said that all our records and clothing had already been shipped down to them. He told us to get on the train anyway since the train was going to stop in Frankfurt and we could join our new unit there. We convinced him before we got to Frankfurt that we could probably pick up our records and our clothing and go home with the rest of the high-pointers. When we got to Frankfurt we got a hold of an MP jeep to take us to the triple-nickel headquarters and there we were informed that they had our personnel files but our clothing and equipment had been shipped out to units in the field. They told us that if we wanted our clothing that we wouldn't be able to catch the train with the 69th. So we decided that we would just pick up our records and forgo all our clothing and equipment. So that's what the three of us did, and that's how I lost all of my souvenirs and clothing. The worst thing I lost was a 8mm camera and about eleven rolls of film that I had taken of the fellows while we were in combat. Well, I lost all of that.

I arrived back in the states in October of 1945 and I was shipped directly to Fort Sheridan, Illinois. From there I was given a seven-day leave to Chicago with orders to report back after seven days. The reason they gave us this leave was because there were so many troops returning that they couldn't process everybody. Those that weren't too far from home they gave a seven-day leave to get them out of the area. By the time we came back our records were processed and we were ready for discharge. The main problem I had when it was time to be discharged was that due to the fact that I came back with the 69th they wanted to record me as being a member of the 69th. I told them no, I was a member of the 95th and got in an argument with the personnel clerks there until a colonel intervened. He said, "What's your problem sergeant!" I told him that they were trying to record me as part of the 69th and that I wanted it to be shown on my discharge that I was with the 95th Division. He said, "I don't blame you," and instructed the clerk to correct my discharge. So I was discharged in October and went back to my home in Chicago.

John G. Little, Jr.
Artilleryman 547th Anti Aircraft Artillery

On April 17, 1945, combat duty for the division in Europe ended and we were settled in the Ruhr Pocket. In June of 1945 we were released from the 95th Infantry Division. By June 13, 1945, we had moved to a little village called Gosselies, Belgium. We were assigned to a military railway security outfit. They were moving depots into Germany. On August 2, 1945, I was transferred to an MP Company. Company A 397 MP Battalion in Chauny, France. The 95th Infantry Division had shipped out to the United States to Camp Shelby, Mississippi. I stayed overseas with the MP Company until January 1946, until I shipped out for the United States.

I want to back up and go back into Germany before we went to Belgium. I hadn't mentioned that bugle lately. When we were in England I had managed to get rid of the bugle to the supply sergeant. It got lost during the war. After the war was over we were in Germany to impress the civilians. We had formation; putting the flag up and they wanted some ceremonies but they couldn't find the bugle. They sent me out to find one. I couldn't find one for several days. They had a non-fraternization order and they suspected me of fraternizing with the young ladies. So the first sergeant said he would get one. He did find a nice one in a case and the battery commander gave it to me. He said I would be borrowing it and when I shipped out to give it back to him. So when I was in Belgium and getting ready to ship out to the MP outfit in France I took it back to him. Captain Oaks said to keep it in remembrance of him. His gift to me.. I thanked him and I still have that little bugle and also my Boy Scout bugle. Oh, by the way the bugle I took overseas with me was made of plastic. It was made cheap just like that submachine gun. It was real cheap but it served the purpose. I still have that bugle in a permanent place with a steel helmet and some American Flags in an entertainment center.

When we got off a boat in New York City we went to Fort Dix, New Jersey. I do not remember the name of the small troop ship we were on. Some of us went on to Georgia and Alabama. We finally got back to Fort McPherson, Georgia where we left from three years before. I signed up for the Army Reserves while I was there. None of the others did. They thought I had lost my mind. They released us in a day or two and I went outside the gate with my duffel bag and rode a bus the whole way from Atlanta, Georgia to Montgomery and to Greenville, Alabama. I got off on the corner, a half block from my home. For several weeks I sat on my front porch and watched several other guys get off that same bus with their duffel bags.

Leon E. Langford
Ordnance 795th Ordnance
(Light Maintenance) Company

We just stayed in Recklinghausen and occupied the place until we eventually got orders to go by truck to Camp Old Gold outside of Le Havre, France. I remember about the time we were ready to leave Recklinghausen I got sick. I went on sick call and they gave me a few pills, aspirin or something that didn't really help. My buddies said you got to get on the trucks and go back with us and I said, "You bet!" So one night they put me in my sack and got some of that awful lemon flavored powdered mix and heated up some water with I don't know how much schnapps or "buzz bomb fluid" or whatever it was, but they sweated it out of me. All the way back when we were riding in the truck I had diarrhea. Those ten-minute breaks every hour didn't necessarily work [Laughs].

Consequently, I used my helmet for EVERYTHING in the Army-that was the ultimate! When we got back we were at Camp Old Gold for I don't know, maybe two weeks, then we shipped back to Boston.

Of course, Suz and I had been corresponding back and forth and when I got back we decided, "Let's get married," so we did. We left the 26th of June, I got back in July and we were married on July 12th and we've been married ever since. We had thirty days leave and then I went to Camp Shelby and of course General Twaddle called the division to formation, I think I had duty that day so I didn't get to that formation. I understand that there were quit a few protests about not wanting to go to Japan. Anyway, they dropped the bomb and we were glad for that. The guy that figured my points figured that I had fifty-nine points, you needed sixty to go home and be discharged from there, so instead of going home I was transferred to Fort Bragg after our unit broke up. Oh, in the meantime happy day, all of a sudden some of those old guys had been transferred out of the unit and went home and two weeks I was a sergeant. After spending two and a half years as a private and a PFC I was up to "buck" sergeant [Laughs]; that's what I was discharged as. I spent about two months working in the separation center at Fort Bragg and was discharged a little after Thanksgiving of 1945.

Martin H. Lincoln
Ordnance 795th Ordnance
(Light Maintenance) Company

Right after Recklinghousen the war ended and we got the news we were going to be joining up with General MacArthur. I think we went out of LaHarve and started for Holland. It's funny; they made me an MP on the trip over on the boat. I had more doggone assignments, but we made it across to the United States and landed at Camp Miles Standish again. We got to Camp Miles Standish and the war was over now, all but the war with Japan, and even though my family was right next door to the camp I couldn't get a pass to go home. So they shipped us all the way up to Fort Devans so when I got a pass I had to hitchhike home again from the fort. I did that for a while until one day I got a phone call from one of my friends and he said, "the division is shipping out," and they all shipped out for Camp Shelby Mississippi. There were about six of us that they had left behind so they put me in charge and we had sleeping quarters all the way to Washington DC. When we got there the word came that the atom bomb had been dropped and the war was over. Once we got to Shelby the guys were getting pretty uneasy. They didn't want to go and join MacArthur; they just wanted to go home. They were demonstrating down in New Orleans until General Twaddle got the whole bunch of us together and had a big talk and tried to get the esprit de corps of the division together again, but the guys really wanted to go home. They ended not sending us over to Japan and that's when they sent me home on a 30-day delay in route and then I got word when I was home that I was being discharged from Camp Edwards down on the cape. And that was it. We had a good time and a bad time, it all depended.

Harry T. Hessler
Clerk 95th Quartermaster Company

The war came to an end and I was there until I finally had enough points to go home. I was sent back by way of Marseille, France, where we caught a Liberty ship. I left Germany on Thanksgiving Day, I sailed from France on Pearl Harbor Day and landed in Newport News, Virginia on Christmas Day and was discharged from the Army at Fort Dix, New Jersey on New Years Day. They gave me my way to get back to Buffalo and away I went. The strange thing is that when I got back to Buffalo, my family knew I was back in the States, but when I got off the train my mother was sitting there waiting for me. She had no idea that I was coming home that day, she just had a feeling that was going to be on the train that day and came down to the station.

Annexes

Annex A: 95th Infantry Division Organization

The 95th Infantry Division was organized along the lines of the normal table of organization and equipment for a light infantry division of the time period. The division totaled approximately 14,000 officers and enlisted men when manned at full strength. For command and control purposes, the division was broken down into three principle infantry regiments and other support organizations. The regiments of the 95th Infantry Division were the 377th, 378th and 379th, each composed of approximately 3,000 officers and enlisted men. At the regimental level, there was a headquarters company, cannon company, anti-tank company and service and support company. The principle strength of the regiment was further broken down into three battalions of approximately 850 men each. Numbered from one to three in each regiment, these battalions were organized as headquarters and headquarters company, three rifle companies and a heavy weapons company (D, H and M), each listed alphabetically from A to M, minus J, beginning with the first battalion and ending with the third.

The additional organizations at division level were three light battalions of field artillery; the 920th, 358th, and 359th, and one medium battalion of field artillery, the 360th, providing the division with much needed indirect fire support. Engineer assets came from the 320th Engineer (Combat) Battalion, and the 320th Medical Battalion furnished medical support. The division also had company size assets handling communications, 95th Signal Company, supply, 95th Quartermaster Company, ordnance, 795th Ordnance Company, human intelligence, 95th Reconnaissance Troop and command and control covered under the Headquarters and Headquarters Company 95th Infantry Division. Not to be forgotten is the Military Police platoon that would provide the traditional combat police support. Also normally under division control, but not organic, were the 547 AAA Battalion (anti-aircraft artillery), at least one battalion of tanks and one battalion of tank destroyers. The division would also receive additional assets in a direct support role, directly supporting, but not technically attached, such as Corps artillery or engineers. To fight specific engagements the division could break these assets down into combat teams, short duration force conglomerations designed to fight a specific engagement. When broken down into separate combat teams or task forces, the division may also receive specialized assets from higher headquarters to supplement the team capabilities, as demonstrated by Combat Teams 7, 8 and 9, or Task Forces Twaddle or Faith.

Annex B: 95th Infantry Division Roll-Up

The 95th Infantry Division fought in Europe for nearly 12-months involving 151 days of combat, including a continuous period of more than 100 days. The 95th captured more than 439 towns and cities, to include Germany's ninth largest city, Dortmund. They traveled 738 square miles and in one 14-day dash, spanned no less than four countries: Germany, France, Holland and Belgium. The division left behind a history of heroism, bravery, but unfortunately, they also left behind 6,591 officially recorded casualties.[8]

Although exact figures will never be available, the 95th Infantry Division is credited with eliminating 47,264 German soldiers. Of this total, 31,988 were captured and 15,276 were wounded or killed.

Another staggering feat that assists in quantifying the massive effort undertaken by the division, is the amount of artillery rounds fired in support of the Victory Division. Records account for just over 250,000 artillery rounds fired in Germany and France, with a net explosive weight of more than eleven million pounds. The earlier picture of the artillerymen near Neuss, Germany is the estimated 200,000th round to be fired by the Iron Artillerymen. The artillerymen of the division played a key role as the 95th defeated twelve German divisions and 225 miscellaneous brigade or smaller German units of action.[9]

Activated: 15 July 1942.

Commander: Major General Harry L. Twaddle.

Overseas: 10 August 1944.

Campaigns: Northern France, Rhineland, Central Europe.

Days of combat: 145.

Distinguished Unit Citations: 1.

Awards:
Medal of Honor-1
Distinguished Service Cross-11
Distinguished Service Medal-1
Silver Star-752
Legion of Merit-15
Soldiers Medal-19
Bronze Star Medal-4,281 (This number changed when all Infantrymen that earned the Combat Infantry Badge were authorized the Bronze Star Medal following the war. Unfortunately, many of these men never received their hard earned medals.)
Air Medal-162

Assignments in the European Theater:
27 July 1944: XIII Corps, Ninth Army.

28 August 1944: XIII Corps, Ninth Army, 12th Army Group.

5 September 1944: III Corps.

10 October 1944: XX Corps, Third Army, 12th Army Group.

29 January 1945: VIII Corps.

5 February 1945: Ninth Army (attached to the British 21st Army Group), 12th Army Group.

13 February 1945: Ninth Army (attached to the British 21st Army Group), 12th Army Group, but attached for operations to the British VIII Corps of the British Second Army.

20 February 1945: XIX Corps, Ninth Army (attached to the British 21st Army Group), 12th Army Group.

26 February 1945: XIII Corps.

30 March 1945: XIX Corps.

31 March 1945: XXII Corps, Fifteenth Army, 12th Army Group.

2 April 1945: XIX Corps, Ninth Army (attached to British 21st Army Group), 12th Army Group.

4 April 1945: XIX Corps, Ninth Army, 12th Army Group.

9 April 1945: XVI Corps.[10]

Returned to United States: 29 June 1945.

Inactivated: 15 October 1945.

Annex C: Biographical Summaries

377th Infantry Regiment:

Charles R. Fowler- went home to Oklahoma City following the war. After a few years of working for Wilson and Company and then as a fieldman for the National Angus Association he started his own farm and raised registered Angus cattle. He was married in 1951 and had two boys. Mr. Fowler's first wife past away from cancer in 1964, but he was remarried in 1968 to his wife Virginia. The Fowler family was expanded with the addition of

Virginia and her daughter from a previous marriage to the family. Although his sons have since purchased his farm Mr. Fowler is still very active in the Angus business. Mr. Fowler was awarded the Silver Star, Bronze Star, and two Purple Hearts in addition to the standard European Theater service package.

William Lake- went on to participate in the Korean War before retiring from the Air Force in 1968. Following his retirement from the military he went on to work for United Airlines in San Francisco, California for another 22-years. The Lake's had two sons, both of which served in the military like their Father, and now enjoy the fruits of retirement. Mr. Lake was awarded the Combat Infantry Badge, a Bronze Star and the standard European Theater service package following his service in the Second World War.

Fred B. Love- went home to Ohio and his lovely family after the war. The Love's had two daughters that both went on to be schoolteachers in Owensboro, Kentucky. Mr. Love and his wife have been happily married for almost 60 years. Fred stayed with the oil company for several years but transferred to the Postal Service once the oil industry began to decline. He worked as a letter carrier and postal supervisor until he retired in 1983. Since then he and his wife have been enjoying the retired life. Mr. Love was awarded the Combat Infantry Badge, a Bronze Star, a Purple Heart and the standard European Theater service package.

Daniel F. McCarthy IV- Returned home in 1945. Because of the GI Bill Veterans were able to attend college for up to 48 months with the government paying tuition up to $500 annually. The Veteran would also receive $65 per month sustenance if he had no dependents or $90 if he had one or more. Mr. McCarthy attended Kansas State University where he received a degree in May of 1950. While in college he also met and later married Mary Beth

Needham. The couple went on to have three wonderful children, one of whom was a Major in the 95th Division. Mr. McCarthy was awarded the Bronze Star and Combat Infantryman Badge, in addition to the standard European Theater service package.

Joseph W. Napier- went home to Missouri and farmed for ten years. In 1948, the Napiers had a daughter, Margaret, and a son, Robert, in 1953. The Napiers have been married for fifty-six years and Joe confesses that he has, "loved Rosalie very much all of these years." Mr. Napier took a job with the St. Joseph, Missouri Light and Power Company in 1956 and remained there for the next thirty-four years, spending the last twenty years as a line foreman. On February 8th, 1985, Joe had a heart attack, but recovered and eventually retired in 1990. In 1991, the Napiers went on a camping trip to Colorado where Joe had another heart attack and a subsequent sextuplet bypass. In August 2002, Mr. Napier was presented his long overdue Purple Heart and Bronze Star, adding to his previous awards of the Combat Infantryman Badge, Silver Star, Bronze Star and standard European Theater service package with four battle stars.

Richard H. Schoen- returned to Indiantown Gap, Pennsylvania, in January 1946, but this time to separate from the Army as a Sergeant and return home to Ohio. He went home and used the GI Bill to go back to John Carroll University and finish his degree before going into business with his father and two brothers. They had the Schoen Paving Company, a highway-paving contractor in Ohio. He married Elaine Mayer from Cleveland and between the two the family ended up with 14 children, 7 boys and 7 girls, all college graduates, and an unbelievable 55 grandchildren. Dick still carries a piece of shrapnel around in his back that was too close to his spine to remove.

William W. Taylor Jr.- joined the reserves and went home following the war. William was called to active duty again to train troops for the Korean War. Not long after his activation, he was given a direct commission and went on to fight in Korea and Vietnam as an Infantry officer, commanding a rifle battalion in the latter conflict. His awards include the Combat Infantryman Badge with two stars (which designates the third award of the CIB), Silver Star, Bronze Star and standard European, Korean and Vietnamese Theater service packages. Colonel Taylor highlights the fact that in three wars he never earned the Purple Heart.

Willis E. Young- went home to Illinois after the war and initially worked for Caterpillar. He was married in 1946 and had a daughter prior to his decision in 1952 to "go to farming and get rich [Laughs]." He farmed for the next fifty years, along with carrying the rural mail in Yates City. The Young's also went on to have another daughter after they went to farming. Mr. Young's first wife passed away in 1994 and he later remarried in 1996 to his wife Rosemary during a self-proclaimed romantic ceremony following the National Rodeo Championships. Mr. Young was awarded the Combat Infantryman Badge, Bronze Star, Purple Heart (x2) and Prisoner of War Medal in addition to the standard European Theater service package.

378th Infantry Regiment:

Richard E. Hunton- went home and enrolled in George Washington University and then George Washington Medical School. After his internship in Gallinger Municipal Hospital in Washington he moved to Spartanburg, South Carolina for his residency before going to Greenwood, South Carolina where he practiced with the Scurry Clinic for the next thirty-seven years. Following bypass surgery in 1989, Dr. Hunton retired for about a month. He has been doing *locum tenens*, or fill-in Doctor in English. Dr. Hunton was married to his wife Agnes in 1953 and the couple went on to have a daughter and son. Dr. Hunton was awarded the Combat Infantryman Badge, Bronze Star and Purple Heart, in addition to the standard European Theater service package.

Anthony N. Petraglia- just relaxed for a couple of months after leaving the service before going to work for the Dukane Light Company, where he stayed for 40 plus years. Not long after joining the light company he was almost killed in an electrical accident at a power station. Tony had made it through the war intact, but the transformer had sent a charge of electricity through his arm and body, exiting out his knee that would cost him his thumb and part of his little finger. He married to a lovely girl named Lois and has four wonderful children, three boys and a daughter. As a combat infantryman in the European Theater Tony is entitled to the Combat Infantryman Badge, Bronze Star and Purple Heart (x2), in addition to the standard European Theater service package.

Frank E. Shaffer- went home to Bloomsburg, Pennsylvania. One year after he returned he married and the new couple had three children. Frank retired from the Post Office, where he had worked for 40 years. Frank still resides in Bloomsburg today. Prior to his separation from the service he was awarded the Combat Infantryman Badge, Bronze Star and the standard European Theater service package.

Louis O. Vogt- was drafted from Lewistown, Pennsylvania in 1943. He was an example of the later United States draftees that were shipped to combat, for him in the European Theater, after as little as six weeks of training. Louis went on to complete his duty with the 378th and later to await outprocessing at Fort Mammoth, New Jersey after the division had begun to prepare for deactivation. He had married his wife Joyce prior to receiving his selective service notice, and was thus still a newlywed when he reported for active duty. When he returned from the war he and his wife went on to expand their family to include a son Louis O. Jr., and a daughter Jane. He was a lifelong business partner with his younger brother Carl, purchasing their Father's business in partnership after he returned from the war. He departed the service as a Sergeant, having been awarded the Combat Infantryman Badge, Bronze Star and Purple Heart, in addition to the standard European Theater service package.

Eugene M. Wroblewski- donated the majority of his souvenirs to the German Language Department of Lafayette University in Easton, Pennsylvania after the war. The military instilled in him a passion for travel, initially leading him to hitchhike across the United States prior to returning to MIT after his discharge. He graduated from MIT with the class of 1949 and moved to Minneapolis, Minnesota to begin work. Interestingly, a few years after he began his working career he quite his job and toured Europe on a motor scooter for five months. He returned to Minneapolis where met and married his wife Lorry at the tender age of 35 (although Lorry is considerably younger I might add). The Wroblewski's had three wonderful children: Miles, Peter and Sue. The family moved to Doylestown, Pennsylvania in 1968 where Gene continued his work as an engineer. The Wroblewski's are extremely active in there community, well into their seventies, Gene still runs a small business and teaches computers to seniors while Lorry is a competitive tennis player, coach and participates in far too many activities to add in this limited space. Prior to his separation from the service he was awarded the Combat Infantryman Badge, Bronze Star, Purple Heart and Presidential Unit Citation, in addition to the standard European Theater service package.

379ᵗʰ Infantry Regiment:

Frank Bever- eventually ended up back in Wabash, Indiana. He took advantage of the GI Bill and learned the printing trade, working in that field for the next thirty years. After leaving the printing trade Mr. Bever served as a postmaster near North Manchester, Indiana, for over twenty-two years. Retired now, Mr. Bever was married in 1947 to his wife Olive and the couple went on to have five sons. Mr. Bever was awarded the Combat Infantryman Badge, Bronze Star, Purple Heart and Good Conduct Medal, in addition to the standard European Theater service package. Not everyone received the Good Conduct Medal, but Mr. Bever, who humbly notes that it, "was sort of an embarrassment at the time but as I look back I should feel gratified," was chosen to receive the medal in the California Desert prior to deploying overseas.

Roger A. Bushee- returned home following the war and re-entered Wilson College until he met and married his wife Maxine. The couple went on to have three wonderful daughters. The family spent over forty years in the same house in Palos Heights, Illinois prior to moving to Bella Vista Arkansas following their retirement. Mr. Bushee worked in newspaper production and also rose to the position of chief and later trustee of the volunteer fire department in Palos Heights. For his part in the establishment of the 95ᵗʰ Infantry Division Museum Mr. Bushee was named the first Honorary Colonel of the 379ᵗʰ Infantry Regiment, along with his friends who were also instrumental in the project and also later named honorary colonels. Mr. Bushee left the service a staff sergeant having been awarded the Combat Infantryman Badge, Bronze Star, and Purple Heart, in addition to the standard European Theater service package.

Eldon L. Knuth- returned to civilian life, and finished his Bachelor and Master's degrees in Aeronautical Engineering at Purdue University before going on to finish his Ph.D. in Aeronautics at Cal Tech. He worked for three years in the Aerospace industry before taking a position at UCLA in 1956. He was promoted to Full Professor in 1965 and remained at UCLA until his retirement in 1991. In 1975, Prof. Knuth received from Germany a von Humboldt Senior Scientist Award in honor of his research contributions. These awards were funded by the German government in appreciation of the aid received from the United States via the Marshall Plan. Since 1975, Prof. Knuth has participated annually in a cooperative research program with one of Max-Planck Institutes in Germany; he and his wife travel regularly back and forth to Germany. As a hobby, he pursues his interests in genealogy. For his researches, publications and lectures involving genealogy and emigration, he has received three awards from organizations within Germany. Interestingly, his family is from Saarlautern, now Saarlouis. Fortunately, he was no longer with the division as it fought its way through Saarlautern. Between his wife Margaret and him they have six children. For his Army service, Knuth received the Combat Infantryman Badge and Bronze Star, in addition to the standard European Theater of Operations service package.

Paul H. Madden, Jr.- went home to Shreveport, Louisiana after his discharge. Since Louisiana only had eleven grades at the high school level during those days Mr. Madden had completed high school by the age of sixteen and gone on to college before entering the service. He returned to pick up where he left off and graduated with a BS degree from Centenary College in the summer of 1947. He worked for the United Gas Company and was later given a direct commission as a 2nd lieutenant of artillery in the reserves in 1950. In the meantime Mr. Madden married his wife Phyllis in 1948 and had a son two years later. With no formal training in the artillery Lieutenant Madden was called to active duty in 1951. Mr. Madden had left the infantry as a PFC and later left the artillery a 1st lieutenant and former commander of the 190th Field Artillery Group, full colonel billet. Mr. Madden gave up the reserves a few years after his second discharge, opting instead to become a Scout Master for the Boy Scouts. Mr. Madden transferred to the Union Producing Company as a Landman and had another son after again leaving active duty. Interestingly, Mr. Madden has used his love of research and travel to gain a better understanding of the war in the years since. He was awarded the Combat Infantryman Badge, Bronze Star, and Purple Heart, in addition to the standard European Theater service package.

Adolph Massa- The Massa's remained in Chicago for a year, adding two children to the family following the war. One day Mr. Massa was out looking for a job when he ran into an old Army friend that was on recruiting duty. One thing led to another and he was back in the military and headed for the occupation forces of the Pacific. When the Korean War kicked off he was thrown back into the infantry until the North Koreans were pushed back to a safe area. Master Sergeant Massa retired on January 1st, 1965, having been awarded the Combat Infantryman Badge, Bronze Star, Purple Heart, the Metz Medal and a Korean Medal (Awarded by the Korean Government), in addition to the standard European Theater, Pacific Theater and Korean War service packages.

547th Anti Aircraft Artillery
John G. Little, Jr.- immediately went back to the University of Alabama and was there until he graduated in 1950. Mr. Little was commissioned a 2nd Lieutenant of Quartermaster in 1949 from ROTC and went to work for his father at their sewing factory following graduation. John was married for 32 years and he and his wife had two children. He now lives in Dothan, Alabama near his daughter and three grandchildren, with his oldest grandchild attending Auburn University. Before moving to Dothan, John lived in Stone Mountain, Georgia for thirteen years. Mr. Little keeps in contact with the guys from D Battery 547 AAA. The D Battery veterans have remained close, conducting their

own local reunions in addition to the annual 95th Infantry Division Association reunion throughout the years.

795th Ordnance (Light Maintenance) Company

Leon E. Langford- ended up back at Penn State, graduating as a civil engineer in 1949, and staying on to teach and complete a master's degree in 1951. While Leon was gone, his wife Suz had graduated from Penn State in June of 1945 and then took a teaching position in North Central Pennsylvania. The couple moved to Pittsburgh following Leon's departure from the university. He accepted a position, and eventually was named a partner, with a consulting firm where he remained a partner until 1969. In 1969 Leon and his partners sold the company, but Mr. Langford decided to stay with the company under a different title until 1982. In the same year he joined again with his former partners to form a new company, where he remained until his retirement in 1989. The Langford's had four children and now live a life of ease in North Western Pennsylvania.

Martin H. Lincoln- ended up back at Massachusetts and finally found a job with an insurance company until he passed the BAR. After passing the BAR he went to work for the town of Easton. He married his wife Rita in 1947 and the couple had one son. Mr. Lincoln is retired now and still resides in Massachusetts.

95th Quartermaster Company

Harry T. Hessler- returned home and went back to his job with the New York Central Railroad. After a few years he transferred to the Reading Railroad as a freight agent. Harry later went into the trucking business as a freight agent. After deregulation took effect Harry started his own company, working as a sales agent. Harry's company expanded from just him to later include two of his sons and daughter. Harry was already married before the war. He and his wife Rita went on to have five children.

Rita unfortunately passed away in 1971. In 1984 Harry remarried, but his second wife Cathy also passed away in 1999. Harry still runs his company, and continues to enjoy a working relationship with three of his children.

Selected Bibliography

Books:

Ambrose, Stephen E., *Band of Brothers: E Company, 506th Regiment, 101st Airborne, from Normandy to Hitler's Eagle's Nest.* New York: Simon and Schuster, 1990.

----, *Citizen Soldiers.* New York: Simon and Schuster, 1997.

----, *The Supreme Commander: The War Years of General Dwight D. Eisenhower.* Garden City, NY: Doubleday, 1970.

Army Historical Series, *American Military History.* Washington, DC: Center of Military History United States Army, 1989.

Brokaw, Tom, *The Greatest Generation.* New York and Toronto: Random House Inc., 1998.

Colby, John, *War from the Ground Up: The 90th Division in WWII.* Austin, TX: Nortex Press, 1991.

Doubler, Michael D., *Closing with the Enemy: How GIs Fought the War in Europe, 1944-1945.* Lawrence: University of Kansas Press, 1994.

Egger, Bruce E., and Lee M. Otts, *G Company's War: Two Personal Accounts of the Campaigns in Europe, 1944-1945.* Tuscaloosa: University of Alabama Press, 1992.

Forty, George, *US Army Handbook, 1939-1945.* New York: Barnes & noble, 1995.

Fuermann, George M. and F. Edward Cranz, *Ninety-Fifth Infantry Division History, 1918-1946.* Atlanta, Georgia: Albert Love Enterprises, circa. 1947.

Grossman, Lieutenant Colonel Dave A., *On Killing: The Psychological Cost of Learning to Kill in War and Society.* Boston, New York, London: Little, Brown and Company, 1995.

Haydock, Michael D., *City Under Siege: The Berlin Blockade and Airlift, 1948-1949*. Washington and London: Brassey's, Inc., 1999.

Headquarters Department of the Army, *Army Regulation 600-8-22 Military Awards*. Washington, DC: Government Printing Office, 25 February 1995.

Januszkiewicz, Joseph, Kim Kowalczyk, Barbara Boal and Scott Tucker, *The Battles of General George S. Patton's Lowest Ranks: 'Old Blood and Guts'-His Blood, Our Guts, expanded edition*. United States of America: Data Based Retrieval System, 1997.

Keegan, John, *The Second World War*. Great Britain: Century Hutchinson Ltd., 1989.

Kemp, Anthony, *Metz 1944: One More River to Cross*. Bayeux, Heimdal, 2003.

Kissinger, Henry A., *Diplomacy*. New York: Simon and Schuster, 1994.

Leckie, Robert, *The Wars of America*. Edison, NJ: Castle Books, 1998.

Marshall, S.L.A., *Men Against Fire*. Gloucester, MA: Peter Smith, 1978.

Miller, Francis Trevelyan, *The Complete History of World War II*. Chicago: Progress Research Corporation, 1948.

Parrish, Thomas, *Berlin in the Balance 1945-1949*. Reading, Massachusetts: Perseus Books, 1998.

Paterson, Thomas G., and Dennis Merrill, *Major Problems in American Foreign Relations Volume II: Since 1914, 4th Edition*. Lexington, MA: DC Heath and Company, 1995.

Perret, Geoffrey, *There's a War to Be Won: The United States Army in World War II*. New York: Random House, 1991.

Province, Charles M., *Patton's Third Army: A Daily Combat Diary*. New York: Hippocrene Books, 1992.

Public Relations Office, 95th Infantry, *The 377th Infantry Regiment, 95th Division*. BatonRouge, Louisiana: Army and Navy Publishing Company, 1946.

----, *Victory*. Atlanta, Georgia: Albert Love Enterprises, circa. 1946.

----, *The Victory Division Journal*. Germany. Monday, May 21st, 1945.

Sledge, E.B., and Paul Fussell (Illustrator), *With the Old Breed: At Peleliu and Okinawa*. United Kingdom and Europe: Oxford University Press, Inc., 1990.

Snow, Donald M. and Dennis M. Drew, *From Lexington to Desert Storm: War and Politics in the American Experience*. Armonk, New York, London: M.E. Sharpe Inc. 1994.

Stannard, Richard M., *Infantry: An Oral History of a World War II American Infantry Battalion*. New York: Twayne, 1993.

United States Army Information School, *The Army Almanac: A Book of Facts Concerning the Army of the United States*. Washington, DC: Government Printing Office, 1950.

Weigley, Russell F., *The American Way of War: A History of United States Military Strategy and Policy*. Bloomington: Indiana University Press. 1973.

----, *Eisenhower's Lieutenants: The Campaigns of France and Germany, 1944-1945*. Bloomington: Indiana University Press, 1981.

Web Sites:

CIA World Factbook [on-line], Reference Maps. Available from http://www.cia.gov/cia/publications/factbook/index.html; Internet: accessed July 15, 2002

Cole, Hugh M. [on-line], *The Ardennes: Battle of the Bulge*. CMH Publication 7-8 available from www.Army.mil/cmh-pg/books/wwii/7-8/7-8_CONT.HTM; *Internet; accessed July 22, 2002*.

Grolier Online [on-line], *World War II*. Available from www.grolier.com/wwii/wwii_i.html; Internet: accessed July 7, 2002.

95th Division (Institutional Training) [on-line], *95th Division History*. Available from http://www.usarc.Army.mil/95thdiv/; Internet; accessed July 10, 2002.

95th Infantry Division Memorial [on-line]. Information available from http://www.usarc.army.mil/95thdiv/memorial_pictures.htm; Oklahoma City, internet; accessed July 10, 2002.

Oral Histories, Memoirs, Letters, Documents and Photographs:

Bever, Frank (North Manchester, Indiana)

Bushee, Roger A. (Bella Vista, Arkansas)

Fowler, Charles R. (Ninnekah, Oklahoma)

Hessler, Harry T. (Parma, Ohio)

Richard E. Hunton (Greenwood, South Carolina)

Knuth, Eldon L. (Encino, California)

Lake, William (Livermore, California)

Langford, Leon E. (Cochranton, Pennsylvania)

Lincoln, Martin H. (North Easton, Massachusetts)

Little, John G. Jr. (Dothan, Alabama)

Love, Fred B. (Owensboro, Kentucky)

Madden, Paul H. (Shreveport, Louisiana)

Massa, Adolph (Redding, California)

McCarthy, Daniel IV (Kansas)

Napier, Joseph W. (Savannah, Missouri)

Petraglia, Anthony N. (Pittsburgh, Pennsylvania)

Schoen, Richard H. (Toledo, Ohio)

Shaffer, Frank E. (Bloomsburg, Pennsylvania)

Taylor, William W. Jr. (Alexandria, Virginia)

Vogt, Louis O. (Lewistown, Pennsylvania)

Wroblewski, Eugene M. (Doylestown, Pennsylvania)

Young, Willis E. (Ocala, Florida)

Footnotes

[1] Fuermann, George M. and F. Edward Cranz, *Ninety-Fifth Infantry Division History, 1918-1946.* 1947, Pagny Bridgehead.

[2] Ibid, The German Defense of Metz.

[3] Ibid, The German Defense of Metz.

[4] Ibid, The German Defense of Metz.

[5] Ibid, The Bridge and Bridgeheads.

[6] Sledge, E.B., and Paul Fussell (Illustrator), *With the Old Breed: At Peleliu and Okinawa*. 1990, 143.

[7] Ibid, 260.

[8] 95th Division [on-line], *95th Division History*, accessed July 10, 2002.

[9] Public Relations Office, 95th Infantry, *The Victory Division Journal*. Germany. Monday, May 21st, 1945.

[10] United States Army Information School, *The Army Almanac: A Book of Facts Concerning the Army of the United States*. 1950, pp. 510-592.

Breinigsville, PA USA
18 April 2010
236372BV00001B/46/A